GLOBAL PERSPECTIVES ON CONSTITUTIONAL LAW

GLOBAL PERSPECTIVES ON CONSTITUTIONAL LAW

Edited by

Vikram David Amar

University of California at Davis School of Law

Mark V. Tushnet

Harvard Law School

New York Oxford

OXFORD UNIVERSITY PRESS

2009

Oxford University Press, Inc., publishes works that further
Oxford University's objective of excellence
in research, scholarship, and education.

Oxford New York
Auckland Cape Town Dar es Salaam Hong Kong Karachi
Kuala Lumpur Madrid Melbourne Mexico City Nairobi
New Delhi Shanghai Taipei Toronto

With offices in
Argentina Austria Brazil Chile Czech Republic France Greece
Guatemala Hungary Italy Japan Poland Portugal Singapore
South Korea Switzerland Thailand Turkey Ukraine Vietnam

Published by Oxford University Press, Inc.
198 Madison Avenue, New York, New York 10016
http://www.oup.com

Library of Congress Cataloging-in-Publication Data

Global perspectives on constitutional law / edited by
Vikram David Amar & Mark V. Tushnet.
p. cm.
Includes index.
ISBN 978-0-19-532811-0 (pbk.)
ISBN 978-0-19-532810-3 (hardback)
1. Constitutional law—United States. 2. Constitutional law.
I. Amar, Vikram. II. Tushnet, Mark V., 1945-
KF4550.G56 2008
342.73—dc22 2008019800

Printed in the United States of America
on acid-free paper

CONTENTS

PREFACE

This volume is a "reader"—a companion set of materials to be used (in whole or in part) in conjunction with basic U.S. constitutional law books and classes. The project was prompted by our sense that the leading U.S. constitutional law casebooks (including the two with which we are individually involved) do not contain much in the way of foreign or comparative source materials that might assist students to understand better the distinct legal, cultural, and historical premises that lie beneath—and the resulting choices that are made by—U.S. constitutional law and doctrine; such an understanding is particularly valuable for today's students.

In a sense, all existing U.S. constitutional law courses already have a significant comparative component; instructors typically compare the way the Constitution was understood by earlier generations and Justices with the way it is approached by modern interpreters; we often compare how the constitutional values seem to be understood differently by the Congress, the President, the judiciary, and the American people, respectively; and we compare the way constitutionalism operates at the state level to the way it works at the federal level. But alongside these historical, institutional, and domestic geographical axes, there is an increasingly worthwhile, if largely underutilized, opportunity for foreign comparison.

Our topical coverage is wide, but not all encompassing; we have focused on those subjects where we think there is something particularly valuable—in terms of understanding the form of constitutionalism and the specifics of constitutional law in the United States—to be gained from reflecting on non-U.S. experiences and approaches. We do not regard our choices as the ones every instructor would make, but rather as a helpful starting point for those who wish to supplement their treatment of U.S. constitutional law.

Each chapter is organized in a way that tracks the basic approach used in U.S. constitutional law casebooks. Following introductory comments, the chapters present foreign primary materials on a particular constitutional subject, and conclude with notes and comments designed to encourage readers to reexamine their understanding of U.S. constitutional law in light of the alternatives offered by other systems. Each chapter's author was encouraged to use as much as possible the raw materials—the judicial opinions, constitutional or statutory or treaty provisions, historical documents, and the like—that would permit instructors to exercise maximum teaching flexibility and would encourage students to produce their own comparisons and generalizations from the materials. There are, of course, stylistic differences among the chapters, which we think is valuable in itself, as demonstrating that non-U.S. materials can be used in a variety of ways to illuminate U.S. doctrine. One additional style note: we have omitted footnotes from the cases and other materials without indicating the omission.

One "methodological" point deserves mention: Some chapters focus entirely, or almost so, on domestic constitutional law, while others draw in, to a greater extent, materials from treaty-based decision makers, such as the European Court on Human Rights and the European Court of Justice. Domestic and treaty-based law differ in many ways, and those who use the book may find it useful to point out the differences. But we believe that both types of material are useful for purposes of shedding light on U.S. constitutional law.

The chapter authors are a talented and accomplished group, with deep knowledge and insight about the topics they present. We hope they also reflect the ideological, demographic, and experiential diversity that characterizes the leading teachers and scholars in American constitutional law today. We thank them for their willingness to participate in this project.

Vikram Amar
Mark Tushnet

CONTRIBUTORS

Gregory S. Alexander
A. Robert Noll Professor of Law
Cornell University Law School

Ashutosh Bhagwat
Professor of Law
UC Hastings College of the Law

Alan E. Brownstein
Professor of Law
UC Davis School of Law

Laurence P. Claus
Professor of Law
University of San Diego School of Law

Michael C. Dorf
Robert S. Stevens Professor of Law
Cornell University Law School

Steven G. Gey
David and Deborah Fonvielle and Donald and Janet Hinkle Professor of Law
Florida State University College of Law

Daniel Halberstam
Professor of Law
University of Michigan Law School

Richard L. Hasen
William H. Hannon Distinguished Professor of Law
Loyola Law School Los Angeles

Nan D. Hunter
Professor of Law
Georgetown University Law Center

Vicki C. Jackson
Carmack Waterhouse Professor of Constitutional Law
Georgetown University Law Center

Frank I. Michelman
Robert Walmsley University Professor
Harvard University

Radhika Rao
Professor of Law
UC Hastings College of the Law;
Fulbright Distinguished Professor,
University of Trento, Italy (March to July 2008)

Judith Resnik
Arthur Liman Professor of Law
Yale Law School

Michel Rosenfeld
Justice Sidney L. Robins Professor of Human Rights and Dirnector, Security, Democracy and the Rule of Law
Benjamin N. Cardozo School of Law,
Yeshiva University

Adrien Katherine Wing
Bessie Dutton Murray Professor of Law and Associate Dean for Faculty Development
University of Iowa College of Law

GLOBAL PERSPECTIVES ON CONSTITUTIONAL LAW

1

Abstract and Concrete Review

Michael C. Dorf

The U.S. Supreme Court has interpreted the case-or-controversy language of Article III to impose rigorous standing requirements for adjudication in all federal courts, including constitutional cases in the Supreme Court itself. "At a minimum, the standing requirement is not met unless the plaintiff has 'such a personal stake in the outcome of the controversy as to assure that concrete adverseness which sharpens the presentation of issues upon which the court so largely depends....'" *Allen v. Wright*, 468 U.S. 737, 770 (1984) (quoting *Baker v. Carr*, 369 U.S. 186, 204 (1962)). Standing and related doctrines such as ripeness and mootness implement a broader prohibition on the issuance of advisory opinions. In constitutional litigation, these limits on the powers of Article III courts collectively characterize the American version of a practice that sometimes goes by the name of "concrete review."

The alternatives to American-style concrete review take two basic forms. In what we might call "pure" abstract review, a constitutional court or other tribunal opines on the constitutionality of proposed or enacted legislation without regard to the application of that legislation to any concrete set of facts. Until recently, the French Constitutional Council (Conseil Constitutionnel) was archetypal. Prior to a constitutional amendment authorizing concrete review, adopted in 2008, its constitutional jurisdiction consisted solely of

> abstract proceedings which are optional in the case of ordinary laws or international agreements and mandatory for institutional acts and the rules of procedure of the parliamentary assemblies. This supervision is exercised after Parliament has voted but before promulgation of the law, ratification or approval of an international agreement or entry into force of the rules of procedure of the assemblies. Optional referral can take place on the initiative either of a political authority (President of the Republic, Prime Minister, President of the National Assembly or of the Senate) or of 60 deputies or 60 senators. (Constitutional Council, Powers, *available at* http://www.conseil-constitutionnel.fr/langues/anglais/ang4.htm, last visited May 22, 2007.)

Abstract review can also occur through the application of permissive standing rules. Exactly *how relaxed* standing rules need to be to qualify the resulting enterprise as abstract review rather than concrete review is a semantic question that need not detain us long because we can understand abstract and concrete as relative rather than absolute terms. We might plot the availability of constitutional review in a given legal system by locating its justiciability requirements along a spectrum from concrete to abstract—except that some systems permit both abstract and concrete review. The German Constitutional Court is a leading example. It hears individual rights cases that are effectively appeals from lower court rulings in concrete cases; it accepts referrals from lower courts in cases that call the constitutional status of statutes into question; and it hears pure abstract cases under circumstances similar to those of the French jurisdictional provisions described above. *See* Procedures *available at* http://www.bundesverfassungsgericht.de/en/organization/procedures.html, last visited May 25, 2007.

Although abstract review is forbidden in the federal courts of the United States, some state courts permit it. Thus, in Massachusetts, the Supreme Judicial Court issues opinions on the constitutionality of proposed laws in much the same way that the Conseil Constitutionnel does in France. *See* Mass. Const. Article LXXXV.

The materials in this chapter illustrate both "pure" abstract review and abstract review as accomplished through relaxed standing rules in concrete cases. As you read these materials, ask whether the relative advantages and disadvantages of various forms of review can be calculated without regard to other features of the constitutional system in which constitutional review occurs.

"PURE" ABSTRACT REVIEW

Article 191 of the Constitution of the Republic of Poland permits, inter alia, fifty or more deputies of the lower house of the Polish Parliament, or Sejm, to petition the Constitutional Tribunal for a ruling that a statute or international agreement is incompatible with the Constitution. Deputies who opposed Poland's membership in the European Union ("EU") brought an abstract case, alleging that a wide variety of obligations of EU membership violated a large number of provisions of the Polish Constitution. At its core, the case raised the question whether Poland had unconstitutionally ceded its sovereignty to the EU by placing European law above Polish law.

Poland's Membership in the European Union (Accession Treaty)

Judgment of 11 May, 2005, K 18/04[1]

1. The accession of Poland to the European Union did not undermine the supremacy of the Constitution over the whole legal order within the field of

[1] This summary of the "principal reasons for the ruling" comes from the official web site of the Polish Constitutional Tribunal, and is available at http://www.

sovereignty of the Republic of Poland. The norms of the Constitution, being the supreme act which is an expression of the Nation's will, would not lose their binding force or change their content by the mere fact of an irreconcilable inconsistency between these norms and any Community provision. In such a situation, the autonomous decision as regards the appropriate manner of resolving that inconsistency, including the expediency of a revision of the Constitution, belongs to the Polish constitutional legislator.

2. The process of European integration, connected with the delegation of competences in relation to certain matters to Community (Union) organs, has its basis in the Constitution. The mechanism for Poland's accession to the European Union finds its express grounds in constitutional regulations and the validity and efficacy of the accession are dependent upon fulfilment of the constitutional elements of the integration procedure, including the procedure for delegating competences....

4. When reviewing the constitutionality of the Accession Treaty as a ratified international agreement, including the Act concerning the conditions of accession (constituting an integral component of the Accession Treaty), it is... permissible to review the Treaties founding and modifying the Communities and the European Union, although only insofar as the latter are inextricably connected with application of the Accession Treaty....

6. It is insufficiently justified to assert that the Communities and the European Union are "supranational organisations"—a category that the Polish Constitution, referring solely to an "international organisation," fails to envisage. The Accession Treaty was concluded between the existing Member States of the Communities and the European Union and applicant States, including Poland. It has the features of an international agreement, within the meaning of Article 90(1) of the Constitution. The Member States remain sovereign entities—parties to the founding treaties of the Communities and the European Union. They also, independently and in accordance with their constitutions, ratify concluded treaties and have the right to denounce them under the procedure and on the conditions laid down in the Vienna Convention on the Law of Treaties 1969....

9. [T]he constitutional review of delegating certain competences should take into account the fact that, in the Preamble of the Constitution, emphasising the significance of Poland having reacquired the possibility to determine her fate in a sovereign and democratic manner, the constitutional legislator declares, concomitantly, the need for "cooperation with all countries for the good of a Human Family," observance of the obligation of "solidarity with others" and universal values, such as truth and justice. This duty refers not only to internal but also to external relations.

---

trybunal.gov.pl/eng/summaries/documents/K_18_04_GB.pdf, last visited May 29, 2007, but only the Polish language text is authoritative.

10. ...Article 8(1) of the Constitution, which states that the Constitution is the "supreme law of the Republic of Poland," is accompanied by the requirement to respect and be sympathetically predisposed towards appropriately shaped regulations of international law binding upon the Republic of Poland (Article 9). Accordingly, the Constitution assumes that, within the territory of the Republic of Poland—in addition to norms adopted by the national legislator—there operate regulations created outside the framework of national legislative organs.

11. Given its supreme legal force (Article 8(1)), the Constitution enjoys precedence of binding force and precedence of application within the territory of the Republic of Poland. The precedence over statutes of the application of international agreements which were ratified on the basis of a statutory authorisation or consent granted (in accordance with Article 90(3)) via the procedure of a nationwide referendum, as guaranteed by Article 91(2) of the Constitution, in no way signifies an analogous precedence of these agreements over the Constitution.

12. The concept and model of European law created a new situation, wherein, within each Member State, autonomous legal orders co-exist and are simultaneously operative. Their interaction may not be completely described by the traditional concepts of monism and dualism regarding the relationship between domestic law and international law. The existence of the relative autonomy of both, national and Community, legal orders in no way signifies an absence of interaction between them. Furthermore, it does not exclude the possibility of a collision between regulations of Community law and the Constitution.

13. Such a collision would occur in the event that an irreconcilable inconsistency appeared between a constitutional norm and a Community norm, such as could not be eliminated by means of applying an interpretation which respects the mutual autonomy of European law and national law. Such a collision may in no event be resolved by assuming the supremacy of a Community norm over a constitutional norm. Furthermore, it may not lead to the situation whereby a constitutional norm loses its binding force and is substituted by a Community norm, nor may it lead to an application of the constitutional norm restricted to areas beyond the scope of Community law regulation. In such an event the Nation as the sovereign, or a State authority organ authorised by the Constitution to represent the Nation, would need to decide on: amending the Constitution; or causing modifications within Community provisions; or, ultimately, on Poland's withdrawal from the European Union.

14. The principle of interpreting domestic law in a manner "sympathetic to European law," as formulated within the Constitutional Tribunal's jurisprudence, has its limits. In no event may it lead to results contradicting the explicit wording of constitutional norms or being irreconcilable with the minimum guarantee functions realised by the Constitution. In particular, the norms of the Constitution within the field of individual rights and

freedoms indicate a minimum and unsurpassable threshold which may not be lowered or questioned as a result of the introduction of Community provisions....

24. The requirement to observe the law of the Republic of Poland, as expressed in Article 83 of the Constitution, also encompasses provisions of ratified international agreements and Community Regulations....

[The decision went on to find no incompatibility between the Constitution and specific EU obligations under challenge.]

Notes and Questions

1. Given that the challenge to Poland's EU accession was fundamentally about sovereignty, a petition by legislators seems a particularly appropriate vehicle for bringing the case before the Constitutional Tribunal. Should abstract review also be available by legislators' petition in cases challenging a law as inconsistent with individual rights?

2. In the United States, legislator standing is not permitted unless the legislator has a personal rather than a merely institutional stake in the litigation. *Compare Raines v. Byrd*, 521 U.S. 811 (1997) *with Powell v. McCormack*, 395 U.S. 486 (1969). However, litigation by political units themselves may stand on a different footing. In *Massachusetts v. E.P.A.*, 127 S. Ct. 1438 (2007), the Court indicated that it may be easier for a state to satisfy the requirements of Article III injury than for a private party to do so. *See id.* at 1454–55.

3. The ability of interested persons and entities to obtain a ruling on the constitutionality of a proposed law or course of conduct can be very useful in avoiding wasteful investment of time and resources in administering and complying with the law or policy, only to have it held invalid (perhaps years) later. Accordingly, in systems without abstract review, a number of mechanisms have developed to bring constitutional challenges before rather than after a law's implementation. In the U.S. federal courts, three of the most common mechanisms are facial challenges, class actions, and anticipatory relief. However, none of these mechanisms, even if used in combination with one or both of the others, perfectly substitutes for abstract review. Under no circumstances do federal courts issue rulings on proposed legislation *before* enactment, and even after enactment, a litigant bringing what we might call a *quasi-abstract* case must still establish Article III standing. *See, e.g.*, Declaratory Judgment Act, 28 U.S.C. § 2201 (authorizing a federal court to grant declaratory relief "[i]n a case of actual controversy within its jurisdiction....").

   Moreover, the term "facial" challenge is something of a misnomer. A federal court ruling that a law is invalid on its face does not result in its removal from the statute books, nor does such a ruling even prevent the law's enforcement in future cases involving different parties, except to the extent that the ruling establishes a binding precedent. Thus, for example, a ruling by the U.S. Court of Appeals for the Ninth Circuit that a California law is unconstitutional and therefore cannot be enforced by the City of Los Angeles would not prevent prosecution in state court of persons who violate the law by the City of San Francisco: San Francisco was not a party to the federal court action and rulings of the lower federal courts are merely persuasive precedent for the state courts. Parties seeking a ruling with broader scope may attempt to bring a constitutional challenge in the form of a class action or to join multiple defendants, but they will then encounter constitutional and subconstitutional limits on class relief and joinder. For discussions of the scope and limits on facial challenges, *see* Michael C. Dorf, *Facial Challenges to State and Federal Statutes*, 46 STAN. L. REV. 235 (1994); Richard H. Fallon, Jr., *As-Applied and Facial Challenges and Third-Party Standing*, 113 HARV. L. REV. 1321 (2000).

4. Although not directly relevant to the precise issues raised in this chapter, the merits of the Polish Constitutional Tribunal's ruling raise important questions about the relation between supranational and domestic constitutional law. The Tribunal's assertion of a power to review EU law for conformity with the Polish Constitution, and similar assertions by other constitutional courts in Europe, have set the stage for a showdown because the European Court of Justice, the principal judicial organ of the EU (formerly the European Community), "has pronounced an uncompromising version of supremacy: in the sphere of application of Community law, any Community norm, be it an article of the Treaty (the Constitutional Charter) or a minuscule administrative regulation enacted by the Commission, 'trumps' conflicting national law whether enacted before or after the Community norm." J.H.H. Weiler, *The Transformation of Europe*, 100 YALE L.J. 2403, 2414 (1991). Similar issues will likely arise in this country as the United States continues to enter into international agreements that purport to supersede domestic law. *See* Henry P. Monaghan, *Article III and Supranational Judicial Review*, 107 COLUM. L. REV. 833 (2007).

ABSTRACT REVIEW THROUGH RELAXED STANDING RULES

Section 38 of the Constitution of the Republic of South Africa provides

> Enforcement of rights
>
> Anyone listed in this section has the right to approach a competent court, alleging that a right in the Bill of Rights has been infringed or threatened, and the court may grant appropriate relief, including a declaration of rights. The persons who may approach a court are:
>
> (a) Anyone acting in their own interest;
> (b) anyone acting on behalf of another person who cannot act in their own name;
> (c) anyone acting as a member of, or in the interest of, a group or class of persons;
> (d) anyone acting in the public interest; and
> (e) an association acting in the interest of its members.

On its face, subsection (d) would seem to allow anyone to challenge legislation on Bill-of-Rights grounds, regardless of whether or not that person had suffered, or could allege a likelihood that she would suffer, any injury from the enforcement of that legislation. However, the South African Constitutional Court has not construed it as quite so far-reaching. Consider

Ferreira v. Levin NO & Others (1995), a case involving the privilege against self-incrimination that arose under the 1994 Interim Constitution, which was substantially similar to the Final Constitution that emerged in 1996 after the full transition from the prior apartheid regime. The Court reached the merits, and ruled for the plaintiffs, without relying on the provision granting standing to "anyone acting in the public interest." Concurring, Justice Kate O'Regan had this to say about Section 7(4) of the Interim Constitution, which was, in relevant respects, identical to Section 38 of the Final Constitution:

> The applicants allege that section 417(2)(b) [of the challenged Companies Act] constitutes a breach of the rights of accused persons, in that it permits the admission of evidence in a criminal trial which has been compelled from those accused persons in a section 417 enquiry. The difficulty the applicants face is that they have not yet been charged, nor is there any allegation on the record to suggest that they consider that there is a threat that a prosecution may be launched against them, after they have given evidence at the section 417 enquiry, in which that evidence will be used against them.
>
> ...[The majority] finds that persons acting in their own interest (as contemplated by section 7(4)(b)(i) [which was identical in terms to section 38(a) of the Final Constitution]) may only seek relief from the court where their rights, and not the rights of others, are infringed. I respectfully disagree with this approach. It seems clear to me from the text of section 7(4) that a person may have an interest in the infringement or threatened infringement of the right of another which would afford such a person the standing to seek constitutional relief. In addition, such an interpretation fits best contextually with the overall approach adopted in section 7(4).
>
> There are many circumstances where it may be alleged that an individual has an interest in the infringement or threatened infringement of the right of another. Several such cases have come before the Canadian courts. In *R v. Big M Drug Mart Ltd* [1985] 13 CRR 64, a corporation was charged in terms of a statute which prohibited trading on Sundays. The corporation did not have a right to religious freedom, but nevertheless it was permitted to raise the constitutionality of the statute which was held to be in breach of the Charter. A similar issue arose in *Morgentaler, Smoling and Scott v. R* [1988] 31 CRR 1 in which male doctors, prosecuted under antiabortion provisions, successfully challenged the constitutionality of the legislation in terms of which they were prosecuted. In both of these cases, the prosecution was based on a provision which itself directly infringed the rights of people other than the accused. The Canadian jurisprudence on standing is not directly comparable to ours, however, for their constitutional provisions governing standing are different, but the fact that situations of this nature arise is instructive of the need for a broad approach to standing.
>
> In this case, however, although the challenge is [to] section 417(2)(b) in its entirety, the constitutional objection lies in the condition that evidence given under compulsion in an enquiry, whether incriminating or not, may be used in a subsequent prosecution. There is no allegation on the record of any actual or threatened prosecution in which such evidence is to be led.
>
> There can be little doubt that section 7(4) provides for a generous and expanded approach to standing in the constitutional context. The categories

of persons who are granted standing to seek relief are far broader than our common law has ever permitted.

...This expanded approach to standing is quite appropriate for constitutional litigation. Existing common law rules of standing have often developed in the context of private litigation. As a general rule, private litigation is concerned with the determination of a dispute between two individuals, in which relief will be specific and, often, retrospective, in that it applies to a set of past events. Such litigation will generally not directly affect people who are not parties to the litigation. In such cases, the plaintiff is both the victim of the harm and the beneficiary of the relief. In litigation of a public character, however, that nexus is rarely so intimate. The relief sought is generally forward-looking and general in its application, so that it may directly affect a wide range of people. In addition, the harm alleged may often be quite diffuse or amorphous. Of course, these categories are ideal types: no bright line can be drawn between private litigation and litigation of a public or constitutional nature. Not all non-constitutional litigation is private in nature. Nor can it be said that all constitutional challenges involve litigation of a purely public character: a challenge to a particular administrative act or decision may be of a private rather than a public character. But it is clear that in litigation of a public character, different considerations may be appropriate to determine who should have standing to launch litigation. In recognition of this, section 7(4) casts a wider net for standing than has traditionally been cast by the common law.

Section 7(4) is a recognition too of the particular role played by the courts in a constitutional democracy. As the arm of government which is entrusted primarily with the interpretation and enforcement of constitutional rights, it carries a particular democratic responsibility to ensure that those rights are honoured in our society. This role requires that access to the courts in constitutional matters should not be precluded by rules of standing developed in a different constitutional environment in which a different model of adjudication predominated. In particular, it is important that it is not only those with vested interests who should be afforded standing in constitutional challenges, where remedies may have a wide impact.

However, standing remains a factual question. In each case, applicants must demonstrate that they have the necessary interest in an infringement or threatened infringement of a right. The facts necessary to establish standing should appear from the record before the court. As I have said, there is no evidence on the record in this case which would meet the requirements of section 7(4)(b)(i). The applicants have alleged neither a threat of a prosecution in which compelled evidence may be led against them, nor an interest in the infringement or threatened infringement of the rights of other persons.

...In the special circumstances of this case, it appears to me that the applicants may rely upon section 7(4)(b)(v) [which was identical in terms to section 38(d) of the Final Constitution], as applicants acting in the public interest. The possibility that applicants may be granted standing on the grounds that they are acting in the public interest is a new departure in our law. Even the old *actiones populares* of Roman Law afforded a right to act in the public interest only in narrowly circumscribed causes of action. Section 7(4)(b)(v) is the provision in which the expansion of the ordinary rules of standing is most obvious and it needs to be interpreted in the light of the special role that the courts now play in our constitutional democracy.

This court will be circumspect in affording applicants standing by way of section 7(4)(b)(v) and will require an applicant to show that he or she is genuinely acting in the public interest. Factors relevant to determining whether a person is genuinely acting in the public interest will include considerations such as: whether there is another reasonable and effective manner in which the challenge can be brought; the nature of the relief sought, and the extent to which it is of general and prospective application; and the range of persons or groups who may be directly or indirectly affected by any order made by the court and the opportunity that those persons or groups have had to present evidence and argument to the court. These factors will need to be considered in the light of the facts and circumstances of each case.

[A]pplicants under section 7(4)(b)(v) need not point to an infringement of or threat to the right of a particular person. They need to allege that, objectively speaking, the challenged rule or conduct is in breach of a right enshrined in [the Interim Constitution's Fundamental Rights]. This flows from the notion of acting in the public interest. The public will ordinarily have an interest in the infringement of rights generally, not particularly.

In this case, it is clear from the referral that the applicants consider that section 417(2)(b) is, objectively speaking, in breach of [fundamental rights]. Although the challenge could be brought by other persons, a considerable delay may result if this court were to wait for such a challenge. It is also clear that the challenge is to the constitutionality of a provision contained in an Act of Parliament and that the relief sought is a declaration of invalidity. It is relief which falls exclusively within the jurisdiction of this court and it is of a general, not particular, nature. In addition, adequate notice of the constitutional challenge has been given and a wide range of different individuals and organisations have lodged memoranda and amicus curiae briefs in the matter. At the hearing also, the matter of the constitutionality of section 417 was thoroughly argued. There can be little doubt that those directly interested in the constitutionality of section 417 have had an opportunity to place their views before the court.

...In these special circumstances, it seems to me that the applicants have established standing to act in the public interest to challenge the constitutionality of section 417(2)(b).

Notes and Questions

1. According to Justice O'Regan, do the expansive standing provisions of the Interim and Final Constitutions of South Africa do more than lift what American constitutional lawyers would call prudential limits on third-party standing? Do they authorize litigation by persons who have not suffered the equivalent of an Article III injury?

2. Section 38 of the Final Constitution confers standing on "anyone acting in the public interest" only where that person makes a claim under the Bill of Rights. Claims of unconstitutionality under the structural provisions of the South African Constitution must meet the stricter limits for standing that otherwise apply. Is this a sensible distinction? Could one argue that there is a *greater* need for "public

interest" standing to enforce structural constitutional principles because particular individuals are more likely to come forward with complaints about infringements of their rights and because the impact of structural provisions is felt more generally than the impact of rights provisions? Is it even sensible to have relaxed standing rules in constitutional cases rather than other kinds of cases? Note that in the United States, the Article III standing requirements do not vary based on the type of claim. But note as well that unlike the Supreme Court of the United States, the Constitutional Court of South Africa hears *only* constitutional questions.

3. Justice O'Regan describes "public interest" standing as a justified departure from common law rules of standing in constitutional cases. The Supreme Court of India has reached a similar conclusion even without express language in the Indian Constitution granting public interest standing. It routinely permits public interest standing in constitutional cases. Consider, for example, *M.C. Mehta v. Union of India*, 1988 S.C.R. (2) 530. There, the Court accepted a petition complaining that insufficient efforts had been made by the government to clean up the Ganges River, in violation of statutory and constitutional duties. No particularized injury was alleged but public interest standing was nonetheless found. The Court explained:

   > The petitioner in the case before us is no doubt not a riparian owner. He is a person interested in protecting the lives of the people who make use of the water flowing in the river Ganga and his right to maintain the petition cannot be disputed. The nuisance caused by the pollution of the river Ganga is a public nuisance, which is wide spread in range and indiscriminate in its effect and it would not be reasonable to expect any particular person [to bring] proceedings to stop it as distinct from the community at large. The petition has been entertained as a Public Interest Litigation. On the facts and in the circumstances of the case we are of the view that the Petitioner is entitled to move this Court in order to enforce the statutory provisions which impose duties on the municipal authorities and the Boards constituted under the Water Act.

4. Justice O'Regan contends that "public interest" standing is warranted because "of the particular role played by the courts in a constitutional democracy." Her use of the plural *courts* rather than the singular *court* is deliberate, because both Section 38(d) of the Final Constitution and Section 7(4)(b)(v) of the Interim Constitution authorize public interest standing in any competent court, not only in the Constitutional Court. In this respect, her argument should apply not only in a legal system that utilizes the "Austrian" model of centralized constitutional review but also in countries that utilize the "American" model of decentralized judicial review. South Africa itself, of course, is a hybrid, permitting constitutional issues to be raised both in ordinary litigation before the lower courts and in original actions in the Constitutional Court.

5. Although this chapter has presented pure abstract review and loose standing rules as different means of achieving the same end, in an important respect they are polar opposites. Pure abstract review, where it exists, typically permits petitions to be brought only by a small and well-defined set of institutional actors, such as some minimum number of legislators. By contrast, under loosened standing rules, such as South Africa's Section 38(d), virtually anybody can bring a constitutional complaint. This latitude raises the concern that the litigants before the

Constitutional Court will not adequately present the relevant issues. To address that concern, Justice O'Regan would "require an applicant to show that he or she is genuinely acting in the public interest." Do the factors Justice O'Regan lists as relevant to that determination really ensure that the applicant is acting in the public interest and presenting the issues as well as possible? Does her test do a better or worse job of filtering litigants than the U.S. Supreme Court's standing rules?

6. Another cost of relaxed standing rules is docket crowding. In Germany, where anyone can, in principle, bring a constitutional complaint to the Constitutional Court, the success rate of such complaints is 2.5 percent, and the Court has accordingly adopted screening procedures to deny full consideration to most complaints. *See* Constitutional Complaint, *available at* http://www.bundesverfassungsgericht.de/en/organization/verfassungsbeschwerde.html, last visited May 25, 2007; Donald Kommers, The Constitutional Jurisprudence of the Federal Republic of Germany 17 (1989). The Supreme Court of India construes its jurisdictional grant as extraordinarily broad, so that even a letter to the editor of a newspaper or a postcard to a Justice has initiated a case. *See* Jamie Cassels, *Judicial Activism and Public Interest Litigation in India: Attempting the Impossible?*, 37 Am. J. Comp. L. 495, 499 (1989). Not surprisingly, broad jurisdiction has led to docket crowding and the need for jurisprudential triage. *See* Carl Baar, *Social Action Litigation in India: The Operation and Limits of the World's Most Active Judiciary, in* Comparative Judicial Review and Public Policy 77, 80–82 (Donald W. Jackson & C. Neal Tate, eds., 1992).

7. The U.S. Supreme Court faced similar problems before 1988, when Congress abolished nearly all of its mandatory appellate jurisdiction. *Compare* 28 U.S.C. § 1257 (1988) *with* 28 U.S.C. § 1257 (1964). In prior years, the Court addressed docket crowding through summary dispositions and dismissals of cases within its nominally mandatory jurisdiction, effectively converting it into discretionary jurisdiction. *See Hogge v. Johnson*, 526 F.2d 833, 836 (4th Cir. 1975) (Clark, retired Justice sitting by designation). Was this tactic legitimate? *See* Herbert Wechsler, *The Appellate Jurisdiction of the Supreme Court: Reflections on the Law and the Logistics of Direct Review*, 34 Wash. & Lee L. Rev. 1043, 1061 (1977) (lamenting the Court's "lawless" approach to its jurisdiction).

   A decade after the reduction in the Court's caseload, the Justices stated what had been true for considerably longer, that the "Court cannot devote itself to error correction." *Calderon v. Thompson*, 523 U.S. 538, 569 (1998). Instead, the Court grants petitions for a writ of certiorari in those cases that present important issues of law with consequences beyond the concerns of the parties. Given that fact, would not the Court be better served by the possibility of abstract review? If so, does this mean that the prohibition on advisory opinions is a mistaken interpretation of Article III? Or would adoption in the United States of procedures like those employed by the Conseil Constitutionnel directly contradict the Framers' rejection of James Madison's proposed Council of Revision? *See Flast v. Cohen*, 392 U.S. 83, 130 (1968) (Harlan, J., dissenting).

8. Articles 103 and 107 of the Mexican Constitution authorize courts to issue writs of *amparo*, a vehicle for aggrieved individuals to complain about government action. "*Amparo*" literally means shelter or protection. Unlike the Anglo-American writ

of habeas corpus, which only permits a court to examine the legality of a prisoner's detention, *amparo* is usually available to protect the legal rights of any person who comes to court. Although pioneered in Mexico, *amparo* and variations on it, such as the writ of *tutela* in Colombia, have proved popular in Latin America and Spain. *See* Justice Manuel José Cepeda-Espinosa, *Judicial Activism in a Violent Context: The Origin, Role, and Impact of the Colombian Constitutional Court*, 3 Wash. U. Global Stud. L. Rev. 529, 552–55 (2004); Hector Fix Zamudio, *A Brief Introduction to the Mexican Writ of "Amparo,"* 9 Cal. W. Int'l L.J. 306 (1979).

The classic writ of *amparo* requires the complainant to demonstrate a legal injury to his individual rights. *See* Ley de Amparo (Amparo Law), *as amended*, Diario Oficial de la Federación (D.O.), Article 73, sec. V, 24 de abril de 2006 (Mex.), *available at* http://www.diputados.gob.mx/LeyesBiblio/pdf/20.pdf, last visited May 29, 2007 ("El juicio de amparo es improcedente...contra actos que no afecten los intereses jurídicos del quejoso" or roughly, "amparo actions are inadmissible against acts that do not affect the legal interests of the petitioner."). *Amparo* thus counts as a form of concrete review. However, because social and economic rights tend to be justiciable in the countries that authorize *amparo* or *tutela*, these writs have been used to seek judicially mandated changes in circumstances in which U.S. courts have been unwilling to find Article III redressability. For example, in one *amparo* action, the Mexican Supreme Court held that the Mexican Institute of Social Security had a duty to implement the right to health by providing antiretroviral treatment for HIV-infected persons. *See Salud. El Derecho A Su Protección*, Pleno de la Suprema Corte de Justicia [S.C.J.N.] [Supreme Court], Semanario Judicial de la Federación y su Gaceta, Novena Epoca, tomo XI, Marzo de 2000, Tesis P. XIX/2000, Pagina 112 (Mex.), *available at* http://www.scjn.gob.mx/ius2006//UnaTesislnkTmp.asp?nIus=192160&cPalPrm=SALUD,DERECHO,&cFrPrm=, last visited May 29, 2007. Does the possibility of broad institutional relief going well beyond the concerns of the individual petitioner act as a kind of substitute for relaxed standing rules? Does it act as a substitute for abstract review?

2

Judicial Independence

Judith Resnik

Around the world, constitutions and transnational conventions now insist that judges be "independent" from the authorities that employ them. Consider first a few such statements.

Constitution of the Republic of South Africa, 1996
Section 165. Judicial authority...

2. The courts are independent and subject only to the Constitution and the law, which they must apply impartially and without fear, favour or prejudice.
3. No person or organ of state may interfere with the functioning of the courts.
4. Organs of state, through legislative and other measures, must assist and protect the courts to ensure the independence, impartiality, dignity, accessibility and effectiveness of the courts.
5. An order or decision issued by a court binds all persons to whom and organs of state to which it applies.

United States Constitution

Article III, Section 1. The judicial Power of the United States, shall be vested in one Supreme Court, and in such inferior Courts as the Congress may from time to time ordain and establish. The Judges, both of the supreme and inferior Courts, shall hold their Offices during good Behaviour, and shall, at stated Times, receive for their Services a Compensation, which shall not be diminished during their Continuance in Office....

Council of Europe
European Convention on Human Rights (ECHR)
November 4, 1950

Article 6, 1. In the determination of his civil rights and obligations or of any criminal charge against him, everyone is entitled to a fair and public hearing within a reasonable time by an independent and impartial tribunal established by law. Judgement shall be pronounced publicly...

Basic Principles on the Independence of the Judiciary endorsed, United Nations, General Assembly Resolutions 40/32 and 40/146 (1985)

1. The independence of the judiciary shall be guaranteed by the State and enshrined in the Constitution or the law of the country. It is the duty of all

governmental and other institutions to respect and observe the independence of the judiciary.

2. The judiciary shall decide matters before them impartially, on the basis of facts and in accordance with the law, without any restrictions, improper influences, inducements, pressures, threats or interferences, direct or indirect, from any quarter or for any reason.
3. The judiciary shall have jurisdiction over all issues of a judicial nature and shall have exclusive authority to decide whether an issue submitted for its decision is within its competence as defined by law.
4. There shall not be any inappropriate or unwarranted interference with the judicial process, nor shall judicial decisions by the courts be subject to revision. This principle is without prejudice to judicial review or to mitigation or commutation by competent authorities of sentences imposed by the judiciary, in accordance with the law.
5. Everyone shall have the right to be tried by ordinary courts or tribunals using established legal procedures. Tribunals that do not use the duly established procedures of the legal process shall not be created to displace the jurisdiction belonging to the ordinary courts or judicial tribunals.
6. The principle of the independence of the judiciary entitles and requires the judiciary to ensure that judicial proceedings are conducted fairly and that the rights of the parties are respected.
7. It is the duty of each Member State to provide adequate resources to enable the judiciary to properly perform its functions.

As you review these provisions, consider the distinctive ideas about what "judicial independence" could mean and how to protect it. One aspect relates to aspirations for impartial judgments in individual cases; the idea is that a judge should be able to make specific decisions without fear of suffering personal sanctions. A contemporary example of a dramatic breach of this norm occurred in Pakistan in 2007 when the Chief Justice and then other justices of that country's highest court were suspended—after making decisions the government disliked and before the court could rule on the legality of General Pervez Musharraf's dual role as president and army chief.

The literature on judicial independence distinguishes a second set of issues, focused on the institutional setting in which judges work—how they are appointed, their length of tenure, mechanisms for removal, their salaries, budgets, facilities, and jurisdiction, as well as whether they run their own internal affairs and set their own procedures. Institutional independence aims to generate environments that equip courts with the resources to render the volume of decisions now expected of them as well as to shape a culture supportive of a unique role for judges.

Although the concept of institutional independence seems straightforward, the demand for judging and the resultant proliferation of working structures for judges raise questions about what forms of bureaucratic organization are appropriate. For example, in the United States, the federal courts have more than 2000 life-tenured judges, aided by some 1600 statutory judges serving for terms. That group in turn has about 30,000 staff working in more than 500 facilities spread across the country and dealing with about 350,000 civil and criminal filings each year. Each state in turn has its own court system, often with many tiers or a varied set of courts with special jurisdiction. In the aggregate, state courts have more than 30,000 judges and respond to filings numbering in the tens of millions.

These institutional configurations give rise both to more dependence on other branches of government for monetary support and to questions about the kind of institutional position judiciaries ought to have. Who should be the advocates for the funding to sustain judicial facilities and staff and to argue for sufficient compensation for the judges themselves? Should judges go directly to other branches to request budgets and raises? And what about responding to pending legislation that would give courts more or different cases? Should judges provide commentary on bills proposing new crimes or altering the punishment or the factors to be considered when sentencing, or requiring a minimum number of years for incarceration? Should judges opine on legislation to widen or limit their jurisdiction over civil cases, or to change detainees' access to habeas corpus? Could taking positions on such proposals undermine the ability or legitimacy to rule on their legality? As these questions suggest, many hard problems are at the intersection of judicial independence at the individual level and at the structural level. Responses in turn depend on political and legal theories of how powers are separated among judicial, legislative, and executive branches.

The excerpts from South Africa, the United States, the Council of Europe, and the United Nations make plain that overlapping but differing mechanisms are used to protect both forms of judicial independence.To parse the various aspects, one needs to begin with a focus on how one becomes a judge—the techniques used to select and retain judges and how such provisions either protect or undercut judicial independence. As the readings below suggest, terms of office may be too short, or perhaps too long. The next set of issues concerns conditions of work. What are the financial structures and incentives at both the individual and the structural levels? Does the judiciary have a "right" to a budget or to a certain level of salaries?

Another set of questions revolves around the power accorded to judges. What are the parameters of judicial authority in general? Are courts creatures of constitutional text or does their existence depend on legislative or executive action? Can judges set their own jurisdiction? Can they decide any kind of case that comes before them and provide the remedies they believe appropriate, or has a legislature limited access to courts and the kinds of solutions that courts can provide?

Note that historically, discussion of "threats" to judicial independence focused on harms coming from other branches of government, and the questions laid out above about support and jurisdiction reflect that focus. But, during the twentieth century, two new "friends" or "foes" of judicial independence have come to the fore—the media and "repeat player" litigants.

Consider first the role of what used to be called "the press" and is now more broadly the media, sending out information through a range of technologies and especially over the internet. Some commentators see courts and the media as interdependent institutions in democratic orders. Many jurisdictions' systems express commitments to the freedom of the media, unfettered from government control and working in conjunction with courts to shape a lively public debate about legal and social norms. The media thus have an important role to play as an intermediary, interpreting judicial rulings and bringing wanted (or uncomfortable) attention to issues related to courts. Further, technologies such as television and the internet can enable courts to try to put themselves directly before the public eye.

Another set of relevant actors are what social scientists have termed "repeat players"—such as government lawyers, public interest litigators, bar associations, or business and corporate entities appearing regularly before judges. In many countries, such groups try to affect selection of judges, the rules of procedure, and the coverage of decisions by the press. Hence, attitudes toward courts and judicial authority are shaped not only by legal texts and practices but through the lenses provided by court users and observers.

Furthermore, as judiciaries in some countries have transformed themselves into multitasking dispute resolution centers, new questions have emerged about whether judges ought to be accorded unique forms of insulation. If, in the provision of "alternative dispute resolution," judges serve as mediators or settlement advisors, ought they be specially insulated? Features of adjudication—its presumptively public processes and the rendering of decisions disseminated to the public—can be used to sustain commitments to, or provide justifications for, judicial independence. Alternatively, new modes of decision making that rely on more private processes may undercut such commitments.

A substantial body of law addresses the range of challenges flagged above. Below are three examples in which judges themselves have reasoned about a few of these issues.

Starrs v. Ruxton

[2000] J.C. 208 (H.C.J.) (Scot.)

Lord Justice-Clerk (Cullen), Lord Prosser, Lord Reed

[The Lord Advocate of Scotland became, pursuant to new legislation in 1998, a member of the Scottish Executive, and subject under Scottish law to the European Convention for the Protection of Human Rights and Fundamental Freedoms (hereinafter "the Convention.") A challenge was brought under the Convention to his power to appoint judges (called Sheriffs) for one year terms. Under the process, the Secretary of State also had the power to recall such an appointment.

The argument was that such appointments violated the rights of the accused under Article 6(1) of the Convention to fair trial by "an independent and impartial tribunal." In terms of the process, in "1998 there were 77 applications; 26 candidates were interviewed, 23 appointments were made, and in addition 3 persons were appointed without being interviewed. In each case appointments were made in December for one year only, being the following calendar year."]

Opinion of the Lord Justice-Clerk (Cullen):

20. The Solicitor General was unable to explain why a period of one year had been chosen....

23. [Explanations to candidates included] the following:

> 7. Permanent Appointments: whilst, in recent years, many of those successful in obtaining appointments to the permanent shrieval Bench have earlier served as Temporary Sheriffs, it should be noted that, at any point in time, the number of Temporary Sheriffs interested in a permanent appointment very substantially exceeds the number of vacancies and there is no guarantee whatsoever that service as a Temporary Sheriff will eventually lead to a permanent appointment.

...[This issue is addressed in a] number of decisions of the European Court of Human Rights and of the European Commission. In *Findlay v. United Kingdom* (1997) 24 E.H.R.R. 221 at para. 73 the court stated that:

> In order to establish whether a tribunal can be considered as "independent," regard must be had *inter alia* to the manner of appointment of its members and their term of office, the existence of guarantees against outside pressures and the question whether the body presents an appearance of independence....

24. ...[W]hether a tribunal is independent and impartial embraces the question whether it presents the appearance of independence from an objective standpoint. For example in *De Cubber v. Belgium* (1984) 7 E.H.R.R. 326 the fact that one of the judges of the court which had given judgment on the charges against the applicant had previously acted as investigating judge gave rise to the misgivings as to the court's impartiality....

In a number of cases the court has found that lack of independence and lack of impartiality are inter-linked. Thus, in *Bryan v. United Kingdom* [(1995) 21 E.H.R.R. 342] the court recognised that the fact that the appointment of an inspector, who had the power to determine a planning appeal in which the policies of the appointing minister might be in issue, could be revoked by the minister at any time gave rise to a question as to his independence and impartiality. In the circumstances, it did not fall foul of Article 6(1) by reason of the scope of review which was available to the High Court in England. In *Findlay v. United Kingdom* the court was satisfied that there was objective justification for doubts as to the independence and impartiality of the members of a court martial where they were subordinate to the convening officer who acted as the prosecutor. In that case the process of review did not provide an adequate guarantee. In Çiraklar v. Turkey [(2001) 32 E.H.R.R. 23], the court observed that it was difficult to disassociate impartiality from independence where the members of a national security court included a military judge. While there were certain constitutional safeguards, the members of the court were still servicemen and remained subject to military discipline and assessment. Their term of office was only four years. In these circumstances the court held (at para. 40) that there was a legitimate fear of their being influenced by considerations which had nothing to do with the nature of the case. There was objective justification for fear of lack of independence and impartiality....

27. ...In *Att.-Gen. v. Lippé,* [[1991] 2 S.C.R. 114 (Can.)] Lamer C.J., whose judgment in this respect was concurred in by the other members of the court, said at page 139:

> The overall objective of guaranteeing judicial independence is to ensure a reasonable perception of impartiality; judicial independence is but a "means" to this"end." If judges could be perceived as "impartial" without judicial "independence," the requirement of "independence" would be unnecessary. Independence is the cornerstone, a necessary prerequisite, for judicial impartiality.

He went on to say at page 140:

> Notwithstanding judicial independence, there may also exist a reasonable apprehension of bias on an institutional or structural level. Although the concept of institutional impartiality has never before been recognised by this court, the constitutional guarantee of an "independent and impartial tribunal" has to be broad enough to encompass this. Just as the requirement of judicial independence has both an individual and institutional aspect..., so too must the requirement of judicial impartiality.

In Ref. re Territorial Court Act (N.W.T.) (1997) 152 D.L.R. (4th) 132, Vertes J. expressed the same idea when he stated at page 146 in regard to concepts of independence and impartiality:

> Recent jurisprudence has recast these concepts as separate and distinct values. They are nevertheless still linked together as attributes of each other. Independence is the necessary precondition to impartiality. It is the *sine qua non* for attaining the objective of impartiality. Hence there is a concern with the status, both individual and institutional, of the decision-maker. The decision-maker could be independent and yet not be impartial (on a specific case basis) but a decision-maker that is not independent cannot by definition be impartial (on a institutional basis)....

[In the case of Scotland's one year appointments, factors interact.] The first of them was the fact that the term of office of a temporary sheriff was limited to one year. The period for which the appointment of a tribunal subsisted was plainly a relevant factor in considering its independence. In Campbell and *Fell v United Kingdom* [(1984) 7 E.H.R.R. 165], which was concerned with a prison board of visitors, a term of three years or less as the Home Secretary might appoint was regarded as "admittedly short," though it was accepted by the court that there were understandable reasons for that. In *Çiraklar v Turkey* the four year term of office, which was renewable, was plainly one of the factors which led the court to conclude that there was a lack of objective independence and impartiality.... [T]he Latimer House Guidelines for the Commonwealth which were adopted by the Commonwealth Parliamentary Association on 19 June 1998...stated...

> Judicial appointments should normally be permanent; whilst in some jurisdictions, contract appointments may be inevitable, such appointments should be subject to appropriate security of tenure....

33. [The government has argued] that a fixed-term appointment was not objectionable provided that there were sufficient guarantees of the independence and impartiality of the judge who held such an appointment....

In the present case it was important to note that the temporary sheriff took a judicial oath. There was no question of the Lord Advocate attempting to influence temporary sheriffs in what they did. The fact that their commission was in respect of every sheriffdom in Scotland had the effect of distancing the Lord Advocate from particular cases, and he had no part in deciding in what sheriff court they served. The limitation of their commission to one year at a time simply reflected the temporary nature of their appointment....

44. It is clear that in other parts of the world time-limited appointments of judges have given cause for concern. In the present case it might have been a reassurance if the reasons for this period were at least consistent with concepts of independence and impartiality. However,... the Solicitor-General was not able to give any reason why that period had been selected. He suggested that it might have been due to the possibility of a drop in the number of temporary sheriffs who were needed. That suggestion lacks plausibility in view of the manifest expansion in the use of temporary sheriffs as the demands on the system as a whole have increased over the years. Rather than a control over numbers, the use of the one year term suggests a reservation of control over the tenure of office by the individual, enabling it to be brought to an end within a comparatively short period. This reinforces the impression that the tenure of office by the individual temporary sheriff is at the discretion of the Lord Advocate. It does not, at least prima facie, square with the appearance of independence.

45. Then there are what I have referred to as the restrictions applied by the Lord Advocate in determining whether a temporary sheriff qualifies for re-appointment. I refer to the minimum period of work which the temporary sheriff is expected to perform and the age limit of 65 years. For present purposes it does not matter that these do not form part of the terms of his appointment. What matters is that they clearly form part of the basis on which the temporary sheriff's prospective tenure of office rests. Neither is sanctioned by statute. They are matters of ministerial policy. They may change as one Lord Advocate succeeds another. As the Solicitor-General made clear, his description of the policy applied by the present Lord Advocate cannot be regarded as binding a successor. How such restrictions

are applied is evidently a matter for his discretion, as the practice of the present Lord Advocate in regard to the age limit demonstrates. The tendency of these restrictions is significant. The first tends, if anything, to eliminate the temporary sheriff who would prefer to sit only occasionally, and to encourage the participation of those who are interested in promotion to the office of permanent sheriff, or at least in their re-appointment as a temporary sheriff. The second may also have a similar effect.

46. There was, in my view, some force…that the terms of appointment might tend to encourage the perception that temporary sheriffs who were interested in their advancement might be influenced in their decision-making to avoid unpopularity with the Lord Advocate….

49. …[T]he power of recall…is incompatible with the independence and appearance of independence of the temporary sheriff….I regard the one year limit to the appointment as being a further critical factor arriving at the same result. As regards the difference in the basis of payment as between a temporary and a permanent sheriff, I would not be disposed to regard this in itself as critical. Rather it illustrates the difference in status to which I have already referred. I also accept that in this case there is a link between perceptions of independence and perceptions of impartiality, of the kind which has been categorised in Canada as institutional impartiality. I consider that there is a real risk that a well-informed observer would think that a temporary sheriff might be influenced by his hopes and fears as to his perspective advancement. I have reached the view that a temporary sheriff, such as Temporary Sheriff Crowe, was not an "independent and impartial tribunal" within the meaning of Article 6(1) of the Convention….

Tumey v. Ohio

273 U.S. 510 (1927)

Justices: Taft, C.J. and Holmes, Van Devanter, McReynolds, Brandeis, Sutherland, Butler, Sanford, and Stone JJ.

Opinion of the Court by Chief Justice Taft:

…All questions of judicial qualification may not involve constitutional validity. Thus matters of kinship, personal bias, state policy, remoteness of interest, would seem generally to be matters merely of legislative discretion….But it certainly violates the Fourteenth Amendment, and deprives a defendant in a criminal case of due process of law, to subject his liberty or property to the judgment of a court, the judge of which has a direct, personal, substantial, pecuniary interest in reaching a conclusion against him in his case.

The mayor of the Village of North College Hill, Ohio, had a direct, personal, pecuniary interest in convicting the defendant who came before him for trial, in the twelve dollars of costs imposed in his behalf, which he would not have received if the defendant had been acquitted.

...[I]n determining what due process of law is, under the Fifth or Fourteenth Amendment, the Court must look to those settled usages and modes of proceeding existing in the common and statute law of England before the emigration of our ancestors, which were shown not to have been unsuited to their civil and political condition by having been acted on by them after the settlement of this country. Counsel contend that in Ohio and in other States, in the economy which it is found necessary to maintain in the administration of justice in the inferior courts by justices of the peace and by judicial officers of like jurisdiction, the only compensation which the state and county and township can afford is the fees and costs earned by them, and that such compensation is so small that it is not to be regarded as likely to influence improperly a judicial officer in the discharge of his duty, or as prejudicing the defendant in securing justice even though the magistrate will receive nothing if the defendant is not convicted.

We have been referred to no cases at common law in England, prior to the separation of colonies from the mother country, showing a practice that inferior judicial officers were dependant upon the conviction of the defendant for receiving their compensation. Indeed, in analogous cases it is very clear that the slightest pecuniary interest of any officer, judicial or quasi-judicial, in the resolving of the subject-matter which he was to decide, rendered the decision voidable....

As early as 12 Richard II, A. D. 1388, it was provided that there should be a commission of the justices of the peace, with six justices in the county once a quarter, which might sit for three days, and that the justices should receive four shillings a day "as wages," to be paid by the sheriffs out of a fund made up of fines and amercements, and that that fund should be added to out of the fines and amercements from the Courts of the Lords of the Franchises which were hundred courts allowed by the king by grant to individuals....

The wages paid were not dependant on conviction of the defendant. They were paid at a time when the distinction between torts and criminal cases was not clear...and they came from a fund which was created by fines and amercements collected from both sides in the controversy....

From this review we conclude, that a system by which an inferior judge is paid for his service only when he convicts the defendant has not become so embedded by custom in the general practice either at common law or in this country that it can be regarded as due process of law, unless the costs usually imposed are so small that they may be properly ignored as within the maxim de minimis non curat lex.

The Mayor received for his fees and costs in the present case $12, and from such costs under the Prohibition Act for seven months he made about $100 a month in addition to his salary. We cannot regard the prospect of receipt or loss of such an emolument in each case as a minute, remote, trifling, or insignificant interest. It is certainly not fair to each defendant brought before the mayor for the careful and judicial consideration of his guilt or innocence, that the prospect of such a prospective loss by the Mayor should weigh against his acquittal.

These are not cases in which the penalties and the costs are negligible. The field of jurisdiction is not that of a small community, engaged in enforcing its own local regulations. The court is a state agency, imposing substantial punishment, and the cases to be considered are gathered from the whole county by the energy of the village marshals, and detectives regularly employed by the village for the purpose. It is not to be treated as a mere village tribunal for village peccadilloes. There are doubtless mayors who would not allow such a consideration as $12 costs in each case to affect their judgment in it; but the requirement of due process of law in judicial procedure is not satisfied by the argument that men of the highest honor and the greatest self-sacrifice could carry it on without danger of injustice. Every procedure which would offer a possible temptation to the average man as a judge to forget the burden of proof required to convict the defendant, or which might lead him not to hold the balance nice, clear, and true between the State and the accused, denies the latter due process of law....

Reference re Remuneration of Judges of the Provincial Court (P.E.I.)

[1997] 3 S.C.R. 3 (Can.)
Justices present: Lamer, C.J. and La Forest, L'Heureux-Dubé, Sopinka, Gonthier, Cory, and Iacobucci, JJ.

Opinion by Chief Justice Lamer (La Forest, J. dissenting in part):

1. The four appeals handed down today—*Reference re Remuneration of Judges of the Provincial Court of Prince Edward Island* (No. 24508), *Reference re Independence and Impartiality of Judges of the Provincial Court of Prince Edward Island* (No. 24778), *R. v. Campbell, R. v. Ekmecic and R. v. Wickman* (No. 24831), and *Manitoba Provincial Judges Assn. v. Manitoba (Minister of Justice)* (No. 24846)—raise a range of issues relating to the independence of provincial courts, but are united by a single issue: whether and how the guarantee of judicial independence in s. 11(*d*) of the Canadian Charter of Rights and Freedoms [which provides that " Any person charged with an offence has the right...(d) to be presumed innocent until proven guilty according to law in a fair and public hearing by an independent and impartial tribunal"] restricts the manner by and the extent to which provincial governments and legislatures can reduce the salaries of provincial court judges....

118. The three *core characteristics* of judicial independence—security of tenure, financial security, and administrative independence—should be contrasted with what I have termed the *two dimensions* of judicial

independence.... [W]hile individual independence attaches to individual judges, institutional or collective independence attaches to the court or tribunal as an institutional entity. [As Justice Le Dain explained in *Valente* [1985] 2 S.C.R. 673, at 687], the two different dimensions of judicial independence are related in the following way:

> The relationship between these two aspects of judicial independence is that an individual judge may enjoy the essential conditions of judicial independence but if the court or tribunal over which he or she presides is not independent of the other branches of government, in what is essential to its function, he or she cannot be said to be an independent tribunal.

121. ...[F]inancial security has *both* an individual and an institutional or collective dimension. *Valente* only talked about the individual dimension of financial security, when it stated that salaries must be established by law and not allow for executive interference in a manner which could "affect the independence of the individual judge" (p. 706). Similarly, in *Généreux* [[1992] 1 S.C.R. 259], this Court...held that performance-related pay for the conduct of judge advocates and members of a General Court Martial during the Court Martial violated s. 11(*d*), because it could reasonably lead to the perception that those *individuals* might alter their conduct during a hearing in order to favour the military establishment.

122. ...[T]o determine whether financial security has a collective or institutional dimension, and if so, what collective or institutional financial security looks like, we must first understand what the institutional independence of the judiciary is.... [T]he conclusion...builds upon traditional understandings of the proper constitutional relationship between the judiciary, the executive, and the legislature....

131. ...[F]inancial security for the courts as an institution has three components, which all flow from the constitutional imperative that, to the extent possible, the relationship between the judiciary and the other branches of government be *depoliticized*.... [T]his imperative demands that the courts both be free and appear to be free from political interference through economic manipulation by the other branches of government, and that they not become entangled in the politics of remuneration from the public purse....

133. *First*, as a general constitutional principle, the salaries of provincial court judges can be reduced, increased, or frozen, either as part of an overall economic measure which affects the salaries of all or some persons who are remunerated from public funds, or as part of a measure which is directed at provincial court judges as a class. However, any changes to or freezes in judicial remuneration require prior recourse to a special process, which is independent, effective, and objective, for determining judicial remuneration, to avoid the possibility of, or the appearance of, political

interference through economic manipulation. What judicial independence requires is an independent body, along the lines of the bodies that exist in many provinces and at the federal level to set or recommend the levels of judicial remuneration. Those bodies are often referred to as commissions, and for the sake of convenience, we will refer to the independent body required by s. 11(*d*) as a commission as well. Governments are constitutionally bound to go through the commission process. The recommendations of the commission would not be binding on the executive or the legislature. Nevertheless, though those recommendations are non-binding, they should not be set aside lightly, and, if the executive or the legislature chooses to depart from them, it has to justify its decision—if need be, in a court of law.... [W]hen governments propose to single out judges as a class for a pay reduction, the burden of justification will be heavy.

134. *Second,* under no circumstances is it permissible for the judiciary —not only collectively through representative organizations, but also as individuals—to engage in negotiations over remuneration with the executive or representatives of the legislature. Any such negotiations would be fundamentally at odds with judicial independence.... [S]alary negotiations are indelibly political, because remuneration from the public purse is an inherently political issue. Moreover, negotiations would undermine the appearance of judicial independence, because the Crown is almost always a party to criminal prosecutions before provincial courts, and because salary negotiations engender a set of expectations about the behaviour of parties to those negotiations which are inimical to judicial independence.... Negotiations over remuneration and benefits, in colloquial terms, are a form of "horse-trading." The prohibition on negotiations therefore does not preclude expressions of concern or representations by chief justices and chief judges, and organizations that represent judges, to governments regarding the adequacy of judicial remuneration.

135. Third, and finally, any reductions to judicial remuneration, including de facto reductions through the erosion of judicial salaries by inflation, cannot take those salaries below a basic minimum level of remuneration which is required for the office of a judge. Public confidence in the independence of the judiciary would be undermined if judges were paid at such a low rate that they could be perceived as susceptible to political pressure through economic manipulation, as is witnessed in many countries....

La Forest, J. (dissenting in part):

296. The primary issue raised in these appeals is a narrow one: has the reduction of the salaries of provincial court judges, in the circumstances of each of these cases, so affected the independence of these judges that persons "charged with an offence" before them are deprived of their right to "an independent and impartial tribunal" within the meaning of s. 11(*d*) of the *Canadian Charter of Rights and Freedoms*?... I cannot concur with his conclusion that s. 11(*d*) forbids governments from changing judges' salaries without first having recourse to the "judicial compensation commissions."....

Furthermore, I do not believe that s. 11(*d*) prohibits salary discussions between governments and judges. In my view, reading these requirements into s. 11(*d*) represents both an unjustified departure from established precedents and a partial usurpation of the provinces' power to set the salaries of inferior court judges pursuant to ss. 92(4) and 92(14) of the *Constitution Act, 1867*....

329. ...While both salary commissions and a concomitant policy to avoid discussing remuneration other than through the making of representations to commissions may be desirable as matters of legislative policy, they are not mandated by s. 11(*d*) of the *Charter*....By its express terms, s. 11(*d*) grants the right to an independent tribunal to persons "charged with an offence." The guarantee of judicial independence inhering in s. 11(*d*) redounds to the benefit of the judged, not the judges....Section 11(*d*), therefore, does not grant judges a level of independence to which they feel they are entitled. Rather, it guarantees only that degree of independence necessary to ensure that accused persons receive fair trials....

335. I agree that financial security has a collective dimension. Judicial independence must include protection against interference with the financial security of the court *as an institution*. It is not enough that the right to a salary is established by law and that individual judges are protected against arbitrary changes to their remuneration. The possibility of economic manipulation also arises from changes to the salaries of judges as a class.

336. The fact that the potential for such manipulation exists, however, does not justify the imposition of judicial compensation commissions as a constitutional imperative. As noted above, s. 11(*d*) does not mandate "any particular legislative or constitutional formula": *Valente, supra,* at p. 693....This Court has repeatedly held that s. 11(*d*) requires only that courts exercising criminal jurisdiction be reasonably perceived as independent. In *Valente, supra,* Le Dain, J. wrote the following for the Court at p. 689:

> Although judicial independence is a status or relationship resting on objective conditions or guarantees, as well as a state of mind or attitude in the actual exercise of judicial functions, it is sound, I think, that the test for independence for the purposes of s. 11(*d*) of the *Charter* should be, as for impartiality, whether the tribunal may be reasonably perceived as independent. Both independence and impartiality are fundamental not only to the capacity to do justice in a particular case but also to individual and public confidence in the administration of justice. Without that confidence the system cannot command the respect and acceptance that are essential to its effective operation. It is, therefore, important that a tribunal should be perceived as independent, as well as impartial, and that the test for independence should include that perception. The perception must, however, as I have suggested, be a perception of whether the tribunal enjoys the essential objective conditions or guarantees of judicial independence, and not a perception of how it will in fact act, regardless of whether it enjoys such conditions or guarantees....

337. In my view, it is abundantly clear that a reasonable, informed person would not perceive that, in the absence of a commission process,

all changes to the remuneration of provincial court judges threaten their independence. I reach this conclusion by considering the type of change to judicial salaries that is at issue in the present appeals. It is simply not reasonable to think that a decrease to judicial salaries that is part of an overall economic measure which affects the salaries of substantially all persons paid from public funds imperils the independence of the judiciary. To hold otherwise is to assume that judges could be influenced or manipulated by such a reduction. A reasonable person, I submit, would believe judges are made of sturdier stuff than this....

349. I now turn to the question of discussions between the judiciary and the government over salaries. In the absence of a commission process, the only manner in which judges may have a say in the setting of their salaries is through direct dialogue with the executive. The Chief Justice terms these discussions "negotiations" and would prohibit them, in all circumstances, as violations of the financial security component of judicial independence. According to him, negotiations threaten independence because a "reasonable person might conclude that judges would alter the manner in which they adjudicate cases in order to curry favour with the executive" (para. 187).

350. In my view, this position seriously mischaracterizes the manner in which judicial salaries are set. *Valente* establishes that the fixing of provincial court judges' remuneration is entirely within the discretion of the government, subject, of course, to the conditions that the right to a salary be established by law and that the government not change salaries in a manner that raises a reasonable apprehension of interference. There is no constitutional requirement that the executive discuss, consult or "negotiate" with provincial court judges.... Provincial judges associations are not unions, and the government and the judges are not involved in a statutorily compelled collective bargaining relationship. While judges are free to make recommendations regarding their salaries, and governments would be wise to seriously consider them, as a group they have no economic "bargaining power" vis-à-vis the government. The atmosphere of negotiation the Chief Justice describes, which fosters expectations of "give and take" and encourages "subtle accommodations," does not therefore apply to salary discussions between government and the judiciary. The danger that is alleged to arise from such discussions—that judges will barter their independence for financial gain—is thus illusory.

Notes and Questions

1. First, consider questions of appointment illustrated by *Starrs v. Ruxton*. Note also that a decision of the South African Constitutional Court, reviewing the procedures for appointment of magistrates and oversight of them, also relied on *Valente* and, while concluding that problems existed, did not vacate the convictions rendered. *See Van Rooyen v. State* 2002 (5) SA 246 (CC) (S. Afr.).

   If a one-year appointment and possible recall or reappointment by the Lord Advocate undermines the perception of impartiality, what other systems of appointments are problematic? Would it be better to have fixed, nonrenewable appointments of several years, as is provided in the Constitutional Court of Germany and in the Conseil Constitutionnel in France? Should appointing authorities not be able to select judges to "bench climb"—moving from one level of court to another? What about popular elections—as opposed to the official appointment—of a judge for a specified term? What rules should govern those elections? If elected, ought judges be able to stand for reelection?

Consider also a distinction drawn between "impartiality" and the "appearance of impartiality." How coherent is the line between the two? What about the distinction between the fact and the perception of independence? Can one design systems to respond to these concerns?

As one might imagine, the literature on these issues is vast. For a focus on the interaction among factors, *see* Vicki C. Jackson, *Packages of Judicial Independence: The Selection and Tenure of Article III Judges*, 95 GEO. L.J. 965 (2007); for discussion of the relationship of methods of selection and the longevity of service to legitimacy of courts in democracies, *see* Judith Resnik, *Judicial Selection and Democratic Theory: Demand, Supply, and Life Tenure*, 26 CARDOZO L. REV. 579 (2005). The relationship between majoritarianism and judicial elections is discussed by David E. Pozen in *The Irony of Judicial Elections*, 108 COL. L. REV. 265 (2008), and the fall 2008 volume of the *American Academy of Arts and Sciences' Journal, Daedelus*, is devoted to the topic of judicial independence. Analyses of the law in Europe on these issues can be found in HUMAN RIGHTS LAW AND PRACTICE (Lord Lester of Herne Hill & David Pannick eds., 2d ed. 2004); MARTIN KUIJER, THE BLINDFOLD OF LADY JUSTICE: JUDICIAL INDEPENDENCE AND IMPARTIALITY IN LIGHT OF THE REQUIREMENT OF ARTICLE 6 ECHR (Leiden het: E.M. Meijers Institute 2004).

As England and Wales have revamped their selection procedures and critics argue that Canada, Australia, and the United States are in need of doing so as well, many commentaries have been produced. *See, e.g.*, APPOINTING JUDGES IN AN AGE OF JUDICIAL POWER: CRITICAL PERSPECTIVES FROM AROUND THE WORLD (Kate Malleson & Peter H. Russell eds., University of Toronoto Press, 2006); REFORMING THE COURT: TERM LIMITS FOR SUPREME COURT JUSTICES (Roger C. Cramton and Paul D.Carrington, eds., Carolina Academic Press, 2006); Kate Malleson, *Parliamentary Scrutiny of Supreme Court Nominees: A View of the United Kingdom*, 44 OSGOODE HALL L.J. 557 (2006). Some of this discussion points to the South African process, using merit commissions, as a model. *See* Penelope E. Andrews, *The South African Judicial Appointments Process*, 44 OSGOODE HALL L.J. 565 (2006). More generally, interest is focused on comparisons. *See* Lee Epstein, Jack Knight & Olga Shvetsova, *Selecting Selection Systems*, in JUDICIAL INDEPENDENCE AT THE CROSSROADS: AN INTERDISCIPLINARY APPROACH 191 (Stephen B. Burbank & Barry Friedman eds., Sage Publications, 2002).

2. What are the legal mechanisms for protecting independence other than length of service? Review the provisions of the South African and U.S. Constitutions as well as those of the ECHR and of the United Nations. How do they differ? Are they sufficient? Would you rewrite any of them and if so, with what mandates? As you consider these issues, do note that many judges in the federal system in the United States—including those called "magistrate" and "bankruptcy" judges and "administrative law judges" or "hearing officers"—are not appointed through the Article III process or given life tenure. Some sit for fixed terms, some are appointed as line employees, and some are civil servants, protected by statutes.

Consider also the question of culture: how do rules and laws interact with cultures of professionalism and adjudication? How does one develop or sustain commitments to independence? What role do the institutional organizations of lawyers, the press, and the development of special interest groups play in that regard? What roles should judges themselves take in these debates?

3. Consider next the question of payment, both to individual judges and to judiciaries. *Tumey* did not rule out "user fees"—and indeed that form of subsidy for courts, with a pay-as-you-go system, is commonplace. The idea is to price services from filing fees to court time. In 2007, England and Wales amended its fee structure for civil court proceedings to graduate the fees depending on the services provided. *See* Civil Proceedings Fees (Amendment), 2007, S.I. 2007/2176, (L. 16), *available at* http://www.opsi.gov.uk/si/si2007/uksi_20072176_en_1 (last visited July 31, 2008).

4. In 1927, the Court in *Tumey v. Ohio* did not propose that federal constitutional due process requirements of impartiality reached "matters of kinship, personal bias, state policy, remoteness of interest." Such matters, the justices reasoned, were a matter of state law. Ought variation be permitted within a federation on those issues? That part of the *Tumey* judgment is no longer good law as the Supreme Court has found that the U.S. Constitution's insistence on due process requires state and federal courts to insist that certain forms of connection by judges to either the parties or the subject matter of a lawsuit renders them unable to decide them. On most points, (see the discussion below about judicial salaries), *Tumey's* holding about the receipt of funds based on decisions for or against a litigant remains the law in the United States. *See Ward v. Village of Monroeville,* 409 U.S. 57 (1972).

   Furthermore, its principles are now supplemented through statutes in many jurisdictions and by canons of judicial ethics. For example, federal judges are subject to the provisions of 28 U.S.C. § 455, excerpted below and setting forth grounds for disqualification. Consider whether this codification captures all (or too many) concerns and whether its reliance on self-appraisal by the challenged judge is wise.

   (a) Any justice, judge, or magistrate judge of the United States shall disqualify himself in any proceeding in which his impartiality might reasonably be questioned.
   (b) He shall also disqualify himself in the following circumstances:
      (1) Where he has a personal bias or prejudice concerning a party, or personal knowledge of disputed evidentiary facts concerning the proceeding;
      (2) Where in private practice he served as lawyer in the matter in controversy, or a lawyer with whom he previously practiced law served during such association as a lawyer concerning the matter, or the judge or such lawyer has been a material witness concerning it;
      (3) Where he has served in governmental employment and in such capacity participated as counsel, adviser or material witness concerning the proceeding or expressed an opinion concerning the merits of the particular case in controversy;
      (4) He knows that he, individually or as a fiduciary, or his spouse or minor child residing in his household, has a financial interest in the subject matter in controversy or in a party to the proceeding, or any other interest that could be substantially affected by the outcome of the proceeding;
      (5) He or his spouse, or a person within the third degree of relationship to either of them, or the spouse of such a person:

(i) Is a party to the proceeding, or an officer, director, or trustee of a party;
(ii) Is acting as a lawyer in the proceeding;
(iii) Is known by the judge to have an interest that could be substantially affected by the outcome of the proceeding;
(iv) Is to the judge's knowledge likely to be a material witness in the proceeding....

(d) For the purposes of this section the following words or phrases shall have the meaning indicated:
(1) "proceeding" includes pretrial, trial, appellate review, or other stages of litigation;...(4) "financial interest" means ownership of a legal or equitable interest, however small, or a relationship as director, adviser, or other active participant in the affairs of a party, except that:
(i) Ownership in a mutual or common investment fund that holds securities is not a "financial interest" in such securities unless the judge participates in the management of the fund;...

(e) No justice, judge, or magistrate judge shall accept from the parties to the proceeding a waiver of any ground for disqualification enumerated in subsection (b). Where the ground for disqualification arises only under subsection (a), waiver may be accepted provided it is preceded by a full disclosure on the record of the basis for disqualification.

(f) Notwithstanding the preceding provisions of this section, if any justice, judge,—magistrate judge—, or bankruptcy judge to whom a matter has been assigned would be disqualified, after substantial judicial time has been devoted to the matter, because of the appearance or discovery, after the matter was assigned to him or her, that he or she individually or as a fiduciary, or his or her spouse or minor child residing in his or her household, has a financial interest in a party (other than an interest that could be substantially affected by the outcome), disqualification is not required if the justice, judge, magistrate judge, bankruptcy judge, spouse or minor child, as the case may be, divests himself or herself of the interest that provides the grounds for the disqualification.

As you review these grounds, consider whether the statute has it right. Ought a belated discovery (section f) be ignored if the same discovery earlier in a case would have ousted the judge? Ought additional bases to be added? For example, if a judge writes an article expressing a view about a legal issue (for example, that saying prayers in school does not violate religious liberties or that affirmative action ought to be prohibited), should disqualification follow? Consider also who should make decisions about disqualification. Why does the statute ask the challenged judge to decide the question? Should the issue be determined by someone else? By whom? And how?

5. Consider, under the *Tumey* principles, whether federal judges could sit on a case challenging the failure of Congress to give them a cost-of-living ("COLA") salary increase. The judge-plaintiffs argued that they had an Article III right to an undiminished salary and COLAs were part of that guarantee. What judges could sit on that decision? The U.S. Supreme Court has concluded that when cases arise in which all federal judges would be disqualified, all can under a "rule of necessity" sit to hear the case. *See United States v. Will* 449 U.S. 200 (1980). As several commentators have argued, state judges and other alternatives exist.

Does the Canadian approach—of mandating a commission to decide salaries for provincial judges—solve the problem of judicial entanglement? Could the Canadian Court have mandated that its justices' salaries be set that way? Note that in that decision, the majority concluded that the decisions of that commission were subject to judicial review. Consider the parameters, set forth below, outlined in *Reference re Remuneration of Judges of the Provincial Court*, for judicial review of commission decisions.

179. What judicial independence requires is that the executive or the legislature, whichever is vested with the authority to set judicial remuneration under provincial legislation, must formally respond to the contents of the commission's report within a specified amount of time. Before it can set judges' salaries, the executive must issue a report in which it outlines its response to the commission's recommendations. If the legislature is involved in the process, the report of the commission must be laid before the legislature, when it is in session, with due diligence. If the legislature is not in session, the government may wait until a new sitting commences. The legislature should deal with the report directly, with due diligence and reasonable dispatch.

180. Furthermore, if after turning its mind to the report of the commission, the executive or the legislature, as applicable, chooses not to accept one or more of the recommendations in that report, it must be prepared to justify this decision, if necessary in a court of law. The reasons for this decision would be found either in the report of the executive responding to the contents of the commission's report, or in the recitals to the resolution of the legislature on the matter. An unjustified decision could potentially lead to a finding of unconstitutionality. The need for public justification...emerges from one of the purposes of s. 11(*d*)'s guarantee of judicial independence—to ensure public confidence in the justice system. A decision by the executive or the legislature, to change or freeze judges' salaries, and then to disagree with a recommendation not to act on that decision made by a constitutionally mandated body whose existence is premised on the need to preserve the independence of the judiciary, will only be legitimate and not be viewed as being indifferent or hostile to judicial independence, if it is supported by reasons....

183. The standard of justification...is one of simple rationality. It requires that the government articulate a legitimate reason for why it has chosen to depart from the recommendation of the commission, and if applicable, why it has chosen to treat judges differently from other persons paid from the public purse. A reviewing court does not engage in a searching analysis of the relationship between ends and means, which is the hallmark of a s. 1 analysis. However, the absence of this analysis does not mean that the standard of justification is ineffectual. On the contrary, it has two aspects. First, it screens out decisions with respect to judicial remuneration which are based on purely political considerations, or which are enacted for discriminatory reasons. Changes to or freezes in remuneration can only be justified for reasons which relate to the public interest, broadly understood. Second, if judicial review is sought, a reviewing court must inquire into the reasonableness of the factual foundation of the claim made by the government, similar to the way that we have evaluated whether there was an economic emergency in Canada in our jurisprudence under the division of powers (*Reference re Anti-Inflation Act*, [1976] 2 S.C.R. 373).

184. Although the test of justification—one of simple rationality—must be met by all measures which affect judicial remuneration and which depart from the recommendation of the salary commission, some will satisfy that test more easily than others, because they pose less of a danger of being used as a means of economic manipulation, and hence of political interference. Across-the-board measures which affect substantially every person who is paid from the public purse, in my opinion, are *prima facie* rational. For example, an across-the-board reduction in salaries that includes judges will typically be designed to effectuate the government's overall

fiscal priorities, and hence will usually be aimed at furthering some sort of larger public interest. By contrast, a measure directed at judges alone may require a somewhat fuller explanation, precisely because it is directed at judges alone.

185. By laying down a set of guidelines to assist provincial legislatures in designing judicial compensation commissions, I do not intend to lay down a particular institutional framework in constitutional stone. What s. 11(*d*) requires is an institutional sieve between the judiciary and the other branches of government. Commissions are merely a means to that end. In the future, governments may create new institutional arrangements which can serve the same end, but in a different way. As long as those institutions meet the three cardinal requirements of independence, effectiveness, and objectivity, s. 11(*d*) will be complied with....

6. What about financing beyond salaries? How do judiciaries obtain new funds for buildings? Staff? In many countries, it is common for a ministry of justice to serve as the "voice" of the judiciary seeking provisions from legislatures. Until 1939 in the United States, departments within the executive branch took that role, and after the Department of Justice was formed in the second half of the nineteenth century, it did so, even as it was a regular litigant within the federal courts. What are the alternatives? A "chancellor" for judges who is not a judge but independent of other branches of government? Judges, as a collective, shaping agendas and submitting their proposals (or testifying) before legislative or executive committees?

3

Federal Powers and the Principle of Subsidiarity

Daniel Halberstam

Federal systems across the world are generally designed according to the principle of subsidiarity, which in one form or another holds that the central government should play only a supporting role in governance, acting if and only if the constituent units of government are incapable of acting on their own. The word itself is related to the idea of assistance, as in "subsidy," and is derived from the Latin "subsidium," which referred to auxiliary troops in the Roman military. *See* Oxford Latin Dictionary s.v. (1983).

The modern idea of subsidiarity is usually traced to Catholic social doctrine, articulated most clearly in the papal encyclical *Quadragesimo Anno* (1931), which sought to stave off the takeover of civil society by ever-expanding state power:

> Just as it is gravely wrong to take from individuals what they can accomplish by their own initiative and industry and give it to the community, so also it is an injustice and at the same time a grave evil and disturbance of right order to assign to a greater and higher association what lesser and subordinate organizations can do. For every social activity ought of its very nature to furnish help to the members of the body social, and never destroy and absorb them. Para. 79[1]

The current Catechism of the Catholic Church puts the idea more succinctly:

> [A] community of a higher order should not interfere in the internal life of a community of a lower order, depriving the latter of its functions, but rather should support it in case of need and help to co-ordinate its activity with the activities of the rest of society, always with a view to the common good. Catechism of the Catholic Church, Para. 1883

Contrary to its predominant usage in the literature as signifying exclusively a restraint on the central government, subsidiarity thus also stands for the

[1] Available in English at http://www.vatican.va/holy_father/pius_xi/encyclicals/documents/hf_p-xi_enc_19310515_quadragesimo-anno_en.html.

justification of central involvement in affairs that cannot adequately be handled at the local level.

The word "subsidiarity" may well sound foreign to Americans, but the federal power principle it stands for should ring familiar. It corresponds to some of the basic tenets underlying federalism in the United States, beginning with the Virginia Plan, which James Madison wrote and Edmund Randolph introduced on the first day of substantive business in the Constitutional Convention as the blueprint for the Constitution. That plan, for example, proposed that the national legislature be granted the power "to legislate in all cases to which the separate States are incompetent, or in which the harmony of the United States may be interrupted by the exercise of individual Legislation." THE RECORDS OF THE FEDERAL CONVENTION OF 1787 20, 21 (Max Farrand, ed., 1911). The Constitutional Convention adopted this provision before sending it to the Committee of Detail, which used it to draft the more specific enumeration of federal powers we now find in Article I, Section 8.

This general federal power principle in one form or another continues to inform political rhetoric, *see, e.g.*, Executive Order 13132, 64 FED. REG. 43255–43259 (August 10, 1999), but subsidiarity and the Virginia Plan's power formula have not been salient features in the operation of our constitutional law at least since Chief Justice Marshall's opinion in *McCulloch v. Maryland*, 17 U.S. 316 (1819). The State of Maryland argued there that the Necessary and Proper Clause had been inserted to clarify that the new Congress, unlike the Congress of the Confederation, could pass laws with binding effect on citizens. As a result, in Maryland's view, that clause constrained Congress's lawmaking generally, allowing only such legislation as was "necessary and proper." *Id.* at 412. The Court, however, disagreed, holding that the Necessary and Proper Clause does not restrict the enumeration of powers elsewhere, but instead removes all doubts regarding Congress's great mass of (additional) powers incidental to those specifically enumerated elsewhere in the Constitution. *See id.* at 412, 420–421. Moreover, even with regard to the additional power conferred on Congress by the Necessary and Proper Clause, judicial review of the "necessity" of federal action would be highly deferential. The Court thus officially set aside any serious examination of the "necessity" of federal action as a tool of constitutional interpretation or of judicial review in the United States.

Not so elsewhere. Canada's Constitution (formerly the British North America Act of 1867) enumerates both federal and provincial government powers. Section 91, which enumerates the federal government's powers, is far more detailed than Article I, Section 8 of the U.S. Constitution. Next to broad topics such as "[t]he Regulation of Trade and Commerce," Const. Act, 1867, Sec. 91(2), Section 91 includes more specific entries such as "Banking, Incorporation of Banks, and the Issue of Paper Money," Const. Act, 1867, Sec. 91(15), which were in part designed to avoid certain constitutional controversies that had previously consumed the United States. Section 92, in turn, expressly gives the Canadian Provinces exclusive power over a whole range of subjects, from the more circumscribed "Establishment and Tenure of Provincial Offices and the Appointment and Payment of Provincial Officers," Const. Act, 1867, Sec. 92(4), to the potentially broad "Property and Civil Rights in the Province," Const. Act, 1867, Sec. 92(13).

Section 92 also contains a residual category of exclusive provincial power over "Generally all Matters of a merely local or private Nature in the Province." Const. Act, 1867, Sec. 92(16). Finally, and most important for present purposes, Section 91, contains a competing residual clause, authorizing the federal government "to make laws for the Peace, Order, and good Government of Canada, in relation to all Matters not coming within the Classes of Subjects by this Act assigned exclusively to the Legislatures of the Provinces." Const. Act, 1867, Sec. 91.

The following controversy arose over whether the federal Ocean Dumping Control Act, which could not be justified as an exercise of one of the more specific federal powers, fell within the federal government's residual power under the "Peace, Order, and Good Government" ("P.O.G.G.") Clause. In interpreting the scope of federal powers under the P.O.G.G. Clause, the Canadian Supreme Court analyzed the federal law in terms of subsidiarity.

Regina v. Crown Zellerbach Canada Ltd.

Supreme Court of Canada, [1988] 1 S.C.R. 401

Per Le Dain, J. (Dickson, C.J.C., McIntyre and Wilson, JJ., concurring): In issue is the validity of s. 4(1) of the Ocean Dumping Control Act, S.C. 1974–75–76, c. 55, which prohibits the dumping of any substance at sea except in accordance with the terms and conditions of a permit, the sea being defined for the purposes of the Act as including the internal [provincial] waters of Canada other than fresh waters....

I

The respondent carries on logging operations on Vancouver Island in connection with its forest products business in British Columbia.... On 16th and 17th August 1980 the respondent, using an 80-foot crane operating from a moored scow, dredged wood waste from the ocean floor immediately adjacent to the shoreline at the site of its log dump in Beaver Cove and deposited it in the deeper waters of the cove approximately 60 to 80 feet seaward of where the wood waste had been dredged. The purpose of the dredging and dumping was to allow a new A-frame structure for log dumping to be floated on a barge to the shoreline for installation there and to give clearance for the dumping of bundled logs from the A-frame structure into the waters of the log dump area. The wood waste consisted of waterlogged logging debris such as bark, wood and slabs. There is no evidence of any dispersal of the wood waste or any effect on navigation or marine life....

II

[T]he Act, viewed as a whole, may be properly characterized as directed to the control or regulation of marine pollution.... The chosen, and perhaps only effective, regulatory model makes it necessary, in order to prevent marine pollution, to prohibit the dumping of any substance without a permit. Its purpose is to require a permit so that the regulatory authority may determine before the proposed dumping has occurred whether it may be permitted upon certain terms and conditions[.]. The Act is concerned with the dumping of substances which may be shown or presumed to have an adverse effect on the marine environment. The Minister and not the person proposing to do the dumping must be the judge of this....

IV

It is necessary... to consider the national dimensions or national concern doctrine (as it is now generally referred to) of the federal peace, order and good government power as a possible basis for the constitutional validity of s. 4(1) of the Act, as applied to the control of dumping in provincial marine waters.

The national concern doctrine was... given its modern formulation by Viscount Simon in *A.G. Ont. v. Can. Temperance Fed.*, [1946] A.C. 193, [205–206]... [:]

> In their Lordships' opinion, the true test must be found in the real subject matter of the legislation: if it is such that it goes beyond local or provincial concern or interests and must from its inherent nature be the concern of the Dominion as a whole (as, for example, in the Aeronautics case and the Radio case), then it will fall within the competence of the Dominion Parliament as a matter affecting the peace, order and good government of Canada, though it may in another aspect touch on matters specially reserved to the provincial legislatures. War and pestilence, no doubt, are instances; so, too, may be the drink or drug traffic, or the carrying of arms. In *Russell v. The Queen*, Sir Montague Smith gave as an instance of valid Dominion legislation a law which prohibited or restricted the sale or exposure of cattle having a contagious disease. Nor is the validity of the legislation, when due to its inherent nature, affected because there may still be room for enactments by a provincial legislature dealing with an aspect of the same subject in so far as it specially affects that province....

In [*Labatt Breweries of Canada Ltd. v. Attorney General of Canada*, [1980] 1 S.C.R. 914, 944–45],... Estey J., with whom Martland, Dickson and Beetz JJ.

concurred,...summed up the doctrine with respect to that basis of federal legislative jurisdiction as falling into three categories: (a) the cases "basing the federal competence on the existence of a national emergency"; (b) the cases in which "federal competence arose because the subject matter did not exist at the time of Confederation and clearly cannot be put into the class of matters of a merely local or private nature," of which aeronautics and radio were cited as examples; and (c) the cases in which "the subject matter" goes beyond local or provincial concern or interest and must, from its inherent nature, be the concern of the Dominion as a whole," citing Can. Temperance Fed. Thus Estey J. saw the national concern doctrine enunciated in Can. Temperance Fed. as covering the case, not of a new subject matter which did not exist at Confederation, but of one that may have begun as a matter of a local or provincial concern but had become one of national concern. He referred to that category as "a matter of national concern transcending the local authorities' power to meet and solve it by legislation," and quoted in support of this statement of the test a passage from Professor Hogg's Constitutional Law of Canada, 1st ed. (1977), at p. 261, in which it was said that "the most important element of national dimension or national concern is a need for one national law which cannot realistically be satisfied by cooperative provincial action because the failure of one province to cooperate would carry with it grave consequences for the residents of other provinces."...

From this survey of the opinions expressed in this court concerning the national concern doctrine of the federal peace, order and good government power I draw the following conclusions as to what now appears to be firmly established:

1. The national concern doctrine is separate and distinct from the national emergency doctrine of the peace, order and good government power, which is chiefly distinguishable by the fact that it provides a constitutional basis for what is necessarily legislation of a temporary nature;

2. The national concern doctrine applies to both new matters which did not exist at Confederation and to matters which, although originally matters of a local or private nature in a province, have since, in the absence of national emergency, become matters of national concern;

3. For a matter to qualify as a matter of national concern in either sense it must have a singleness, distinctiveness and indivisibility that clearly distinguishes it from matters of provincial concern and a scale of impact on provincial jurisdiction that is reconcilable with the fundamental distribution of legislative power under the Constitution;

4. In determining whether a matter has attained the required degree of singleness, distinctiveness and indivisibility that clearly distinguishes it from matters of provincial concern it is relevant to consider what would be the effect on extra-provincial interests of a provincial failure to deal effectively with the control or regulation of the intra-provincial aspects of the matter.

This last factor, generally referred to as the "provincial inability" test and noted with apparent approval in this court in Labatt, Schneider and Wetmore, was suggested...by Professor Gibson in his article, "Measuring 'National Dimensions'" (1976), 7 Man. L.J. 15, [34–35]...:

> "By this approach, a national dimension would exist whenever a significant aspect of a problem is beyond provincial reach because it falls within the jurisdiction of another province or of the federal Parliament. It is important to emphasize however that the entire problem would not fall within federal competence in such circumstances. Only that aspect of the problem that is beyond provincial control would do so. Since the 'P.O. & G.G.' clause bestows only residual powers, the existence of a national dimension justifies no more federal legislation than is necessary to fill the gap in provincial powers. For example, federal jurisdiction to legislate for pollution of interprovincial waterways or to control 'pollution price-wars' would (in the absence of other independent sources of federal competence) extend only to measures to reduce the risk that citizens of one province would be harmed by the non-co-operation of another province or provinces."...

V

Marine pollution, because of its predominantly extra-provincial as well as international character and implications, is clearly a matter of concern to Canada as a whole. The question is whether the control of pollution by the dumping of substances in marine [i.e. salt] waters, including provincial marine waters, is a single, indivisible matter, distinct from the control of pollution by the dumping of substances in other [i.e. fresh] provincial waters....

...In many cases the pollution of fresh waters will have a pollutant effect in the marine waters into which they flow, and this is noted by the United Nations Report, but that report...emphasizes that marine pollution, because of the differences in the composition and action of marine waters and fresh waters, has its own characteristics and scientific considerations that distinguish it from fresh water pollution. Moreover, the distinction between salt water and fresh water as limiting the application of the Ocean Dumping Control Act meets the consideration emphasized by a majority of this court in [prior case law] that in order for a matter to qualify as one of national concern falling within the federal peace, order and good government power it must have ascertainable and reasonable limits, insofar as its impact on provincial jurisdiction is concerned.

For these reasons I am of the opinion that s. 4(1) of the Ocean Dumping Control Act is constitutionally valid as enacted...and...in its application to the dumping of waste in the waters of Beaver Cove....

La Forest, J., (dissenting) (Beetz and Lamer, JJ., concurring):

...Many of th[e] subjects [such as radio, aeronautics, or the capitol region] are new and are obviously of extra- provincial concern. They are thus appropriate for assignment to the general federal legislative power. They are often related to matters intimately tied to federal jurisdiction. Radio (which is relevant to the power to regulate interprovincial undertakings) is an example. The closely contested issue of narcotics control...is intimately related to criminal law and international trade [both of which are enumerated powers of the federal government].

The need to make such characterizations from time to time is readily apparent. From this necessary function, however, it is easy but, I say it with respect, fallacious to go further, and, taking a number of quite separate areas of activity, some under accepted constitutional values within federal, and some within provincial legislative capacity, consider them to be a single indivisible matter of national interest and concern lying outside the specific heads of power assigned under the Constitution. By conceptualizing broad social, economic and political issues in that way, one can effectively invent new heads of federal power under the national dimensions doctrine, thereby incidentally removing them from provincial jurisdiction or at least abridging the provinces' freedom of operation....

...All physical activities have some environmental impact. Possible legislative responses to such activities cover a large number of the enumerated legislative powers, federal and provincial. To allocate the broad subject matter of environmental control to the federal government under its general power would effectively gut provincial legislative jurisdiction....In man's relationship with his environment, waste is unavoidable. The problem is thus not new, although it is only recently that the vast amount of waste products emitted into the atmosphere or dumped in water has begun to exceed the ability of the atmosphere and water to absorb and assimilate it on a global scale....In Canada, both federal and provincial levels of government have extensive powers to deal with these matters. Both have enacted comprehensive and specific schemes for the control of pollution and the protection of the environment. Some environmental pollution problems are of more direct concern to the federal government, some to the provincial government. But a vast number are interrelated, and all levels of government actively cooperate to deal with problems of mutual concern....

To allocate environmental pollution exclusively to the federal Parliament would, it seems to me, involve sacrificing the principles of federalism enshrined in the Constitution....

It is true, of course, that we are not invited to create a general environmental pollution power but one restricted to ocean pollution. But it seems to me that the same considerations apply....In my view, ocean pollution fails to meet th[e] test [of singleness, distinctiveness and indivisibility that would clearly distinguish this matter from those of provincial concern] for a variety of reasons. In addition to those applicable to environmental pollution generally, the following specific difficulties may be noted. First of all, marine waters are not wholly bounded by the coast; in many areas, they extend upstream into rivers for many miles. The application of the Act appears to be restricted to waters beyond the mouths of rivers (and so intrude less on provincial powers), but this is not entirely clear, and if it is so restricted, it is not clear whether this distinction is based on convenience or constitutional imperative. Apart from this, the line between salt and fresh water cannot be demarcated clearly; it is different at different depths of water, changes with the season and shifts constantly[.] In any event, it is not so much the waters, whether fresh or salt, with which we are concerned, but their pollution. And the pollution of marine water is contributed to by the vast amounts of effluents that are poured or seep into fresh waters everywhere[.] There is a constant intermixture of waters; fresh waters flow into the sea and marine waters penetrate deeply inland at high tide only to return to the sea laden with pollutants collected during their incursion inland. Nor is the pollution of the ocean confined to pollution emanating from substances deposited in water. In important respects, the pollution of the sea results from emissions into the air, which are then transported over many miles and deposited into the sea.... I cannot, therefore, see ocean pollution as a sufficiently discrete subject upon which to found the kind of legislative power sought here. It is an attempt to create a federal pollution control power on unclear geographical grounds and limited to part only of the causes of ocean pollution. Such a power then simply amounts to a truncated federal pollution control power only partially effective to meet its supposed necessary purpose, unless of course one is willing to extend it to pollution emanating from fresh water and the air, when for reasons already given such an extension could completely swallow up provincial power, no link being necessary to establish the federal purpose....

...The difficulty with the impugned provision is [furthermore] that it seeks to deal with activities that cannot be demonstrated either to pollute or to have a reasonable potential of polluting the ocean....The prohibition in fact would apply to the moving of rock from one area of provincial property to another. I cannot accept that the federal Parliament has such wide legislative power over local matters having local import taking place on provincially owned property.

Notes and Questions

1. *What qualifies for federal regulation under the P.O.G.G. Clause?* What does or should qualify as a matter of "national concern" under the "provincial inability" test? The court focuses principally on externalities and other collective action problems. Let us call these "inter-jurisdictional difficulties." For example, the court highlights the relevance of "the effect on extra-provincial interests of a provincial failure to deal effectively with the control or regulation of the intra-provincial aspects of the matter," and it discusses the problem of "pollution price-wars," that is, races to the bottom in environmental regulation. Are there other aspects of subsidiarity that this formulation ignores?

   Consider a second category of benefits of centralization: the reduction of transaction costs (including economies of scope and scale). Certain regulatory and other services might be provided more efficiently in a single location as opposed to through multiple smaller agencies. For example, some U.S. scholars have made a case in favor of the involvement of the Department of Justice in handling difficult criminal cases based on the extensive technical resources of a single large investigating unit. *See* Jamie S. Gorelick & Harry Litman, *Prosecutorial Discretion and the Federalization Debate*, 46 HASTINGS L.J. 967 (1995). An argument based purely on economies of scope or scale or the reduction of transaction costs more generally would not, however, seem to make out a sufficient case for federal regulation under the Court's P.O.G.G. Clause doctrine. Why might that be?

Consider a third category of provincial problems—call them "intra-jurisdictional difficulties," that is, local democratic defects, such as majority oppression, minority capture, or corruption. Here, the effects of the defect are felt most intensely by those living inside—not outside—the local jurisdiction, and yet, centralization may help. Indeed, this was Madison's main argument in support of the federal government in Federalist No. 10—that the sieve of federal politics and political pluralism at the national level would provide for better democracy than would exist at the local level. James Madison, *The Federalist No. 10, in* THE FEDERALIST PAPERS 56 (J.E. Cooke, ed., 1961). A similar argument served as the basic justification for the Reconstruction amendments in the United States, which centralized civil rights protection, especially for African Americans. As presented in the *Crown Zellerbach* case, the provincial inability test does not seem sensitive to the problem of intra-jurisdictional difficulties either. Is that wise?

2. *Is the P.O.G.G. Clause instrumental or substantive?* The Canadian Supreme Court begins its application of the provincial inability test to the facts of the case by noting: "Marine pollution, because of its predominantly extra-provincial as well as international character and implications, is clearly a matter of concern to Canada as a whole." Accordingly, the only question the court addresses is whether marine dumping control is single, indivisible, and distinct from dumping control in other provincial waters.

   Although plausible, is this point of departure constitutionally sufficient? Need the court not locate the desire to combat environmental pollution in the provinces themselves? Or can the federal government simply pronounce pollution control as a goal of governance against the wishes of the provinces? Put another way, the court seems to assume that the federal government is merely coordinating localities in the achievement of a mutually desired goal. That may well be true. But perhaps the failure of provincial environmental control is not that British Columbia, for example, lacks the proper incentives to regulate pollution that travels beyond its borders. Maybe British Columbia simply has a different, more sanguine, substantive assessment of the harm of environmental pollution itself. Does (or should) the P.O.G.G. Clause only allow the federal government to help the provinces achieve the provinces' own goals, or does (or should) the P.O.G.G. Clause allow the federal government to impose something as a national goal for the "Peace, Order, and good Government of Canada" against the wishes of the provinces?

   The point can be illustrated more generally and starkly when we shift to ideological "externalities." Just as environmental pollution is "a by-product of everything we do," so, too, every action has ideological valence. A citizen in one jurisdiction may be offended by the actions of a citizen in another. That offense is certainly real, but whether we recognize the offense as a legitimate basis for regulation involves difficult, substantive questions about the nature of rights and harms. *See* Don Herzog, *Externalities and Other Parasites*, 67 U. CHI. L. REV. 895 (2000). Consider, for example, abortion, physician-assisted suicide, or gay marriage. The ideological (and physical) effects of local policies in these areas will often cross jurisdictional lines. Does the principle of subsidiarity in general or the P.O.G.G. Clause in particular authorize the center to address these and other "externalities" against the wishes of local governments?

3. *Subsidiarity and environmental regulation in the United States.* The U.S. Constitution, too, was written before environmental regulation was the coherent and distinct policy objective it is today. In the United States, however, the constitutionality of federal environmental regulation is not generally thought of as based on the "need" for federal regulation in light of the political- or resource-based constraints on the States's ability to regulate the environment effectively. Instead, the constitutionality of federal environmental regulation simply depends on whether Congress is nominally acting within the domain of a specifically enumerated power, such as the power to regulate interstate and foreign commerce or to implement international treaties. Although the U.S. Supreme Court sometimes makes reference to functional considerations sounding in subsidiarity, these considerations rarely provide the actual basis for decision. Consider the following examples:
   (a) *Federal Power and the Clean Water Act:* In reviewing the federal migratory bird rule, which required a federal permit before dredging wetlands used by migratory birds, the U.S. Supreme Court interpreted the federal statute as not reaching isolated wetlands, but only wetlands "that actually abu[t] on a navigable waterway." *Solid Waste Agency of Northern Cook Cty. (SWANCC) v. Army Corps of Engineers*, 531 U.S. 159 (2001); *cf. Rapanos v. United States*, 547 U.S. 715 (2006). Although rendered as a matter of statutory interpretation, the decision had constitutional overtones, given that the Court's narrow interpretation of the act expressly avoided reaching the question of the outer limits of Congress's powers. Does the distinction between wetlands that abut navigable waterways and isolated wetlands serve any functional purpose when judged against the principle of subsidiarity? Is the distinction any less defensible than the Canadian Supreme Court's distinction between freshwater and saltwater, which enters toward the end of the otherwise functional Canadian judgment?

      In dissent, Justice Stevens interpreted the statute as reaching isolated wetlands and then noted that there were several functional reasons why Congress should have the power to pass the migratory bird rule:

      > The destruction of aquatic migratory bird habitat, like so many other environmental problems, is an action in which the benefits (e.g., a new landfill) are disproportionately local, while many of the costs (e.g., fewer migratory birds) are widely dispersed and often borne by citizens living in other States. In such situations, described by economists as involving "externalities," federal regulation is both appropriate and necessary. (SWANCC, 531 U.S. at 195–96 (citing Richard L. Revesz, Rehabilitating Interstate Competition: Rethinking the "Race-to-the-Bottom" Rationale for Federal Environmental Regulation, 67 N.Y.U. L. Rev. 1210, 1222 (1992)) (Stevens, J., dissenting)

      Should it be important for Commerce Clause purposes that these costs are economic as opposed to, say, ideological?
   (b) *Federal Power and the Migratory Bird Treaty:* In *Missouri v. Holland*, 252 U.S. 416 (1920), Justice Holmes upheld Congress's power to implement the Migratory Bird Treaty. In light of the Court's pre-New Deal jurisprudence, there was serious doubt at the time whether the Commerce Clause extended to the

regulation of migratory birds. *See* Charles A. Lofgren, *Missouri v. Holland in Historical Perspective*, 1975 SUP. CT. REV. 77. The Court in *Missouri v. Holland*, however, held that, regardless of the Commerce Clause, implementing the Treaty with Canada was within Congress's powers under the Necessary and Proper Clause as combined with the federal government's power to make treaties. In upholding the treaty and the implementing act, Justice Holmes noted that "the States individually are incompetent to act" and that the treaty served "a national interest of very nearly the first magnitude... [that] can be protected only by national action in concert with that of another power." 252 U.S. at 433, 435. Despite the functional rhetoric in this case, however, the Supreme Court has never invoked the absence of functional justifications as a reason to strike down a Treaty. Would it ever be appropriate for the Court to strike down a treaty that was actually concluded with a foreign government as beyond the federal government's powers under the Treaty Clause? *See* Mark Tushnet, *Federalism and International Human Rights in the New Constitutional Order*, 47 WAYNE L. REV. 841 (2001).

4. *Subsidiarity as enumeration versus subsidiarity as interpretive guide?* In Canada, subsidiarity functions as enumeration, that is, the Canadian Supreme Court interprets the P.O.G.G. Clause as incorporating subsidiarity into the basic constitutional enumeration of federal powers. In *SWANCC* and in *Missouri v. Holland*, in contrast, subsidiarity might have served as an interpretive guide to determine the meaning of the otherwise vague grants of federal power over interstate commerce and treaty making, respectively. Over Justice Stevens's objection, the *SWANCC* majority refused to entertain this idea, holding firmly to the formal distinction between wetlands that abut navigable waterways and isolated wetlands. Justice Holmes's purported functionalism in *Missouri v. Holland* has not proven decisive in later treaty cases either.

   Is it possible, however, to read other U.S. Supreme Court decisions as implicitly relying on subsidiarity as interpretive guide to otherwise vaguely defined powers? In *United States v. Darby*, 312 U.S. 100 (1941), for example, the Court upheld federal minimum wage and maximum hour regulations on manufacturers of goods shipped in interstate commerce, expressly deferring to Congress's view that "interstate commerce should not be made the instrument of competition in the distribution of goods produced under substandard labor conditions, which competition is injurious to the commerce and to the states from and to which the commerce flows." *Id.* at 115. *Cf. General Motors of Canada Ltd. v. City National Leasing*, [1989] 1 S.C.R. 641 (upholding Canada's national Combines Investigation Act as within the federal "trade and commerce power" in part because "provincial legislation cannot be an effective regulator.")

   Might *United States v. Lopez*, 514 U.S. 549 (1995), and *United States v. Morrison*, 529 U.S. 598 (2000), be justified along similar lines? As a matter of doctrine, the Court's opinions here, as so frequently elsewhere, refuse to analyze in functional terms what is needed to make the federal system work as a productive whole, focusing instead on formal jurisdictional "entitlements" received at the Founding. *See* Daniel Halberstam, *Of Power and Responsibility: The Political Morality of Federal Systems*, 90 VA. L. REV. 732, 795–97 (2004). The decisions simply posit that only activities of an "economic nature" can be regulated under the substantial effects prong of Congress's interstate commerce jurisdiction. *See Morrison*, 529 U.S. at 610–12. But perhaps some functional idea of subsidiarity might yet justify shielding policy areas such as violent crime, family law, and education from federal intervention. Such a decision might include the substantive judgments (1) that non-economic activities are intimately connected with communal self-expression and fundamental rights, (2) that federal market regulation alleviates collective action problems posed by individual state regulation, and (3) that a common market serves to integrate the body politic. *See* Roderick M. Hills, Jr., *The Individual Right to Federalism in the Rehnquist Court*, 74 GEO. WASH. L. REV. 888 (2006). *But see* Judith Resnik, *Categorical Federalism: Jurisdiction, Gender, and the Globe*, 111 YALE L.J. 619 (2001). Would such broader functional considerations support or challenge the Court's subsequent holding in *Gonzales v. Raich*, 545 U.S. 1 (2005) (upholding federal ban on personal cultivation and use of marijuana)?

5. *Subsidiarity as side constraint.* Moving beyond subsidiarity as enumeration and subsidiarity as interpretive guide, consider a third and final use of subsidiarity: subsidiarity as side constraint. The European Union provides an instructive example in this regard. The Treaty on European Community contains an express limitation on the Community's exercise of enumerated concurrent powers:

> In areas which do not fall within its exclusive competence, the Community shall take action, in accordance with the principle of subsidiarity, only if and in so far as the objectives of the proposed action cannot be sufficiently achieved by the Member States and can therefore, by reason of the scale or effects of the proposed action, be better achieved by the Community. TREATY ON EUROPEAN COMMUNITY, Art. 5.

Notice that this provision, unlike the Canadian P.O.G.G. Clause, clearly assumes that the central level of governance has (by enumeration elsewhere) the express power to determine the regulatory policy goal. According to Article 5 EC, the substantive policy decision lies with the Community and subsidiarity operates as a purely instrumental side constraint. Put another way, the assumption is that the Community, acting pursuant to its concurrent powers, has taken aim at a particular regulatory goal. The only remaining question under Article 5 EC is instrumental: can the Member States achieve the Community defined goal just as well as the Community itself could?

The European Court of Justice has been highly reluctant to adjudicate this form of subsidiarity (i.e., as a side constraint on Community action). In *Germany v. Parliament and Council*, C-233/94, [1997] ECR I-2405, for example, Germany had challenged an EC Directive requiring each Member State to set up a bank deposit guarantee scheme within each territory. Germany argued that the Community institutions had failed to give reasons for its action (which is a general requirement under Article 190, now 253, EC) by failing to address the issue of subsidiarity. The Court ruled (at ¶¶ 26–28):

> In the present case, the Parliament and the Council stated in the...preamble to the Directive that "consideration should be given to the situation which might arise if deposits in a credit institution that has branches in other Member States became unavailable" and that it was "indispensable to ensure a harmonized minimum level of deposit protection wherever deposits are located in the Community." This shows that, in the Community legislature's view, the aim of its action could, because of the dimensions of the intended action, be best achieved at Community level....[F]rom [this] it is clear that the decision regarding the guarantee scheme which is competent in the event of the insolvency of a branch situated in a Member State other than that in which the credit institution has its head office has repercussions which are felt outside the borders of each Member State.
>
> Furthermore, in the [preamble to the Directive] the Parliament and the Council stated that the action taken by the Member States in response to the Commission's Recommendation has not fully achieved the desired result. The Community legislature therefore found that the objective of its action could not be achieved sufficiently by the Member States.

> Consequently, it is apparent that, on any view, the Parliament and the Council did explain why they considered that their action was in conformity with the principle of subsidiarity and, accordingly, that they complied with the obligation to give reasons as required under Article 190 of the Treaty. An express reference to [the] principle [of subsidiarity] cannot be required.

Does the Court's examination of the justification for central government involvement in this case take subsidiarity seriously? How might that be done? *Cf.* George A. Bermann, *Taking Subsidiarity Seriously: Federalism in the European Community and the United States*, 94 COLUM. L. REV. 332, 391 (1994); Halberstam, *supra*, at 827–32; Vicki Jackson, *Narratives of Federalism: Of Continuities and Comparative Constitutional Experience*, 51 DUKE L.J. 223, 285 (2001).

6. *Subsidiarity and the politics of federalism.* In *Crown Zellerbach*, the majority and dissent disagree over whether the regulation of marine dumping falls within the P.O.G.G. Clause. There is, of course, a third possibility: to refuse judicial review altogether and rely instead on the political safeguards of federalism.

   Most prominently associated with Herbert Wechsler, but followed, modified, and elaborated upon by scholars such as Jesse Choper, Larry Kramer, and Mark Tushnet, the theory of the political safeguards of federalism is based on the following three ideas. First, the formal representation of state interests in the U.S. Senate, the Electoral College, and the informal solicitude of federal politicians for the views of their state counterparts will generally suffice to protect the States against federal overreaching. Second, even if those safeguards allow for the strong assertion of federal power, the Supreme Court lacks the institutional capacity to arbitrate cases of reasonable disagreement among the federal government and the States. Third, the Court, in any event, is not able to stop a determined and unified federal government in cases of serious disagreement and blatant violation of state prerogatives. So far, these theories have been developed with an exclusive focus on the United States. *See, e.g.*, MARK TUSHNET, TAKING THE CONSTITUTION AWAY FROM THE COURTS 123 (1999); Larry D. Kramer, *Understanding Federalism*, 47 VAND. L. REV. 1485 (1991); JESSE H. CHOPER, JUDICIAL REVIEW AND THE NATIONAL POLITICAL PROCESS (1980); Herbert Wechsler, *The Political Safeguards of Federalism: The Role of the States in the Composition and Selection of the National Government*, 54 COLUM. L. REV. 543 (1954).

   A comparative perspective, however, may help inform our assessment of these conclusions. *See generally* Daniel Halberstam, *Comparative Federalism and the Role of the Judiciary*, *in* THE OXFORD HANDBOOK OF LAW AND POLITICS (Keith Whittington et al. eds., forthcoming 2008). With the exception of Switzerland, which has a strong tradition of popular referenda, federal systems other than the United States provide for judicial review of federalism disputes. To be sure, in some systems, such as Belgium and the newly devolved United Kingdom (if we count it as a federal system), the political branches have not yet turned to the judiciary for the settlement of federalism disputes. And in other systems, such as Australia, the high court has effectively turned many substantive power issues into a political question. And yet, in many systems, such as Canada, the European Union, and Germany, central review of federalism disputes persists. And this despite the fact that the structural safeguards of federalism are far stronger in some of these systems as compared to those in the United States.

   Germany and the European Union, for example, are both "vertical" federal systems, that is, central government laws are largely carried out by the constituent states; constituent state governments are formally represented in an upper house at the central level of government, and the power of taxation is shared. Contrast this with the "horizontal" systems of federalism in the United States, Canada, and Australia, where central and constituent state governments are independent political organizations sitting alongside one another, each with a full complement of powers. In horizontal systems of federalism, each level of government has an independent democratic base, an independent fiscal base, as well as the ability to formulate, execute, and generally adjudicate its own policies. As a structural matter, vertical systems protect constituent state interests far more robustly than do horizontal systems. *See, e.g.*, Daniel Halberstam and Roderick M. Hills, Jr., *State Autonomy in Germany and the United States*, 574 ANNALS AM. ACAD. POL. & SOC. SCI. 158 (March 2001). In vertical as compared to horizontal systems, constituent states have greater formal control over the central government's regulatory activity and distribution of resources, as a formal matter as well as informally by virtue of the central government's dependence on the constituent states in the routine implementation of federal policies.

The German Federal Constitutional Court originally abdicated judicial review of federal compliance with the German constitution's "necessity clause," which had imposed subsidiarity considerations as a side constraint on the federal exercise of concurrent powers. In response, Germany's *Länder* (the constituent states)—especially the *Länder* parliaments—lobbied for over 20 years until, finally, in 1994 the *Grundgesetz* (Germany's constitution) was amended to include a new, justiciable necessity clause. In 2005, the German Federal Constitutional Court rendered its first decision striking down a federal law for failure to make out the necessity for a particular piece of federal legislation.

In the European Union, in which constituent state control over the central level of governance is even stronger than in Germany, dissatisfaction with the current state of subsidiarity control led to the inclusion of a specific subsidiarity protocol in the proposed constitutional treaty. *See* Draft Treaty Establishing a Constitution for Europe, Protocol on the Application of the Principles of Subsidiarity and Proportionality (not ratified). The new protocol would have established an early warning system by which one-third of the Member State parliaments could force the Commission to reconsider its legislative proposal in light of the principle of subsidiarity. Although the Commission could still proceed with the proposed legislation, such a "yellow card" system, as it has been called, raises the political stakes considerably. Derrick Wyatt, *Could a "Yellow card" for national parliaments strengthen judicial as well as political policing of subsidiarity?*, 2 CROATIAN Y.B. EUR. L. & POL'Y 1 (2006); Stephen Weatherill, *Using national parliaments to improve scrutiny of the limits of EU action*, 28 EUR. L. REV. 909 (2003). After the defeat of the constitutional treaty, a similar protocol was included in the Treaty of Lisbon (not yet ratified).

Do the German and European examples suggest that some form of judicial involvement or at least some specific procedural mechanism to address federal compliance with the principle of subsidiarity is desirable in all federal systems to prevent the federal government from overreaching? Would an EU style "early warning system" be useful in the United States? If there is to be judicial involvement, should the judiciary ultimately adjudicate the subsidiarity question or merely insist on the democratic transparency of the legislature's consideration of subidiarity by enforcing clear statement rules? For further discussion, *see* Wyatt, *supra;* Weatherill, *supra*; Halberstam, *Comparative Federalism and the Role of the Judiciary*, *supra*; Bermann, *supra*; Jackson, *supra*.

4

Separation of Powers and Parliamentary Government

Laurence P. Claus

Government under the U.S. Constitution is not *parliamentary.* To be certain of this, we need notice only two features of American government. First, the person primarily responsible for administering the American government is chosen independently of the national legislature in most circumstances. Second, that person does not depend for continuation in office on majority support in the House of Representatives.

During the century of the American founding, the British government was evolving a practice whereby the national legislature's choice of persons to administer the nation from day to day was consistently accepted by the monarch. Those who could assemble majority support in the elected chamber of the British Parliament were appointed by the monarch as his ministers. Those appointees served formally at the monarch's pleasure, but in fact their appointments depended on parliamentary support and did not last longer than Parliament's confidence in them. Parliamentary systems of government are distinguished by their conformity with the British prototype in four respects, the first two essential and the other two usual. First, the choice of those who will administer government is directly or indirectly determined by a legislature in most circumstances, and second, the chosen ministers depend for their continuation in office on continued majority support in the legislature. Where a legislature is bicameral, control over who will administer government belongs to the legislative chamber that is most representative of the whole population. In addition, in most parliamentary systems, those who will administer government are chosen from among incumbent legislators, and the office of national chief executive is a formal one that does not normally involve actual administrative decision making. There is said to be a separation of "head of state" from "head of government."

Beyond these generally shared characteristics, parliamentary systems vary widely. Some are constituted under documents that cannot be amended by ordinary legislative action. Others, like the British original, function under a general principle of "parliamentary supremacy." Some are federal systems. Others are not. Some explicitly separate the judiciary from the rest of government. Others do not. In all of these respects, British parliamentary government differs sharply from government under the U.S. Constitution.

In this chapter, we will explore two salient features of British parliamentary government that help to illuminate the strengths and weaknesses of the American founders' institutional choices.

PARLIAMENTARY SUPREMACY IN THE UNITED KINGDOM

The U.S. Constitution claims to be created by "We the People of the United States" and provides for "[a]ll legislative powers herein granted" to "be vested in a Congress of the United States." No comparable document creates or controls the British Parliament. As British courts and executive departments now receive their powers from Parliament, British constitutional law presents a puzzle: Is there anything that Parliament *cannot* lawfully do? When Justice Robert Jackson observed that the U.S. Constitution must not be construed as a "suicide pact" (*Terminiello v. Chicago*, 337 U.S. 1, 36 (1949)), he was referring to the risk that the Constitution's limitations on government power might cause the American form of government to collapse into anarchy. British constitutionalism poses the obverse question of self-preservation: Might the *lack* of limitations on Parliament's power cause the British form of government to collapse into tyranny? Consider that question as you read Dicey's classic account of parliamentary supremacy.

Albert Venn Dicey, Introduction to the Study of the Law of the Constitution, 39–40, 61 n. 2, 91 38–39, 59 n. 1, 87 (10th ed. London: Macmillan, 1965) (first edition published 1885):

Parliament means, in the mouth of a lawyer (though the word has often a different sense in ordinary conversation), the King, the House of Lords, and the House of Commons; these three bodies acting together may be aptly described as the "King in Parliament," and constitute Parliament.

The principle of Parliamentary sovereignty means neither more nor less than this, namely, that Parliament thus defined has, under the English constitution, the right to make or unmake any law whatever; and, further, that no person or body is recognised by the law of England as having a right to override or set aside the legislation of Parliament.

A law may, for our present purpose, be defined as "any rule which will be enforced by the courts." The principle then of Parliamentary sovereignty may, looked at from its positive side, be thus described: Any Act of Parliament, or any part of an Act of Parliament, which makes a new law, or repeals or modifies an existing law, will be obeyed by the courts. The same principle, looked at from its negative side, may be thus stated: There is no person or body of persons who can, under the English constitution, make rules which override or derogate from an Act of Parliament, or which (to express the same thing in other words) will be enforced by the courts in contravention of an Act of Parliament. Some apparent exceptions to this rule no doubt suggest themselves. But these apparent exceptions, as where, for example, the Judges of the High Court of Justice make rules of court repealing Parliamentary enactments, are resolvable into cases in which Parliament either directly or indirectly sanctions subordinate legislation. …

Another limitation has been suggested more or less distinctly by judges such as Coke (*Bonham's Case* (1610) 8 Co. Rep. 118, and *Case of Proclamations* (1610) 12 Co. Rep. 74, at p. 76; K. & L. 78, and *see* Hearn, *Government of England* (2nd ed., 1887), pp. 48, 49); an Act of Parliament cannot (it has been intimated) overrule the principles of the common law. This doctrine once had a real meaning (see Maine, *Early History of Institutions* (7th ed., 1905), pp. 381, 382), but it has never received systematic judicial sanction and is now obsolete….

These then are the three traits of Parliamentary sovereignty as it exists in England: first, the power of the legislature to alter any law, fundamental or otherwise, as freely and in the same manner as other laws; secondly, the absence of any legal distinction between constitutional and other laws; thirdly, the non-existence of any judicial or other authority having the right to nullify an Act of Parliament, or to treat it as void or unconstitutional.

These traits are all exemplifications of the quality which my friend Mr. Bryce has happily denominated the "flexibility" of the British constitution. Every part of it can be expanded, curtailed, amended, or abolished, with equal ease. It is the most flexible polity in existence, and is therefore utterly different in character from the "rigid" constitutions (to use another expression of Mr. Bryce's) the whole or some part of which can be changed only by some extraordinary method of legislation.

If Parliament can by statute "make or unmake any law whatever," can Parliament change itself?

H.M. Government White Paper, House of Lords: Reform, ¶¶ 3.6, 3.26, 4.18, 6.1, 7.1, 10.11, 12.2 (February, 2007):

The crisis over the Lords' rejection of the 1909 budget led to the Parliament Act 1911, which was passed only under the threat of the creation of a large number of Liberal peers. The Act ensured that a Money Bill could receive Royal Assent without the approval of the House of Lords, if not passed by the Lords without amendment within one month. The Act also provided that any other Public Bill (except one extending the life of a Parliament) would receive Royal Assent without the consent of the House of Lords, if it had been passed by the Commons in three successive sessions, as long as two years had elapsed between its second reading in the first session and its final passage in the Commons. The Act also shortened the maximum length of a Parliament from seven to five years……..

In 1999, the Government introduced the House of Lords Bill to remove the hereditary peers, as the first stage of Lords reform……..

The Government is committed to holding a free vote on composition of the House of Lords in both Houses….

The Government believes that there are certain principles that should underpin a reformed House of Lords, whatever its composition:

- Primacy of the House of Commons
- Complementarity of the House of Lords
- A More Legitimate House of Lords

- No Overall Majority for Any Party
- A Non Party-Political Element
- A More Representative House of Lords
- Continuity of Membership…

Broadly speaking, there are three main options, an all-appointed House, an all-elected House, or a hybrid of the two.… The Government has been clear that in a modern democracy it is unacceptable that individuals still qualify for a seat in Parliament on the basis of their ancestry. The transitional arrangements made in 1999 should therefore come to an end by formally ending the right of the remaining hereditary members to membership of the second Chamber.…

The Government believes that the centre of gravity on opinions for a reformed House lies around the hybrid option, with elections run on a partially-open list system in European constituencies at the same time as European elections. A hybrid House can deliver a second chamber which is a complement to the House of Commons, and delivers the important principles of representation which are essential for an effective House of Lords.

Notes and Questions

1. During the nineteenth and twentieth centuries, Parliament extended the franchise for electing the House of Commons, redrew and reapportioned electoral districts for the House of Commons, reduced the powers of the unelected House of Lords, and altered the rules for creation and duration of peerages. Each of these changes served to make Parliament more representative of the British people. Could Parliament just as validly change itself into a *less* representative body? Could Parliament, for example, by statute provide for incumbent members of the House of Commons to hold their positions for life? If there are intrinsic limits on Parliament's ability to change itself into a less representative body, might Parliament not even be able to repeal the nineteenth- and twentieth-century statutes by which it made itself more representative?

2. *Regina (Jackson and others) v. Attorney General*, [2006] 1 A.C. 262 (House of Lords, decided October 13, 2005). The Parliament Act 1911 converted the absolute veto formerly enjoyed by the House of Lords over proposed legislation into a power in the House of Lords to do no more than delay the adoption of statutes on which the House of Commons insisted. The Parliament Act 1949 amended the 1911 Act to shorten the maximum period of delay, and was adopted without the consent of the House of Lords pursuant to the provisions of the 1911 Act. In 2004 a statutory ban on fox hunting received royal assent pursuant to the 1949 Act, having passed the House of Commons but not the House of Lords. In the course of rejecting a challenge to the 2004 statute, the Law Lords addressed the question whether the 1949 Act violated basic constitutional principles. The question was phrased in this way: "The Parliament Act 1949 is not an Act of Parliament and is consequently of no legal effect." The Law Lords held that the 1949 Act was an Act of Parliament because the 1911 Act's provision for reducing the power of the House of Lords could be relied on when passing an act that further reduced the Lords' power.

   The 1911 Act also reduced the maximum period between elections for the House of Commons to five years and provided that any bill to extend that period would still require the House of Lords' consent. Note the Law Lords' discussion of whether Parliament's provision for enacting statutes without the consent of the House of Lords could be amended without the consent of the Lords to cover attempts to enact statutes extending the maximum period between parliamentary elections. Consider also the following extract from the speech of Lord Steyn:

> ¶102...The classic account given by Dicey of the doctrine of the supremacy of Parliament, pure and absolute as it was, can now be seen to be out of place in the modern United Kingdom. Nevertheless, the supremacy of Parliament is still the *general* principle of our constitution. It is a construct of the common law. The judges created this principle. If that is so, it is not unthinkable that circumstances could arise where the courts may have to qualify a principle established on a different hypothesis of constitutionalism. In exceptional circumstances involving an attempt to abolish judicial review or the ordinary role of the courts, the Appellate Committee of the House of Lords or a new Supreme Court may have to consider whether this is a constitutional fundamental which even a sovereign Parliament acting at the behest of a complaisant House of Commons cannot abolish.

Were a future British judiciary to declare an ostensible Act of Parliament invalid in the exceptional circumstances to which Lord Steyn referred, would their decision be legally justified? How would any legal basis for their decision differ from the legal basis of U.S. Supreme Court decisions that declare Acts of Congress invalid? Is the legal basis of such U.S. Supreme Court decisions stronger? If so, why?

RESPONSIBLE GOVERNMENT AND REMOVAL OF EXECUTIVE OFFICERS IN THE UNITED KINGDOM

Although current legislation sets the maximum period between parliamentary elections at five years, the monarch has discretion, exercisable on the advice of incumbent ministers, to dissolve Parliament sooner, leading to fresh elections for the House of Commons. Prime ministers sometimes seek early dissolution simply because they consider their electoral prospects particularly favorable at the time of the request. But a constitutionally compelling reason to seek early dissolution of Parliament is a majority vote in the House of Commons that the incumbent ministry has lost the confidence of the House. This may occur in times of political crisis where governing multiparty coalitions break down or where a party that hitherto held a majority in the House suffers defections or a loss of factional discipline. It may also occur due to a governing party's loss of majority status through deaths and resignations of members. Another situation in which an incumbent ministry may lose the confidence of the House arises where a "minority government" loses the support of those members of the House who, though not members of a governing coalition, had previously contributed to majority support for the government.

Votes of no confidence may be directed by the House of Commons against an entire incumbent ministry, requiring fresh elections unless a majority of members coalesce in support of an alternative ministry. Each of the last century's three successful "no confidence" votes was framed as a vote against the whole government. Votes of no confidence may alternatively be directed against particular ministers, and might appear to permit an incumbent government to continue sans the censured ministers, much as the U.S. Constitution contemplates that an administration may continue even though particular "civil Officers of the United States" have been removed through impeachment proceedings. In practice, a vote of no confidence, at least when based on government policy, is treated by an incumbent ministry as a vote against them all. When in 1895 the House passed a motion to reduce the salary of the Secretary of War, the whole ministry resigned. Consider the following colloquy concerning an attempt to target Prime Minister Tony Blair individually by instead invoking the impeachment mechanism.

Hansard, House of Commons, September 9, 2004, Columns 871–872:

Adam Price (East Carmarthen and Dinefwr) (PC): When the Leader of the House chaired the Young Liberals he supported a campaign to impeach the then Lord Advocate of Scotland. Does he still believe that impeachment is a sanction available to the House when seeking to hold Ministers to account, or will he oppose any moves to introduce a motion for debate under that procedure?

Mr. Hain: The hon. Gentleman is an admirable researcher who digs up all sorts of facts, some of which are uncomfortable for the Government. I cannot for the life of me recall that campaign, which was over 30 years ago. However, he has dug it up from a file somewhere, so I acknowledge his research expertise.

The House of Commons has already voted overwhelmingly to back the Government's position on Iraq. That was the House's clear decision. For the first time, the Government brought to the House a motion on a decision to go to war, and gave it an opportunity to authorise it or not. That decision was made, but the hon. Gentleman is seeking to circumvent it.

I am advised by the Clerk of the House that impeachment effectively died with the advent of full responsible parliamentary government, perhaps to be dated from the second Reform Act of 1867, and a motion of no confidence would be the appropriate modern equivalent. The Joint Committee on Parliamentary Privilege in 1999 concluded that

"The circumstances in which impeachment has taken place are now so remote from the present that the procedure may be considered obsolete."

Perhaps the hon. Gentleman should research the matter more carefully.

William Searle Holdsworth, A History of English Law 379–385, Vol. 1 (3d ed. Boston: Little, Brown, 1922):

An impeachment is a criminal proceeding initiated by the House of Commons against any person. The person impeached is tried before the whole House of Lords presided over by the Lord High Steward if a peer is impeached for treason or felony, or by the Lord Chancellor or Lord Keeper in all other cases. The judgment is given in accordance with the vote of the majority of the House, and, on the demand of the House of Commons made through its Speaker, the House passes sentence. The last instance of an impeachment was the case of Lord Melville in 1805; and, as it is improbable that this procedure will ever be revived, it might almost be regarded as another case of the obsolete jurisdiction of the House of Lords. On the other hand it is still legally possible, so that, whatever may the political probabilities, it is impossible to treat it as wholly obsolete....

The Origin of Impeachments.—Impeachment means accusation and the word gradually acquired the narrower technical meaning of an accusation made by the House of Commons to the House of Lords. The first impeachment comes from the year 1376, and the practice of impeachment originated in the prevalent political ideas and conditions of that period. Firstly, at that period, and indeed all through the Middle Ages, political thinkers and writers throughout Western Europe taught that the ideal to be aimed at by all rulers and princes and their officials was government in accordance with law. Secondly, the House of Commons and the House of Lords were united in desiring to limit the activities of the royal officials or favourites and to prevent them from breaking the law. Thirdly, the limits of jurisdiction of the House of Lords were ill defined. It was open to receive petitions and complaints from all and sundry; and it could deal with them judicially or otherwise as it saw fit. It was essentially a court for great men and great causes; and it occasionally seems to have been thought that it could apply to such causes a *lex Parliamenti*—a law which could do justice even when the ordinary law failed. Probably some such thought as this was at the back of the minds of those who in Edward III.'s Statute of Treason gave the king and Parliament a power to declare certain acts to be treasonable.

It was thus only natural that the Commons, when they discovered that royal officials or others had broken the law, and that the government of the state was therefore badly conducted, should make a complaint to the House of Lords, which took the form of an accusation against the delinquents; and that the Lords should entertain and deal with it. Probably therefore the practice of impeachment arose partly from the prevalent political ideal—government according to law, partly from the alliance of the two Houses to secure the sanctity of the law as against royal officials or favourites, and partly from the wide and indefinite jurisdiction which the House of Lords exercised at that time....

The Constitutional Importance of Impeachments.—The last mediaeval impeachment was in 1459. During the Wars of the Roses the place of impeachments was taken by Acts of Attainder, which were used by the rival factions much as criminal appeals had been used in Richard II's reign. During the Tudor period these Acts of Attainder were used to get rid of the ministers whom the king had ceased to trust, or of persons considered to be dangerous to the state. But, in the later period, the accused was often heard in his defence; and, at a time when the legislative and judicial function of Parliament were not clearly distinguished, it was possible to regard them, as Coke regarded them, as judgments of the full Parliament—a point of view which is still maintained by modern writers. The practice of impeachment was revived in 1620–1621 with the impeachment of Sir Giles Mompesson. Between that date and 1715 there were fifty cases of impeachments brought to trial. Since that date there have only been four. Thus the great period of impeachments was the seventeenth and the early years of the eighteenth centuries. It is therefore in the impeachments of this period, and more especially in the impeachments of the period before the Revolution of 1688, that we must seek reasons for their constitutional importance.

The Parliamentary opposition in the reigns of the two first Stuart kings was, as we shall see, essentially a legal opposition, based on precedents drawn from the records of the mediaeval Parliaments, and aiming at the attainment of the mediaeval ideal—the maintenance of the common law. Under these circumstances the impeachment was its natural weapon. By means of it the greatest ministers of state could be made responsible, like humbler officials, to the law. Thus the greatest services rendered by this procedure to the cause of constitutional government have been, firstly the establishment of the doctrine of ministerial responsibility to the law, secondly its application to all ministers of the crown, and, thirdly and consequently the maintenance of the supremacy of the law over all. The two impeachments which have contributed most to the attainment of these results are Buckingham's impeachment in Charles I's and Danby's impeachment in Charles II's reign; and of the two the latter is the most important. It was Buckingham's impeachment which decisively negatived Charles I's contention that not only was he personally above the law, but also his ministers acting under his orders. It was Danby's impeachment which decided that the king could not by use of his power to pardon stop an impeachment.[1] A pardon could be pleaded to an indictment; but an indictment was a proceeding taken in the king's name. An impeachment was a proceeding taken in the name of the Commons; and he could no more stop it by granting a pardon than he could stop a criminal appeal brought by a private person. It was also resolved in *Danby's Case* that, though the House, if a peer is impeached for treason, sits under the presidency of the Lord High Steward, it has "power enough to proceed to trial though the king should not name a High Steward;" and this fact was emphasized by a change in the form of the High Steward's commission. Thus although the trial nominally takes place before the king in Parliament, the king plays no active part. As we have seen, this elimination of the crown from all active share in the judicial functions of Parliament was taking place concurrently in the case of Parliament's civil jurisdiction. The influence of the crown being thus eliminated, impeachments became as the Commons said in 1679, "the chief institution for the preservation of the government."

Thus the practice of impeachment has had a large share in establishing English constitutional law upon its modern basis. But its efficacy was or should have been strictly limited to prosecuting offenders against the law. It is because its efficacy was thus limited that, during the eighteenth century, it has fallen into disuse.

The Disuse of Impeachments.—So soon as the aim of the Commons came to be, not only to secure the observance of the law by the king's ministers, but also to secure their adhesion to the line of policy which they approved,

[1] Maitland took a different view, and argued that Parliament's subsequent provision in the Act of Settlement 1701 against royal pardons stopping impeachments was transformative, not declaratory: FREDERIC WILLIAM MAITLAND, THE CONSTITUTIONAL HISTORY OF ENGLAND 318, 480 (Cambridge, 1931) (first published 1908). The House of Commons in Danby's Case had compromised the precedential value of its action by switching tactics from impeachment to attainder. Even after the Act of Settlement, royal pardons could prevent execution of sentences imposed by the House of Lords for conviction on impeachment.

the weakness of impeachments as a constitutional weapon began to appear. This further aim of the House of Commons was clearly manifested in the Long Parliament; and the weakness of this weapon appeared in the case of the Earl of Strafford. The success of his policy would have been fatal to constitutional government, but it was impossible to prove that its pursuit was treasonable. That the House saw this weakness in their favourite remedy is clear from the clause of the Grand Remonstrance, in which it was pointed out to the king, "that it may often fall out that the Commons may have just cause to take exception at some men for being councillors and yet not charge these men with crimes, for there be grounds of diffidence which lie not in proof." But, until the growth of the system of Cabinet government, impeachment was the only remedy open to them. The king chose his ministers; and, unless they could be convicted of crimes, there was no way of getting rid of them. It is for this reason that the charges made against unpopular ministers in the latter half of the seventeenth century were often supported by very little evidence. It is for this reason that claims were sometimes made to put ministers on their trial for offences created for that purpose by Parliament. Mediaeval precedents might no doubt have been invoked for taking such a course, but they were obviously inapplicable in an age which had learnt to draw the modern distinction between judicial and legislative acts. Clearly the weapon of impeachment was breaking down; and it ceased to be necessary to use it for political purposes when it became possible to get rid of ministers by an adverse vote of the House of Commons. The four last impeachments—those of Lord Macclesfield (1724), Lord Lovat (1746), Warren Hastings (1787), and Lord Melville (1805)—were not occasioned by the political conduct of the accused, who were all charged with serious breaches of the criminal law.

The case of Warren Hastings showed that the remedy of impeachment was far too clumsy and dilatory a remedy in a case of any complication; and therefore it is improbable that it will ever be used again, even in a case where it is desired to put a minister on his trial for a criminal offence. But, if the procedure upon it could be altered to suit modern needs, it might still be a useful weapon in the armoury of the constitution. It does embody the sound principle that ministers and officials should be made criminally liable for corruption, gross negligence, or other misfeasances in the conduct of the affairs of the nation. And this principle requires to be emphasized at a time when the development of the system of party government pledges the party to defend the policy of its leaders, however mistaken it may be, and however incompetently it may have been carried out; at a time when party leaders are apt to look indulgently on the most disastrous mistakes, because they hope that the same indulgence will be extended to their own mistakes when they take office; at a time when the principle of the security of the tenure of higher permanent officials is held to be more important than the need to punish their negligences and ignorances. If ministers were sometimes made criminally responsible for gross negligence or rashness, ill considered activities might be discouraged, real statesmanship might be encouraged, and party violence might be moderated. Ministers preparing a legislative programme or advocating a policy would be forced to look beyond the immediate election or the transient notoriety which they hope to win by this means, because they would be forced to remember that they might be called to account for neglecting to consider the probable consequences of their policy. If officials

> were sometimes made similarly responsible for their errors, it might do something to freshen up that stagnant atmosphere of complacent routine, which is and always has been the most marked characteristic of government departments.

What structural factors might have contributed to impeachment's demise in Britain even as a mechanism for removing ministers whose misconduct does *not* relate to government policy? Motions of no confidence have not visibly filled the function of policing *non-policy* conduct. How do you think that the British system would address conduct by a minister of the kind for which President William Jefferson Clinton was subjected to impeachment proceedings in the United States? Having regard to the basis on which ministers acquire and hold office in Britain, what features of that basis might make British ministers more likely to leave office preemptively, before any prospective parliamentary censure occurs?

As we have noticed, parliamentary dissatisfaction with government *policy* is now addressed through motions of no confidence. But what causes a government that loses a no-confidence vote to resign or to submit to a new election for the House of Commons?

Albert Venn Dicey, Introduction to the Study of the Law of the Constitution, 10th ed., 449–51 (1965) (first edition published 1885):

> [L]et us consider for a moment the effect of disobedience by the government to one of the most purely conventional among the maxims of constitutional morality, the rule, that is to say, that a Ministry ought to retire on a vote that they no longer possess the confidence of the House of Commons. Suppose that a Ministry, after the passing of such a vote, were to act at the present day as Pitt acted in 1783, and hold office in the face of the censure passed by the House. There would clearly be a prima facie breach of constitutional ethics. What must ensue is clear. If the Ministry wished to keep within the constitution they would announce their intention of appealing to the constituencies, and the House would probably assist in hurrying on a dissolution.... Suppose then that, under the circumstances I have imagined, the Ministry either would not recommend a dissolution of Parliament, or, having dissolved Parliament and being again censured by the newly elected House of Commons, would not resign office. It would, under this state of things, be as clear as day that the understandings of the constitution had been violated. It is however equally clear that the House would have in their own hands the means of ultimately forcing the Ministry either to respect the constitution or to violate the law. Sooner or late the moment would come for passing the Army (Annual) Act or the Appropriation Act, and the House by refusing to pass either of these enactments would involve the Ministry in all the inextricable embarrassments which (as I have already pointed out) immediately follow upon the omission to convene Parliament for more than a year. The breach, therefore, of a purely conventional rule, of a maxim utterly unknown and indeed opposed to the theory of English law, ultimately entails upon those who break it direct conflict with the undoubted law of the land.... The conventions of the constitution are not laws, but, in so far as they really possess binding force, derive

their sanction from the fact that whoever breaks them must finally break the law and incur the penalties of a law-breaker.

Notes and Questions

The U.S. Constitution empowers the U.S. Congress to remove "[t]he President, Vice President and all civil Officers of the United States" by impeaching for and convicting of "Treason, Bribery, or other high Crimes and Misdemeanors." U.S. CONST. art. II § 4, read with art. I § 2 cl. 5 and § 3 cl. 6. Does the impeachment power, or any other feature of the Constitution, protect against executive officers whose conduct is not criminally proscribed, but merely unethical, misguided, or dangerously ineffectual? The 25th Amendment's provision to protect against Presidential "inability" did not arrive until 1967, and requires an initiative from within the Executive. Did the American founders mean to create an Executive that was *more* entrenched in office than were those who held executive power in England? Consider the extent to which the American founders relied on purported descriptions of the British system when designing the U.S. Constitution's provisions for interbranch checks and balances. *See* Laurence Claus, *Montesquieu's Mistakes and the True Meaning of Separation*, 25 OXFORD J. LEGAL STUDIES 419 (2005). Is protection from misuse of power by political actors better achieved by the U.S. Constitution's provision for impeaching the Executive, or by the British Constitution's convention that executive officers serve only for so long as they have the confidence of the House of Commons? (Include within your conception of political actors the members of each branch of government.)

5

Property Rights

Gregory S. Alexander

Most written constitutions (or entrenched Bills of Rights) have clauses expressly protecting property. Recent history favors this trend. Although Canada and New Zealand rejected property clauses in their Charters of Rights of 1982 and 1990, respectively, a substantial number of other post-1980 constitutions include clauses expressly protecting "property" or "ownership" against uncompensated state expropriations.

Although constitutional property clauses are not all identical, certain features are common to all of them. All recognize that the state may "expropriate" or "take"[1] property. Moreover, all place restrictions on the state's power to expropriate property. The two notable restrictions that nearly all constitutional property clauses share are, first, that expropriations are permitted only for "public purposes" or for "public use" and, second, that such expropriations be compensated, at least to some degree.[2]

Beyond these common features, certain important textual differences exist among various constitutional property clauses. Textual differences are important because they can and in some cases do influence the substantive reach of the social obligation norm. Of these textual differences, by far the most important concerns the social-obligation norm itself. The American Constitution's property clause, the Takings Clause of the Fifth Amendment, contains no social-obligation provision as such. It acknowledges the limited

---

[1] The term "expropriate" is far more common than the American Constitution's highly ambiguous term "take."

[2] Compensation practices differ, sometimes in very important ways. In the United States, for example, the courts have interpreted the constitutional requirement of "just compensation" as requiring payment to the owner of the full market value to the expropriated asset. In South Africa, on the other hand, the Constitution expressly limits the compensation requirement by providing that "[t]he amount of the compensation and the time and manner of payment must be just and equitable, reflecting an equitable balance between the public interest and the interests of those affected, having regard to all relevant circumstances [defined to include not solely market value but also such factors as "the history of the acquisition and use of the property" and "the nation's commitment to land reform"]. Constitution of the Republic of South Africa, Ch. 2 §25(3). The South African Constitution clearly contemplates that less than full fair market value may be paid in some cases.

character of the American constitutional right of property only indirectly, by permitting the state to expropriate property under particular circumstances. Beyond this, there is no formal textual recognition of social obligation of property.

Some constitutions go further, however. They acknowledge, textually and affirmatively, that the constitutional right of property is limited by an overriding obligation that property serve the needs of society. The German Basic Law is an example of such a constitutional property clause. It states, in relevant part, that "Ownership [*Eigentum*] entails obligations. Its use should also serve the public interest."[3] This social-obligation provision explicitly acknowledges, as the American Takings Clause does not, that owners of property have social responsibilities to society. Other national constitutions include similar language in their property clauses, and some, such as South Africa's Constitution, have textually extended the social-obligation provision beyond that of the German clause. Such text has facilitated judicial interpretations of both the German and South African property clauses that place significant limits on the scope and substance of the constitutional right of property. The absence of such a social-obligation textual provision in the American takings clause is one of the single most important difference between that clause from modern property clauses.

The South African Constitution is unusual. Immediately following its property clause (section 25), it expressly guarantees certain socioeconomic rights, such as housing, food, and health care. Thus, although it does not subsume socioeconomic rights within the meaning of property as such, the Constitution clearly does contemplate that a direct linkage between the two exists. Moreover, the property clause itself includes certain positive guarantees, including restitution of land to persons dispossessed by past racially discriminatory laws and legally secure land tenure, which are parts of the same basic framework as the socioeconomic rights. Although the socioeconomic rights sections of the Constitution are considered to be cognate provisions with the property clause, a tension exists between them and section 25's protection of private property rights. The following case presented an opportunity for the Constitutional Court to clarify the relationship between section 25 and one of these rights, the right to housing, guaranteed under section 26.

Port Elizabeth Municipality v. Various Occupiers

2005 (1) SA 217 (CC) (S. Afr.)

Sachs, J.

The applicant in this matter is the Port Elizabeth Municipality (the Municipality). The respondents are some 68 people, including 23 children,

[3] Constitution of the Federal Republic of Germany, Art. 14(2).

who occupy 29 shacks they have erected on privately owned land (the property) within the Municipality. Responding to a petition signed by 1600 people in the neighbourhood, including the owners of the property, the municipality sought an eviction order against the occupiers in the South Eastern Cape Local Division of the High Court (High Court).

[The High Court issued an eviction order after finding that the occupiers, some of whom had lived on the land for eight years, were unlawfully occupying the property and that eviction was in the public interest. The Supreme Court of Appeal (SCA) set aside the eviction order, determining that the occupiers were not seeking preferential treatment for municipally provided housing but only that land be identified where they could place their shacks. The court stressed that the existence of a suitable alternative was especially important here because of the length of time they had occupied the land. On appeal by the Municipality, the Constitutional Court affirmed.]

. . .

I. The Constitutional and Statutory Context

The Prevention of Illegal Squatting Act 52 of 1951

In the pre-democratic era the response of the law to a situation like the present would have been simple and drastic. In terms of the Prevention of Illegal Squatting Act 52 of 1951 (PISA), the only question for decision would have been whether the occupation of the land was unlawful. Once it was determined that the occupiers had no permission to be on the land, they not only faced summary eviction, they were liable for criminal prosecution. Expulsion from land of people referred to as squatters was accordingly accomplished through the criminal and not the civil courts, and as a matter of public rather than of private law. The process was deliberately made as swift as possible: conviction followed by eviction....

PISA was an integral part of a cluster of statutes that gave a legal/administrative imprimatur to the usurpation and forced removal of black people from land and compelled them to live in racially designated locations....The Native Urban Areas Consolidation Act, 25 of 1945, was premised on the notion of Africans living in rural reserves and coming to the towns only as migrant workers on temporary sojourn. Through a combination of spatial apartheid, permit systems and the creation of criminal offences the Act strictly controlled the limited rights that Africans had to reside in urban areas. People living outside of what were defined as native locations were regarded as squatters and, under PISA, were expelled from the land on which they lived.

Differentiation on the basis of race was accordingly not only a source of grave assaults on the dignity of black people. It resulted in the creation of large, well-established and affluent white urban areas co-existing side by side with crammed pockets of impoverished and insecure black ones. The principles of ownership in the Roman–Dutch law then gave legitimation in an apparently neutral and impartial way to the consequences of manifestly racist and partial laws and policies.... It was against this background and to deal with these injustices that section 26(3) of the Constitution was adopted and new statutory arrangements made.

The Prevention of Illegal Eviction from and Unlawful Occupation of Land Act 19 of 1998

The Prevention of Illegal Eviction from and Unlawful Occupation of Land Act 19 of 1998 (PIE) was adopted with the manifest objective of overcoming the above abuses and ensuring that evictions in future took place in a manner consistent with the values of the new constitutional dispensation....

PIE not only repealed PISA but in a sense inverted it: squatting was decriminalised and the eviction process was made subject to a number of requirements, some necessary to comply with certain demands of the Bill of Rights. The overlay between public and private law continued, but in reverse fashion, with the name, character, tone and context of the statute being turned around.... The former objective of reinforcing common law remedies while reducing common law protections, was reversed so as to temper common law remedies with strong procedural and substantive protections; and the overall objective of facilitating the displacement and relocation of poor and landless black people for ideological purposes was replaced by acknowledgement of the necessitous quest for homes of victims of past racist policies. While awaiting access to new housing development programmes, such homeless people had to be treated with dignity and respect.

...The courts now had a new role to play, namely, to hold the balance between illegal eviction and unlawful occupation. Rescuing the courts from their invidious role as instruments directed by statute to effect callous removals, the new law guided them as to how they should fulfil their new complex and constitutionally ordained function: when evictions were being sought, the courts were to ensure that justice and equity prevailed in relation to all concerned.

The Broad Constitutional Matrix for the Interpretation of PIE

...PIE has to be understood, and its governing concepts of justice and equity have to be applied, within a defined and carefully calibrated constitutional matrix.

As with all determination about the reach of constitutionally protected rights, the starting and ending point of the analysis must be to affirm the values of human dignity, equality and freedom. One of the provisions of the Bill of Rights that has to be interpreted with these values in mind, is section 25[.]...[4] As Ackermann J pointed out in [*First National Bank of SA*

---

[4] [Section] 25 reads as follows: Property

(1) No one may be deprived of property except in terms of law of general application, and no law may permit arbitrary deprivation of property.

Ltd v. Commissioner, South African Revenue Service, 2002 (4) SA 768 (CC) (S. Afr.)], subsections (4) to (9) of section 25 underlined the need for and aimed at redressing one of the most enduring legacies of racial discrimination in the past, namely the grossly unequal distribution of land in South Africa. The details of these provisions…emphasised that under the Constitution the protection of property as an individual right was not absolute but subject to societal considerations. His judgment went on to state:

When considering the purpose and content of the property clause it is necessary, as *Van der Walt* (1997) [A.J. van der Walt, *The Constitutional Property Clause* (1997), p. 15–16] puts it

> to move away from a static, typically private-law conceptualist view of the constitution as a guarantee of the status quo to a dynamic, typically public-law

---

(2) Property may be expropriated only in terms of law of general application
(a) for a public purpose or in the public interest; and
(b) subject to compensation, the amount of which and the time and manner of payment of which have either been agreed to by those affected or decided or approved by a court.
(3) The amount of the compensation and the time and manner of payment must be just and equitable, reflecting an equitable balance between the public interest and the interests of those affected, having regard to all relevant circumstances, including
(a) the current use of the property;
(b) the history of the acquisition and use of the property;
(c) the market value of the property;
(d) the extent of direct state investment and subsidy in the acquisition and beneficial capital improvement of the property; and
(e) the purpose of the expropriation.
(4) For the purposes of this section
(a) the public interest includes the nation's commitment to land reform, and to reforms to bring about equitable access to all South Africa's natural resources; and
(b) property is not limited to land,
(5) The state must take reasonable legislative and other measures within its available resources, to foster conditions which enable citizens to gain access to land on an equitable basis.
(6) A person or community whose tenure of land is legally insecure as a result of past racially discriminatory laws or practices is entitled to the extent provided by an Act of Parliament, either to tenure which is legally secure or to comparable redress.
(7) A person or community dispossessed of property after 19 June 1913 as a result of past racially discriminatory laws or practices is entitled, to the extent provided by an Act of Parliament, either to restitution of that property or to equitable redress.
(8) No provision of this section may impede the state from taking legislative and other measures to achieve land, water and related reform, in order to redress the results of past racial discrimination, provided that any departure from the provisions of this section is in accordance with the provisions of section 36(1).
(9) Parliament must enact the legislation referred to in subsection (6).

> view of the constitution as an instrument for social change and transformation under the auspices [and I would add 'and control'] of entrenched constitutional values.[5]

The transformatory public-law view of the Constitution referred to by *Van der Walt* is further underlined by section 26, which reads:

Housing

(1) Everyone has the right to have access to adequate housing.

(2) The state must take reasonable legislative and other measures, within its available resources, to achieve the progressive realisation of this right.

(3) No one may be evicted from their home, or have their home demolished, without an order of court made after considering all the relevant circumstances. No legislation may permit arbitrary evictions.

Section 26(3) evinces special constitutional regard for a person's place of abode. It acknowledges that a home is more than just a shelter from the elements. It is a zone of personal intimacy and family security...

Much of this case accordingly turns on establishing an appropriate constitutional relationship between section 25...and section 26....The Constitution recognises that land rights and the right of access to housing and of not being arbitrarily evicted, are closely intertwined. The stronger the right to land, the greater the prospect of a secure home....[S]ections 25 and 26 create a broad overlap between land rights and socio-economic rights, emphasising the duty on the state to seek to satisfy both, as this Court said in *Grootboom* [*Government of the Republic of South Africa v. Grootboom*, 2001 (1) SA 46 (CC) (S. Afr.)].

There are three salient features of the way the Constitution approaches the interrelationship between land hunger, homelessness and respect for property rights. In the first place, the rights of the dispossessed in relation to land are not generally delineated in unqualified terms as rights intended to be immediately self-enforcing. For the main part they presuppose the adoption of legislative and other measures to strengthen existing rights of tenure, open up access to land and progressively provide adequate housing....

A second major feature of this cluster of constitutional provisions is that through section 26(3) they expressly acknowledge that eviction of people living in informal settlements may take place, even if it results in loss of a home.

A third aspect of section 26(3) is the emphasis it places on the need to seek concrete and case-specific solutions to the difficult problems that arise. Absent the historical background outlined above, the statement in the Constitution that the courts must do what courts are normally expected to do, namely, take all relevant factors into account, would appear otiose (superfluous), even odd. Its use in section 26(3), however, serves a

---

[5] *Id.* in paras [50]–[52]. Footnotes omitted.

clear constitutional purpose. It is there precisely to underline how non-prescriptive the provision is intended to be. The way in which the courts are to manage the process has accordingly been left as wide open as constitutional language could achieve, by design and not by accident, by deliberate purpose and not by omission.

In sum, the Constitution imposes new obligations on the courts concerning rights relating to property not previously recognised by the common law. It counterposes to the normal ownership rights of possession, use and occupation, a new and equally relevant right not arbitrarily to be deprived of a home.... The judicial function in these circumstances is not to establish a hierarchical arrangement between the different interests involved, privileging in an abstract and mechanical way the rights of ownership over the right not to be dispossessed of a home, or vice versa. Rather it is to balance out and reconcile the opposed claims in as just a manner as possible taking account of all the interests involved and the specific factors relevant in each particular case.

II. The structure of PIE

PIE provides some legislative texture to guide the courts in determining the approach to eviction now required by section 26 (3) of the Constitution....

Section 6, the governing provi sion [of PIE] in the present matter, reads:

6. Eviction at instance of organ of state.

(1) An organ of state may institute proceedings for the eviction of an unlawful occupier from land which falls within its area of jurisdiction... and the court may grant such an order if it is just and equitable to do so, after considering all the relevant circumstances, and if

(a) the consent of that organ of state is required for the erection of a building or structure on that land or for the occupation of the land, and the unlawful occupier is occupying a building or structure on that land without such consent having been obtained; or

(b) it is in the public interest to grant such an order.

(2) For the purposes of this section, "public interest" includes the interest of the health and safety of those occupying the land and the public in general.

(3) In deciding whether it is just and equitable to grant an order for eviction, the court must have regard to

(a) the circumstances under which the unlawful occupier occupied the land and erected the building or structure;

(b) the period the unlawful occupier and his or her family have resided on the land in question; and

(c) the availability to the unlawful occupier of suitable alternative accommodation or land.

Simply put, the ordinary prerequisites for the Municipality to be in a position to apply for an eviction order are that the occupation is unlawful and the structures are either unauthorised, or unhealthy or unsafe.... If [these facts] are proved, the court then may (not must) grant an eviction order if it is just and equitable to do so. In making its decision it must take account of all relevant circumstances, including the manner in which occupation was effected, its duration and the availability of suitable alternative accommodation or land.

'The circumstances of the occupation of the land'

A distinction could be drawn between occupation with the consent of the landowner but involving structures that [constitute] a health hazard, and occupation in the face of landowner opposition. Different considerations could arise depending on whether the land occupied is public or privately owned.... The motivation for settling on the land could be of importance. The degree of emergency or desperation of people who have sought a spot on which to erect their shelters, would always have to be considered. Furthermore, persons occupying land with at least a plausible belief that they have permission to be there can be looked at with far greater sympathy than those who deliberately invade land with a view to disrupting the organised housing programme and placing themselves at the front of the queue....

'The period the unlawful occupier and his or her family have been on the land'

[PIE's] concern is with time as an element of fairness.... The longer the unlawful occupiers have been on the land, the more established they are on their sites and in the neighbourhood, the more well settled their homes and the more integrated they are in terms of employment, schooling and enjoyment of social amenities, the greater their claim to the protection of the courts. A court will accordingly be far more cautious in evicting well-settled families with strong local ties, than persons who have recently moved on to land and erected their shelters there....

'The availability of suitable alternative accommodation or land'

Section 6(3) states that the availability of a suitable alternative place to go to is something to which regard must be had, not an inflexible requirement. There is therefore no unqualified constitutional duty on local authorities to ensure that in no circumstances should a home be destroyed unless alternative accommodation or land is made available. In general terms, however, a court should be reluctant to grant an eviction against relatively settled occupiers unless it is satisfied that a reasonable alternative is available, even if only as an interim measure pending ultimate access to housing in the formal housing programme.

...It is not enough to have a programme that works in theory....Thus it would not be enough for the municipality merely to show that it has in place a programme that is designed to house the maximum number of homeless people over the shortest period of time in the most cost effective way. The existence of such a programme would go a long way towards establishing a context that would ensure that a proposed eviction would be just and equitable. It falls short, however, from being determinative of whether and under what conditions an actual eviction order should be made in a particular case.

'Considering all the relevant circumstances'

There is nothing in section 6 to suggest that the three specifically identified circumstances are intended to be the only ones to which the court may refer in deciding what is just and equitable. They are peremptory but not exhaustive. It is clear both from the open-ended way in which they are framed and from the width of decision-making involved in the concept of what is just and equitable, that the court has a very wide mandate and must give due consideration to all circumstances that might be relevant....What is just and equitable could be affected by the reasonableness of offers made in connection with suitable alternative accommodation or land, the time scales proposed relative to the degree of disruption involved, and the willingness of the occupiers to respond to reasonable alternatives put before them.

The combination of circumstances may be extremely intricate, requiring a nuanced appreciation of the specific situation in each case....This is precisely why, even though unlawfulness is established, the eviction process is not automatic and why the courts are called upon to exercise a broad judicial discretion on a case by case basis....The proper application of PIE will therefore depend on the facts of each case, and each case may present different facts that call for the adoption of different approaches.

'Must have regard to'

...What the court is called upon to do is to decide whether, bearing in mind the values of the Constitution, in upholding and enforcing land rights it is appropriate to issue an order which has the effect of depriving people of their homes. Of equal concern, it is determining the conditions under which, if it is just and equitable to grant such an order, the eviction should take place. Both the language of the section and the purpose of the statute require the court to ensure that it is fully informed before undertaking the onerous and delicate task entrusted to it....Indeed when the evidence submitted by the parties leaves important questions of fact obscure, contested or uncertain, the court might be obliged to procure ways of establishing the true state of affairs, so as to enable it properly to 'have regard' to relevant circumstances.

'Just and equitable'

In *Port Elizabeth Municipality v Peoples Dialogue on Land and Shelter and Others*,[6] a case with some similarities to the present, section 6 was helpfully analysed by Horn AJ. He pointed out that in matters brought under PIE one is dealing with two diametrically opposed fundamental interests. On the one hand there is the traditional real right inherent in ownership reserving exclusive use and protection of property by the landowner. On the other hand there is the genuine despair of people in dire need of adequate accommodation. It was with this regard that the legislature had by virtue of its provisions of PIE set about implementing a procedure which envisaged the orderly and controlled removal of informal settlements. It is the duty of the court in applying the requirements of the Act to balance these opposing interests and bring out a decision that is just and equitable. He went on to say that the use of the term 'just and equitable' relates to both interests, that is what is just and equitable not only to the persons who occupied the land illegally but to the landowner as well. He held that the term also implies that a court, when deciding on a matter of this nature, would be obliged to break away from a purely legalistic approach and have regard to extraneous factors such as morality, fairness, social values and implications and circumstances which would necessitate bringing out an equitably principled judgment.

The court is thus called upon to go beyond its normal functions, and to engage in active judicial management according to equitable principles of an ongoing, stressful and law-governed social process. This has major implications for the manner in which it must deal with the issues before it, how it should approach questions of evidence, the procedures it may adopt, the way in which it exercises its powers and the orders it might make....

Thus, PIE expressly requires the court to infuse elements of grace and compassion into the formal structures of the law. It is called upon to balance competing interests in a principled way and promote the constitutional vision of a caring society based on good neighbourliness and shared concern. The Constitution and PIE confirm that we are not islands unto ourselves. The spirit of ubuntu, part of the deep cultural heritage of the majority of the population, suffuses the whole constitutional order.[7] It combines individual rights with a communitarian philosophy. It is a unifying motif of the Bill of Rights, which is nothing if not a structured, institutionalised and operational declaration in our evolving new society of the need for human interdependence, respect and concern.

[In Part III, the Court determined that "absent special circumstances it would not ordinarily be just and equitable to order eviction if proper

---

[6] Port Elizabeth Municipality v Peoples Dialogue on Land and Shelter and Others 2000 (2) SA 1074 (SE) at 1079 (S. Afr.)

[7] *Ubuntu*, a word that derives from the Zulu and Xhosa languages, roughly translates as "humaneness."

discussions, and where appropriate, mediation, have not been attempted"; however, it was inappropriate for the Court to order mediation in this instance since it had not already been attempted in the proceedings.]

IV. Should the decision of the SCA be overturned?

[I]n the light of the lengthy period during which the occupiers have lived on the land in question, the fact that there is no evidence that either the Municipality or the owners of the land need to evict the occupiers in order to put the land to some other productive use, the absence of any significant attempts by the Municipality to listen to and consider the problems of this particular group of occupiers, and the fact that this is a relatively small group of people who appear to be genuinely homeless and in need, I am not persuaded that it is just and equitable to order the eviction of the occupiers.

In the circumstances, the application for leave to appeal fails and the Municipality is ordered to pay the costs of the respondents, including the costs of two counsel.

Notes and Comments

1. *Perspectives on* Port Elizabeth. One prominent South African legal scholar has made the following comment about *Port Elizabeth*:

   > The judgment in *Port Elizabeth*...makes it clear that the constitutional court favours a contextual, transformative view of eviction, which means that the [South African Roman-Dutch] common law relating to eviction has to be developed (and new eviction legislation has to be interpreted) in a way that will reflect the constitutional choice for change—in this specific instance, continuity and change have to make way for development and change because of a clearly justified constitutional aspiration directly relating to the abolition and dismantling of the apartheid past and the building of a more equitable and just future land law. As far as eviction is concerned, the common law is subjected to direct influence and change inspired by constitutional provisions and aspirations.

   A.J. van der Walt, *Transformative Constitutionalism and the Development of South African Property Law (Part 1)*, 4 J. FOR S. AFR. L. 655, 677 (2005).

2. *The right to housing*. The *Port Elizabeth* Court was faced with the uneviable task of balancing the right of property under section 25 with the right to housing under 26. The leading case involving section 26 is *Government of the Republic of South Africa v. Grootboom*, 2001 (1) SA 46 (CC) (S. Afr.).

   In *Grootboom*, the Constitutional Court held that the legislature's housing program violated section 26 of the Constitution because the program was unreasonable in failing to address the plight of 900 individuals, more than half of them children, in desperate need of housing after they were evicted from an unlawful informal settlement. 2001 (1) SA 46 paras. 4, n.2, 8, 66. Although the court interpreted section 26 as requiring the state to adopt a reasonable housing program that addresses both short- and long-term housing inadequacies, it rejected the notion that section 26 imposes on the state a minimum core obligation to supply a minimum essential level of housing. 2001 (1) SA 46 paras. 30, 33, 43. The court further clarified that section 28 does not oblige the state to supply children and their parents with shelter if the parents are caring for their children. 2001 (1) SA 46 paras. 77, 79.

Grootboom has had more than its share of critics, most of whom have taken the Court to task for its failure to read section 26 as imposing a minimum core obligation on the state. *See, e.g.*, Theunis Roux, *The Constitutional Protection of Property Rights, in* CONSTITUTIONAL LAW OF SOUTH AFRICA, 46-1, 46-19 (Stuart Woolman et al., eds. 2006).

Professor Alexander has made the following observation regarding *Port Elizabeth* and *Grootboom* taken together:

> *Grootboom* and *Port Elizabeth Municipality* create a unique approach to defining the constitutional dimensional to the social obligation of ownership. This approach has three defining characteristics. First, as *Grootboom* makes clear, the state is under positive duties in relation to both the section 25 property right and to socioeconomic rights. These duties exist in tension with the more conventional negative duties that section 25 also imposes on the state....

Second, the social obligation defined by the socioeconomic rights provisions is limited in a highly important way. The state's obligation...has three components: (1) to undertake reasonable legislative and other measures and (2) to achieve progressive realization of the socioeconomic rights (3) within the range of available resources. An important consequence of this definition of the social obligation is that individuals do not have a constitutional entitlement to demand direct provision of services or benefits from the state.

Third, the social obligation...has primarily been imposed upon the state. This is especially true with respect to positive obligations, which have been the basis for claims in most of the [constitutional] court's socioeconomic rights cases. Whether the socioeconomic rights provisions create causes of action in litigation solely involving private parties has been a highly controversial topic....

GREGORY S. ALEXANDER, THE GLOBAL DEBATE OVER CONSTITUTIONAL PROPERTY: LESSONS FOR AMERICAN TAKINGS JURISPRUDENCE 181–82 (University of Chicago Press, 2006).

3. *Constitutional property and socioeconomic rights (including housing) in comparative perspective*. South Africa's recognition of a constitutional right to housing is highly unusual. Only a few constitutions, most of which have been enacted or revised in recent years, recognize this or any other positive constitutional right. The U.S. Constitution has no counterpart to section 26 or any of the other socioeconomic rights provisions of the South African Constitution. Even Germany's Basic Law, which is not a classical liberal constitution like that of the United States, does not guarantee positive socioeconomic individual rights such as housing.

Positive socioeconomic constitutional rights have been a subject of considerable debate in the United States and elsewhere. One of the objections often raised is that such rights are not justiciable because courts lack the power to enforce them. Positive rights impose affirmative obligations on the state to act on behalf of the individual. They compel the state to reach into its pocket to make provision for certain basic needs, and budgetary and other constraints make courts unsuitable to order such actions. *See, e.g.*, David P. Currie, *Positive and Negative Constitutional Rights*, 53 U. CHI. L. REV. 864 (1986). In *In re Certification of the Constitution of the Republic of South Africa*, 1996(4) SA 744 (CC) (S. Afr.), the South African Constitutional Court rejected this objection, holding that the positive socioeconomic rights in its constitution are, at least to some extent, justiciable.

Acknowledging that enforcement of socioeconomic rights almost invariably is limited by budgetary constraints, the court said that this does not bar justiciability because at a minimum courts can negatively protect such rights from improper invasion. The implication is that although fiscal complications are not a sufficient reason for judicial abstention, they may nevertheless influence the standard of review in individual cases. *See* Sandra Liebenberg, *The Interpretation of Socio-Economic Rights, in* Constitutional Law of South Africa 33-i, 33-5 (Stuart Woolman et al. eds., Juta Publishing, 2d ed. 2004).

In the United States, the Constitution does not expressly recognize positive socioeconomic rights. Some state constitutions, however, do affirmatively guarantee certain specific socioeconomic interests, such as education. *See, e.g.*, N.H. Const., Pt. I, Art. 12. There appeared to be some possibility that the U.S. Supreme Court would recognize socioeconomic interests as property when the Court in *Goldberg v. Kelly*, 397 U.S. 254 (1970), held that the Fourteenth Amendment's Due Process Clause requires that a welfare recipient was entitled to an evidentiary hearing prior to termination of benefits. That possibility was soon dashed, however, when the Court in *Dandridge v. Williams*, 397 U.S. 471 (1970), held that a state family-assistance law was valid even though its cap on maximum payments left many families living at state-recognized poverty levels. Since then, the Court has consistently rejected any possibility of reading a right to substantive protection of socioeconomic interests into the U.S. Constitution.

4. *The "horizontal effect" and the duty to protect*. Alexander's last comment alludes to the possibility that individual rights provisions of the South African Constitution might be given "horizontal effect," as it is sometimes called. The term refers to the idea that constitutional rights provisions impose duties on private actors as well as the state. As Professor Stephen Gardbaum puts it, "The horizontal position expressly rejects a public–private distinction in constitutional law…." Stephen Gardbaum, *The "Horizontal Effect" of Constitutional Rights*, 102 Mich. L. Rev. 387, 395 (2003). For additional discussion, *see infra* chapter 16, State Action Doctrine.

   More recently, the Court seems to have sidestepped the horizontality issue altogether. It did so by introducing the German discourse of a state duty to protect constitutional principles. According to this protective duty theory, the relevant question is, "Do the constitutional duties placed on government include positive ones to prohibit…certain actions by private individuals that touch on constitutional values." Gardbaum, *"Horizontal Effect," supra*, at 390 n.10.

   An important case that seemingly adopted this theory is *Modderklip East Squatters v. Modderklip Boerdery (Pty) Ltd.*, 2004 (8) BCLR 821 (SCA) (S. Afr.), *aff'd sub nom., President of the Republic of South Africa v Modderklip Boerdery (Pty) Ltd.*, 2005 (5) SA 3 (CC) (S. Afr.). In *Modderklip*, some 400 residents of an informal settlement in Johannesburg moved onto adjacent land that they mistakenly thought was owned by the city. In fact, the land was privately owned by Modderklip Farm. Within six months the new settlements included 18,000 people living in 4000 shacks. The owner sought to evict the occupants, relying on the Prevention of Illegal Eviction and Unlawful Occupation of Land (PIE) Act. The lower court granted an eviction order, but the occupants failed to vacate. Meanwhile the Modder East settlement had grown to 40,000 inhabitants. The sheriff was ordered to evict trespassers, but she insisted that the owner pay a large sum of money to cover the cost of eviction. The owner was unwilling to pay the sum because it exceeded the estimated value of the land. Modderklip then sought assistance from various public bodies, including the President of South Africa, who referred the matter to the Department of Land Affairs, which referred the matter to the Department of Housing, which did not respond. Understandably frustrated, Modderklip once again went to court and obtained a declaratory order forcing all of the relevant government officials to take all necessary steps to remove the unlawful occupants.

The state officials and the police treated the case solely a matter of private law, enforcement of a simple eviction order. The Supreme Court of Appeal took a different view of the situation. It observed that this attitude "does not reflect an adequate appreciation of the wider social and political responsibilities [that the *Grootboom* Court] identified in respect of persons such as the present occupiers." 2004 (8) BCLR at 828. The case posed an apparent conflict between two constitutional duties of the state: its duty to protect Modderklip's ownership rights under section 25 and its duty to provide access to adequate housing under section 26. The court's resolution of this apparent conflict was premised on its assumption that the state was under a constitutional duty to break the impasse by removing the main obstacle to enforcement of the eviction order, namely, the lack of available alternative land for the occupants. The court treated the state's failure in this regard as simultaneously a breach of the occupants' section 26 housing right and Modderklip's section 25 property right. The basis for this conclusion was section 7(2) of the Constitution, which provides that the state is under a duty to "respect, protect, promote and fulfill the rights in the Bill of Rights." In the court's view, by failing to provide the occupants with alternative housing in accordance with section 26, the state failed to protect the owner's section 25 property right, as section 7(2) requires. The court stated:

> [I]n a material respect the state failed in its constitutional duty to protect the rights of Modderklip: it did not provide the occupiers with land which would have enabled Modderklip (had it been able) to enforce the eviction order. Instead, it allowed the burden of the occupiers need for land to fall on an individual....

Id. at 834. Failure to protect one right, in other words, meant failure to protect another right.

On appeal, the Constitutional Court affirmed the relief ordered by the Supreme Court of Appeal. It did so on a theory other than the protective duty theory but without directly rejecting that theory. The status of both the horizontal effect question and the protective duty theory in South African constitutional law remains unclear. The possibility remains open that the Constitutional Court will recognize some version of either of these doctrines.

5. Additional readings. The best sources on South African constitutional property law include A.J. van der Walt, Constitutional Property Law (2005); Theunis Roux, *Property, in* South African Constitutional Law: The Bill of Rights 429 (M.H. Cheadle, D.M. Davis & N.R.L. Haysom eds., 2002); Theunis Roux, *Section 25, in* Constitutional Law of South Africa ch. 46 (Stuart Woolman et al. eds., 2d ed. 2003); Geoff Budlender, *The Constitutional Protection of Property Rights: Overview and Commentary, in* Juta's New Land Law ch. 1 (Geoff Budlender, Johan Latsky & Theunis Roux eds., 1998).

6

Abortion Rights

Radhika Rao

As one legal scholar observes, "it has been striking to watch the United States Supreme Court wrestle with the problems of abortion as though pregnancy were a phenomenon unique to the United States."[1] Other legal systems confront the same basic questions of when life begins, whether a fetus is a person entitled to legal protection, and who should possess the power to decide. Their choices illustrate alternate possibilities and illuminate the character of American law. Comparative study demonstrates that abortion rights may stem from a constitution, a statute, local law, or even international obligations. They may be conceptualized as procedural or substantive, and they may take the form of negative rights or affirmative obligations. Comparative study also highlights the divergence between the articulation of a right and its realization.

Justice Scalia claims that American abortion law is "out of step" with the rest of the world because the United States is "one of only six countries that allow abortion on demand until the point of viability."[2] Technically, he may be correct: only five other countries expressly permit abortion until viability (estimated to occur between 20 and 24 weeks) or a later point in pregnancy.[3] Yet 56 countries, containing almost 40% of the world's population, currently allow abortion for any reason in the early stages of pregnancy (generally the first trimester).[4] Moreover, close study of comparative abortion law reveals that the reality is too complex to be captured in a series of statistics. Even in

---

1 John Langbein, *The Influence of Comparative Procedure in the United States*, 43 AM. J. COMP. L. 545, 550 (1995).

2 Norman Dorsen (ed.), *The Relevance of Foreign Legal Materials in U.S. Constitutional Cases: A Conversation Between Justice Antonin Scalia and Justice Stephen Breyer*, 3 INT'L J. CONST. L. 519, 521 (2005); Roper v. Simmons, 543 U.S. 551, 625 (2005) (Scalia, J., dissenting).

3 The five include Canada, China, Korea, the Netherlands, and Vietnam, although Sweden and Singapore could also be added to this list because they permit abortion for any reason up until eighteen weeks and twenty-four weeks of pregnancy, respectively. See Center for Reproductive Rights, The World's Abortion Laws (May 2007) (http://www.reproductiverights.org/pub_fac_abortion_laws.html) (last accessed March 2008).

4 See Center for Reproductive Rights, The World's Abortion Laws (May 2007) (http://www.reproductiverights.org/pub_fac_abortion_laws.html) (last accessed March 2008).

those countries where abortion appears to be illegal in principle, the reality often belies the language of the law. French law, for example, limits abortion to women who are "in distress" but authorizes women to judge their own situation. German abortion law is frequently invoked as diametrically opposed to that of the United States. As you read the following materials, consider whether this is an accurate assessment.

Abortion I Case[5]

Constitutional Court of Germany
39 BVerfGE I (1975)

[This case arose as an abstract judicial-review proceeding—a procedure by which a state government or one-third of the Bundestag (the popularly elected branch of the legislature) may directly challenge the constitutionality of a statute immediately after its passage into law. Five state governments and 193 members of the Bundestag (primarily from Christian parties) petitioned the Constitutional Court to review the Abortion Reform Act of 1974 on grounds that it violated the right-to-life and human dignity clauses of the Basic Law (the German Constitution). The statute liberalized abortion law by providing that an abortion would not be punished if performed during the first twelve weeks of pregnancy by a physician with the consent of the pregnant woman after preventive counseling. However, criminal penalties would continue to be enforced with respect to abortions performed after twelve weeks, unless necessary to protect the woman's life or health or justified by genetic indications.]

Guiding principles

1. The life developing within the mother's womb is an independent legal value which enjoys the protection of the constitution. The State's duty to protect forbids not only direct state attacks against developing life, but also requires the state to protect and foster this life.

2. The obligation of the state to protect the developing life exists even against the mother.

3. The protection of life of the child *en ventre sa mere* takes precedence as a matter of principle for the entire duration of the pregnancy over the

---

[5] Edited from *West German Abortion Decision: A Contrast to* Roe v. Wade, translated by Robert E. Jonas and John D. Gorby, 9 John Marshall J. PRAC. & PROC. 605 (1976) and DONALD P. KOMMERS, THE CONSTITUTIONAL JURISPRUDENCE OF THE FEDERAL REPUBLIC OF GERMANY 336–46 (2nd ed. 1997).

right of the pregnant woman to self-determination and may not be placed in question for any particular time.

4. The legislature may express the legal condemnation of the termination of pregnancy required by the Basic Law through measures other than the threat of punishment. The decisive factor is whether the totality of the measures serving the protection of the unborn life guarantees an actual protection which in fact corresponds to the importance of the legal value to be guaranteed. In the extreme case, if the protection required by the constitution cannot be realized in any other manner, the legislature is obligated to employ the criminal law to secure the developing life.

5. A continuation of the pregnancy is not to be exacted (legally) if the termination is necessary to avert from the pregnant woman a danger to her life or the danger of serious impairment of her health. Beyond that the legislature is at liberty to designate as non-exactable other extraordinary burdens for the pregnant woman, which are of similar gravity and, in these cases, to leave the interruption of pregnancy free of punishment.

The Federal Constitutional Court...[holds that the Abortion Reform Act of 1974]...is incompatible with...the Basic Law and is void insofar as it exempts termination of pregnancy from punishment in cases where no reasons exist which...have priority over the value order contained in the Basic Law....

C

The question of the legal treatment of the interruption of pregnancy has been discussed publicly for decades from various points of view....It is the task of the legislature to evaluate the many sided and often opposing arguments.... The statutory regulation...can be examined by the Constitutional Court only from the viewpoint of whether it is compatible with the Basic Law, which is the highest valid law in the Federal Republic....

I

1. Article 2 (2)[1] of the Basic Law also protects the life developing within the mother's womb as an independent legal interest.

a) Unlike the Weimar Constitution, the express incorporation of the self-evident right to life in the Basic Law may be explained principally as a reaction to the "destruction of life unworthy to live," to the "final solution" and the "liquidations" that the National Socialist Regime carried out as measures of state. Article 2(2)[1] of the Basic Law implies..." an affirmation of the fundamental worth of human life and of a state concept which emphatically opposes the views of a political regime for which the individual life had little significance and which therefore practiced unlimited abuse in the name of the arrogated right over life and death of the citizen."

b) In construing Article 2(2)[1] of the Basic Law, one should begin with its language: "Everyone has a right to life...." Life, in the sense of the developmental existence of a human individual begins, according to established biological–physiological knowledge, on the 14th day after conception.... The process of development which has begun at that point is a continuing process which exhibits no sharp demarcation.... Therefore, the protection of Article 2(2)[1] of the Basic Law cannot be limited either to the "completed" human being after birth or to the child about to be born which is independently capable of living. The right to life is guaranteed to everyone who "lives"; no distinction can be made here between various stages of the life developing before birth or between prenatal and postnatal life. "Everyone" in the sense of Article 2(2)[1] of the Basic Law... includes the yet unborn human being....

c) ... The security of human existence against encroachments by the state would be incomplete if it did not also embrace the prior step of... unborn life....

2. Therefore, [we] derive the obligation of the state to protect all human life directly from Article 2(2)[1] of the Basic Law. Additionally, [this obligation] follows from the express... protection which Article 1(1) accords to human dignity. Wherever human life exists, it merits human dignity; whether the subject of this dignity is conscious of it and knows how to safeguard it is not of decisive moment. The potential faculties present in the human being from the beginning suffice to establish human dignity....

II

1. The duty of the state to protect is comprehensive. It not only forbids... direct state attacks on developing life but also requires the state to take a position protecting and promoting this life... [and to] preserve it even against illegal attacks by others....

2. The obligation of the state to [protect] developing life... exists, as a matter of principle, even against the mother.... Pregnancy belongs to the sphere of intimacy of the woman, the protection of which is... guaranteed... [by] the Basic Law. Were the embryo to be considered only as a part of the maternal organism the interruption of pregnancy would remain in the area of the private structuring of one's life, where the legislature is forbidden to encroach. Since, however, the one about to be born is an independent human being who stands under the protection of the constitution, there is a social dimension to the interruption of pregnancy which makes it amenable to... regulation....

A compromise... is not possible since the interruption of pregnancy always means the destruction of the unborn life. In the required balancing, "both constitutional values are to be viewed in their relationship to human dignity, the center of the value system of the constitution." A decision oriented to... the Basic Law must come down in favor of the precedence of the protection of life for the child *en ventre sa mere* over the right of the pregnant woman to self-determination.... This precedence exists as a matter of principle for the entire duration of pregnancy....

3. ...[T]he legal order may not make the woman's right to self-determination the sole guideline of its rulemaking.... The condemnation of abortion must be clearly expressed in the legal order. The false impression must be avoided that the interruption of pregnancy is the same social process as, for example, approaching a physician for healing an illness or indeed a legally irrelevant alternative for the prevention of conception....

III

1. ...It is...the task of the state to employ, in the first instance, social, political, and welfare means for securing developing life.... [H]ow the assistance measures are to be structured in their particulars is largely left to the legislature and is generally beyond judgment by the Constitutional Court....

2. ...The legislature is not obligated...to employ the same penal measures for the protection of the unborn life as it considers required...for born life....

a) ...The interruption of pregnancy irrevocably destroys an existing human life. Abortion is an act of killing.... [T]he employment of penal law for the requital of "acts of abortion" is to be seen as legitimate without a doubt; it is valid law in most cultural states...and especially corresponds to the German legal tradition....

b) ...[But t]he legislature is not prohibited...from expressing the legal condemnation of abortion required by the Basic Law in ways other than the threat of punishment. The decisive factor is whether the totality of the measures serving the protection of the unborn life...guarantees an actual protection corresponding to the importance of the legal value to be secured....

3. The obligation of the state to protect the developing life exists...against the mother as well.... [H]owever, the employment of the penal law may give rise to special problems which result from the unique situation of the pregnant woman.... The right to life of the unborn can lead to a burdening of the woman which essentially goes beyond that normally associated with pregnancy. The result is the question of exactability, or, in other words, the question of whether the state...may compel the bearing of the child to term with the means of the penal law....

A continuation of the pregnancy appears to be non-exactable especially when it is proven that the interruption is required "to avert" from the pregnant woman "a danger for her life or the danger of a grave impairment of her condition of health." In this case her own "right to life and bodily inviolability" is at stake, the sacrifice of which cannot be expected of her for the unborn life. Beyond that, the legislature has a free hand to leave the interruption of pregnancy free of punishment in the case of other extraordinary burdens for the pregnant woman, which, from the point of view of non-exactability, are as weighty as those referred to in [the 1974 statute]. In this category can be counted, especially, the cases of the genetic, ethical [rape or incest], and of the social or emergency indication for abortion....

In all other cases the interruption of pregnancy remains a wrong deserving punishment...[and the legislature may dispense with punishment] only on the condition that another equally effective legal sanction stands at its command which would clearly bring out the unjust character of the act (the condemnation by the legal order) and likewise prevent the interruptions of pregnancy as effectively as a penal provision....

D

II

...The [1974] statute is based upon the idea that developing life would be better protected through individual counseling of the pregnant woman than through a threat of punishment.... On this basis the legislature has reached the decision to abandon the criminal penalty entirely for the first twelve weeks of pregnancy under definite prerequisites and, in its place, to introduce...preventive counseling.

...The regulation in question, however, encounters decisive constitutional problems....

1. The...condemnation of [abortion] required by the constitution must clearly appear in the legal order....This absolute condemnation is not expressed in the provisions of the [1974 statute] with regard to the interruption of pregnancy during the first twelve weeks because the statute leaves unclear whether an interruption of pregnancy which is not "indicated" is legal or illegal after the repeal of the criminal penalty.... [T]he impression must arise that s. 218a completely removes, through the absolute repeal of punishability, the legal condemnation—without consideration of the reasons—and legally allows the interruption of pregnancy under the prerequisites listed therein....

The proposed regulation, as a whole, can therefore only be interpreted to mean that an interruption of pregnancy performed by a physician in the first twelve weeks of pregnancy is not illegal and therefore should be allowed (under law)....

2. ...The objection against this is...that the penal sanction is often ineffective....At the same time,...the threat of punishment, by discouraging counseling of women susceptible of influence, impedes saving life in other cases....

a) [T]his concept does not do justice to the essence and the function of the penal law....No doubt, the mere existence of such a penal

> sanction has influence on the conceptions of value and the…behavior of the populace…. An opposite effect will result if, through a general repeal of punishability, even doubtlessly punishable behavior is declared to be legally free from objection….The purely theoretical announcement that the interruption of pregnancy is "tolerated," but not "approved," must remain without effect as long as no legal sanction is recognizable which clearly segregates the justified cases of abortion from the reprehensible. If the threat of punishment disappears in its entirety,…[t]he "dangerous inference of moral permissibility from a legal absence of sanction"…is too near not to be drawn by a large number of those subject to the law….
>
> b) The weighing in bulk of life against life which leads to the allowance of the destruction of a supposedly smaller number in the interest of the preservation of an allegedly larger number is not reconcilable with the obligation of an individual protection of each single concrete life….

…The fundamental legal protection in individual cases may not be sacrificed to the efficiency of the regulation as a whole. The statute is not only an instrument to steer social processes according to sociological judgments and prognoses but is also the enduring expression of socio-ethical…[and] legal evaluation of human acts; it should say what is right and wrong for the individual.

IV

The [1974 statute] at times is defended with the argument that in other democratic countries of the Western World in recent times the penal provisions regulating the interruption of pregnancy have been "liberalized" or "modernized" in a similar or an even more extensive fashion….

These considerations cannot influence the decision to be made here. Disregarding the fact that all of these foreign laws in their respective countries are sharply controverted, the legal standards which are applicable there for the acts of the legislature are essentially different from those of the Federal Republic of Germany.

Underlying the Basic Law are principles for the structuring of the state that may be understood only in light of the historical experience and the spiritual–moral confrontation with the previous system of National Socialism. In opposition to the omnipotence of the totalitarian state which claimed for itself limitless dominion over all areas of social life and which, in the prosecution of its goals of state, consideration for the life of the individual fundamentally meant nothing, the Basic Law of the Federal Republic of Germany has erected an order bound together by values which places the individual human being and his dignity at the focal point of all of its ordinances. At its basis lies the concept…that human beings possess an inherent worth as individuals in order of creation which uncompromisingly demands unconditional respect for the life of every individual human being, even for the apparently socially "worthless," and which therefore excludes the destruction of such life without legally justifiable grounds.

This fundamental constitutional decision determines the structure and the interpretation of the entire legal order....

Dissenting Opinion of Justice Rupp Von Brunneck and Justice Dr. Simon

The life of each individual human being is self-evidently a central value of the legal order. It is uncontested that the constitutional duty to protect this life also includes its preliminary stages before birth. The debates in Parliament and before the Federal Constitutional Court dealt not with the *whether* but rather only the *how* of this protection. This decision is a matter of legislative responsibility....

A-I

The authority of the Federal Constitutional Court to annul the decisions of the legislature demands sparing use, if an imbalance between the constitutional organs is to be avoided. The requirement of judicial self-restraint, which is designated as the "elixir of life" of the jurisprudence of the Federal Constitutional Court, is especially valid when [what is] involved is not a defense from overreaching by state power but rather the making, via constitutional judicial control, of provisions for the positive structuring of the social order....

1. ...The fundamental legal norms standing in the central part of our constitution guarantee as rights of defense to the citizen in relation to the state a sphere of unrestricted structuring of one's life based on personal responsibility. The classical function of the Federal Constitutional Court lies in...[determining whether] the state, generally or to the extent provided, may punish.

In the present constitutional dispute, the inverse question is presented for the first time...namely whether the state *must* punish, whether the abolition of punishment for the interruption of pregnancy in the first three months of pregnancy is compatible with fundamental rights....

2. ...According to [the majority], the fundamental rights not only establish rights of defense of the individual against the state, but also contain at the same time objective value decisions, the realization of which through affirmative action is a permanent task of state power....The majority of this Court insufficiently considers differences in the two aspects of fundamental rights, differences essential to the judicial control of constitutionality.

As defense rights the fundamental rights have a comparatively clear recognizable content; in their interpretation and application, the judicial opinions have developed practicable, generally recognized criteria for the control of state encroachments.... On the other hand, it is regularly a most complex question, *how* a value decision is to be realized through affirmative measures of the legislature....The decision, which frequently presupposes compromises and takes place in the course of trial and error, belongs, according to the principle of division of powers and to the democratic principle, to the responsibility of the legislature directly legitimatized by the people....

II

1. Our strongest reservation is directed to the fact that for the first time in opinions of the Constitutional Court an objective value decision should function as a *duty* of the legislature to enact *penal norms*.... This inverts the function of the fundamental rights into its contrary. If the objective value decision contained in a fundamental legal norm to protect a certain legal value should suffice to derive therefrom the duty to punish, the fundamental rights could underhandedly, on the pretext of securing freedom, become the basis for an abundance of regimentations which restrict freedom....

...In this way the Supreme Court of the United States has even regarded punishment for the interruption of pregnancy, performed by a physician with the consent of the pregnant woman in the first third of pregnancy, as a violation of fundamental rights.[6] This would, according to German constitutional law, go too far indeed. According to the liberal character of our constitution, however, the legislature needs a constitutional justification to punish, not to disregard punishment....

2. ...A contrary standpoint cannot be supported with the argument that...Article 2(2) of the Basic Law unquestionably originated from the reaction to the inhumane ideology and practice of the National Socialist regime. This reaction refers to the mass destruction of human life by the state in concentration camps and, in the case of the mentally ill, sterilizations and forced abortions directed by authorities, to involuntary medical experiments on human beings, to disrespect of individual life and human dignity which was expressed by countless other measures of state.

...[During the Nazi era, the penalty for abortion]...was significantly sharpened.... [P]rofessional abortion was...punished with imprisonment in the penitentiary; and, even with the death penalty, if the perpetrator had "thereby continually injured the vitality of the German people."...[Thus] the reasons which led to the adoption of Article 2(2) of the Basic Law can by no means be adduced in favor of a constitutional duty to punish abortions. Rather, the decisive renunciation completed with the Basic Law of the totalitarian National Socialist state demands rather the reverse conclusion, that is, restraint in employing criminal punishment, the improper use of which in the history of mankind has caused endless suffering.

---

[6] Roe v. Wade, 410 U.S. 113 (1973).

B-I

...The [majority neglects] the *uniqueness of the interruption of pregnancy* in relation to other dangers of human life.... The unusual circumstances that in the person of the pregnant woman there is a unique unity of "actor" and "victim" is of legal significance, because much more is demanded of the pregnant woman than mere omission—as opposed to the demands on the one addressed by penal provisions against homicide....

...According to the view of the undersigned Madame Justice, the refusal of the pregnant woman to permit the child *en ventre sa mere* to become a human being is something essentially different from the killing of independently existing life, not only according to the natural sensitivities of the woman but also legally. For this reason the equating in principle of abortion in the first stage of pregnancy with murder or intentional killing is not allowable from the outset.... [F]or the legal consciousness of the pregnant woman as well as for the general legal consciousness, there is a difference between an interruption of pregnancy which takes place in the first stage of pregnancy and one which takes place in a later phase. This has resulted at all times in domestic and foreign legal systems in a different penal assessment which is tied to such stages which are based on time, as, for example, the Supreme Court of the United States impressively stated....

III

That the decision of the German legislature for the regulation of terms and counseling neither arises from a fundamental attitude which is to be morally or legally condemned nor proceeds from apparently false premises in the determination of the circumstances of life is confirmed by identical or similar *provisions for reform in numerous foreign states*. In Austria, France, Denmark, and Sweden an interruption of pregnancy, performed during the first twelve weeks (in France, ten) of pregnancy by a physician with the consent of the pregnant woman, is not punishable; in Great Britain and in the Netherlands a regulation of indications is in effect which amounts to the same thing in its practical application. These states can boast that they are a part of an impressive constitutional tradition and all-in-all certainly do not lag behind the Federal Republic in unconditional respect for life of each individual human being; some of them likewise have historical experience with an inhuman system of injustice....

Notes and Questions

1. *Abortion and Reunification.* After this case, abortion was permitted in the Federal Republic of Germany (West Germany) only under limited circumstances, such as for medical, genetic, ethical, and serious social "indications." The law also required a physician other than the one performing the abortion to certify the

presence of a legal "indication" and called for counseling of the pregnant woman. In the absence of these "indications," abortion was a criminal offense. At the time of German unification in 1990, abortion on demand at public expense in the first trimester was legal in the German Democratic Republic (East Germany). The Unification Treaty permitted each portion of the country to maintain its own practice on abortion until 1992, when a unified law was to be enacted. However, the Bundestag's first attempt to pass a unified law was struck down again by the Constitutional Court in 1993.

2. *Abortion II Case*, 88 BVerfGE 203 (Germany 1993).[7] According to Professor Donald Kommers, "*Abortion II*... reaffirmed the essential core of *Abortion I* while simultaneously adjusting the character of this protection to meet the needs of post-unification Germany."[8] In a major departure from *Abortion I*, the Constitutional Court in *Abortion II* ruled that nonindicated abortions performed during the first twelve weeks of pregnancy need *not* be punished. Thus the Court upheld the legislature's decision to replace criminal penalties with a system of counseling that allows women themselves to judge whether abortion is justified. Yet the Constitutional Court struck down the provision of the new law labeling "not illegal" abortions performed during the first trimester of pregnancy, holding that abortions not justified by "indications" must remain illegal even though they are not punished. The Court also ruled that abortions without a third-party finding of "indications" cannot constitutionally be covered by Germany's national health plan, although welfare assistance must be provided to poor women who want nonindicated abortions but cannot afford them.

 The full opinion is over 163 pages long, but the headnotes, drafted by the Court itself, contain the following statements:

> 7. The fundamental rights of a woman do not mandate the general suspension of a duty to carry out a pregnancy, even within a limited time frame. However, a woman's constitutional rights permit—and in certain cases might require—recognition of exceptional circumstances under which such a duty shall not be imposed on her....
>
> 8. ...[T]he state is precluded from freely dispensing with criminal punishment and its protective effect on human life....
>
> 11. The legislature acts constitutionally when it adopts a regulatory scheme for the protection of the unborn which uses counseling as a means of inducing pregnant women in conflict during the early stage of pregnancy to carry their pregnancy to term. The legislature also acts within constitutional bounds when it dispenses with criminal prosecution for indicated abortions as well as the determination of such indications by third parties....
>
> 15. Abortions performed in the absence of a determined indication as prescribed by the counseling regulation may not be deemed justified (not unlawful)....[A]n exception can have the effect of a legal justification only if it is incumbent on the state alone to establish the criteria necessary to take the act in question out of the general rule.
>
> 16. It is unconstitutional to create an entitlement to statutory health insurance benefits for the performance of an abortion whose lawfulness has not been established. By contrast, it is not unconstitutional to grant social welfare benefits for abortions not incurring criminal liability under the counseling regulation where a woman lacks financial means....

---

[7] Edited from DONALD KOMMERS, THE CONSTITUTIONAL JURISPRUDENCE OF THE FEDERAL REPUBLIC OF GERMANY 349–51 (2nd ed. 1997)

[8] *Id.* at 349.

In 1995, a new unified law was enacted that adhered to the guidelines given by the Constitutional Court in *Abortion II* by labeling abortion illegal without attaching criminal penalties.

3. Compare the German approach to abortion with that of the United States. Critics of *Roe v. Wade* have accused the U.S. Supreme Court of being "activist" and of writing a "legislative code" rather than a judicial opinion. Are the German abortion decisions less "activist" than those of the U.S. Supreme Court? Are they less "legislative" in character? Consider the specifics of the opinions.
   (a) In contrast to the U.S. Supreme Court, which did not answer the question of when life begins, the German Constitutional Court found that "[l]ife…begins, according to established biological–physiological knowledge, on the 14th day after conception." Moreover, the Basic Law guarantees the right to life of "everyone who lives"—including the unborn—whereas the fetus is not a person protected by the U.S. Constitution. What explains these differences? Is it the text of the respective documents? Both the Basic Law and the U.S. Constitution are silent on this question, although draft reports of the Basic Law suggest that a provision that would have explicitly protected the unborn was defeated because of the prevailing understanding that such protection was already encompassed in the right to life. Can the contrast between German and U.S. constitutional law be evaluated without reference to differences in their history and culture?
   (b) In the United States, women have a fundamental constitutional right to terminate their pregnancies prior to fetal viability, whereas in Germany, the government has a fundamental constitutional duty to protect unborn life by outlawing abortion except under very limited circumstances. This disparity highlights a dramatic difference in the concept of constitutional rights—as negative rights that shield the citizen from state intrusion, or as positive rights that impose affirmative obligations on the government. What do you think of the Constitutional Court's use of constitutional rights as a sword rather than a shield, to compel the government to protect unborn life by criminalizing abortion? Does the German example shed light on the U.S. Supreme Court's reluctance to protect "affirmative" rights by illustrating the dangers of such an approach?
   (c) Despite these theoretical differences, Professor Gerald Neuman states that "[i]n practical terms, the situation in Germany [after *Abortion II*] now resembles the post-*Casey* situation in Pennsylvania" because, in both places, "[a]bortion is available after burdensome preliminaries" such as waiting periods and counseling. Gerald L. Neuman, Casey *in the Mirror: Abortion, Abuse and the Right to Protection in the United States and Germany*, 43 AM. J. COMP. L. 273 (Spring 1995). How should this comparison be evaluated? By observing the results—such as the actual rates of abortion in the two countries? Or by examining the reasoning of the German and U.S. decisions? What do you make of the fact that, in practice, abortion is more widely available in Germany than it is in the United States because the state must pay for the procedure for all women when it is justified by "indications" (through the national health insurance), and for poor women, even when it is not justified, through the welfare system?
   (d) What about the fact that abortion remains illegal in principle in Germany, even though it is not punished so long as the pregnant woman undergoes

counseling? Describing French abortion law, which closely resembles that of Germany after *Abortion II*, Professor Mary Ann Glendon suggests that it is preferable to the American approach because it "*names* the underlying problem as one involving human life, not as a conflict [between] a woman's individual liberty or privacy and a non-person." *See* MARY ANN GLENDON, ABORTION & DIVORCE IN WESTERN LAW 19 (1989). Another commentator observes:

> [T]he distinction between "illegality" of a crime and its punishment represents a concept lawyers have difficulty understanding. This is more true of the average citizen. How illegal is an abortion that goes unpunished not only in exceptional cases but in principle? The illegality of abortion, stressed by the Constitutional Court, may be transformed in reality into an empty legalistic shell.

Udo Werner, *The Convergence of Abortion Regulation in Germany and the United States: A Critique of Glendon's Rights Talk Thesis*, 18 LOYOLA (L.A.) INT. & COMP. L.J. 571, 601 (1996). Do you agree with this criticism? Must criminal law consist of enforceable norms, or does it also possess an expressive and educative function?

4. *Procedure versus substance.* In *Morgentaler, Smoling and Scott v. The Queen*, 1 S.C.R. 30 (Supreme Court of Canada 1988), the Canadian Supreme Court struck down a statute that outlawed abortion but created an exception by which women could obtain legal abortions if a "therapeutic abortion committee" composed of three doctors certified that "the continuation of the pregnancy of such female person...would be likely to endanger her life or health." The Canadian Supreme Court held that this law violates Section 7 of the Canadian Charter of Rights and Freedoms, which provides that "everyone has the right to life, liberty and security of the person and the right not to be deprived thereof except in accordance with the principles of fundamental justice." The Court found the procedures established by Parliament to qualify for the statutory exception to be "illusory or so difficult to attain as to be practically illusory" because, in many parts of the country, it was impossible to satisfy them and obtain a therapeutic abortion. The Court declared it unnecessary to determine whether the Charter guarantees a substantive right to an abortion because "the procedures...for obtaining a therapeutic abortion do not comport with the principles of fundamental justice." After this decision, it was theoretically possible for the Canadian Parliament to enact another law regulating abortion, but thus far it has failed to do so. In 1991, an attempt to reinstate a law criminalizing abortion failed to pass the upper chamber of the Canadian Parliament on a tie vote.

Compare the Canadian approach to abortion with that of the United States. Some scholars suggest that *Morgentaler* is a more narrow ruling than *Roe* because it invalidated the abortion law on procedural grounds without granting a substantive right. In so doing, the Canadian Supreme Court opened a dialogue with the legislature but left Parliament free to enact another abortion law. *See* Daniel O. Conkle, *Canada's* Roe*: The Canadian Abortion Decision and Its Implications for American Constitutional Law and Theory*, 6 CONST. COMMENT. 299, 315–16 (1989). But consider the Canadian Supreme Court's decision to hold the government accountable for the circumstances that made therapeutic abortions practically unavailable to many women. How does this compare with the United States, where abortion is a fundamental constitutional right yet the Supreme Court regards the conditions that prevent many women from actually exercising this right as the result not of government action, but rather of the market, or nature, or even the responsibility of women themselves? *See Maher v. Roe*, 432 U.S. 464 (1977); *Harris v. McRae*, 448 U.S. 297 (1980) (it is constitutional for government to fund childbirth but not abortion because "government may not place obstacles in the path of a woman's exercise of her constitutional right to an abortion, but it need not remove those obstacles not of its own creation"); *Webster v. Reproductive Health Services*, 492 U.S. 490 (1989) (it is constitutional for government to prohibit public employees from performing abortions and to bar access to public facilities).

5. *Framing the abortion question*. There are many different ways to characterize abortion in terms of how the rights are framed, which sources of law are invoked, and—at an even more basic level—whether abortion is conceived as a legal issue at all. In the United States, the debate over the constitutional basis for abortion has focused on the question whether the right should have been grounded in privacy/liberty or in gender equality. Other countries have framed the issue in terms of a woman's constitutional right to "security of the person" (Canada) or the constitutional right to "life" and "human dignity" of the unborn (Germany).

   The Colombian Constitutional Court struck down a statute criminalizing all abortion on grounds that it violated women's rights to health, dignity, and life, which are protected under the Colombian Constitution and international human rights law. In a decision that invalidated one of the most restrictive abortion laws in the world, the Court ruled that abortion must be legally permitted when the life or health (physical and mental) of the woman is in danger, when pregnancy is the result of a crime such as rape or incest, or when grave fetal malformations make life outside the uterus unviable. *See* Decision C-355/2006 (Colombia May 2006).[9] The Court found that "the right to health," even though it is not expressly protected as a fundamental right under the Colombian Constitution, "has a fundamental character when it is in close relation to the right to life." The Court perceived restrictive abortion laws as a threat to women's health and their lives because the large number of illegal abortions performed prior to this decision contributed to Colombia's high rate of maternal mortality. The Court held that the state can protect prenatal life, but only in a way that is compatible with the rights to life and health of women:

   > the state cannot oblige a person, in this case a pregnant woman, to perform heroic sacrifices and give up her own rights for the benefit of others or for the benefit of society in general. Such an obligation is unenforceable, even if the pregnancy is the result of a consensual act, in light of article 49 of the Constitution, which mandates that all persons take care of their own health.

   According to the Constitutional Court,

   > laws criminalizing medical interventions that specially affect women constitute a barrier to women's access to needed medical care, compromising women's right to gender equality in the area of health, and amounting to a violation of states' international obligations to respect those internationally recognized rights.

   Sometimes the abortion issue arises only obliquely in claims involving other constitutional rights. In Ireland, for example, the abortion controversy raises additional questions regarding freedom of speech and freedom of movement to the extent that it involves the ability of Irish women to acquire information about abortion elsewhere and to travel to other countries in order to obtain the procedure. In other contexts, abortion may not even be conceptualized as a

---

[9] Obtained from www.womenslinkworldwide.org, which provides excerpts from the 600-page long opinion.

constitutional issue. For example, abortion in China is not viewed as a matter of "rights" but rather as a method of population control that is occasionally used to enforce the one-child policy. For this reason, Professor Gunter Frankenberg argues that a comparison with a country like China would illuminate the issue by calling into question the very categories used to construct abortion in the West:

> [A] contrasting view from, say, the practice of coerced abortions in China after the first child for the sake of population control...brings to the fore the contours and peculiarities of the categories ("infanticide," "unborn life," "right") and of the sets of relationships ("individual"/"state," "private"/"public") of the domestic world as well as our own normative preferences and emotional reactions. It elucidates options and perspectives not allowed by the traditionally closed systems of comparison. Comparison can show that there are whole other issues, such as population control and other (not necessarily better) solutions. To turn in on the public and legal discourse on abortion in the United States, Canada, West Germany, and Italy from the vantage point of a "radically different" culture like China means to recognize alternatives, to recognize behind moral/legal debates the imposition of "modernization" on a traditional culture there and the sustenance of patriarchy and state authority against women's movements and democratization here. Comparison thus can contribute to learning—beyond the conservative "infanticide"-discourse and the liberal "rights"-discourse on abortion and brings out that birth control is not an essentially legal issue that can be discussed more fully and adequately beyond the horizon of legal regulations and reasoning. (Gunter Frankenberg, *Critical Comparisons: Re-thinking Comparative Law*, 26 HARV. INT'L L.J. 411, 452–53 (1985))

Justice Scalia contends that such comparisons are irrelevant to the interpretation of the U.S. Constitution. He criticizes the Supreme Court for its selective use of foreign law and asks why the Court does not alter its abortion jurisprudence when the United States is "one of only six countries that allow abortion on demand until the point of viability." *Roper v. Simmons*, 543 U.S. 551, 625 (2005) (Scalia, J., dissenting). *See also* Norman Dorsen (ed.), *The Relevance of Foreign Legal Materials in U.S. Constitutional Cases: A Conversation Between Justice Antonin Scalia and Justice Stephen Breyer*, 3 INT'L J. CONST. L. 519, 521 (2005). Is Justice Scalia's characterization of American abortion law still accurate after the Supreme Court's decision in *Gonzales v. Carhart*, 127 S. Ct. 1610 (2007), upholding federal prohibitions on abortion contained in the Partial Birth Abortion Ban Act? What do you think of his argument? Doesn't it reduce comparative abortion law to the level of simple arithmetic, when the reality is much more complicated? In theory, there may not be a constitutional right to an abortion in countries like Germany or Canada, but in practice, abortion is more widely available—particularly to poor women—in many other places than it is in the United States. What does all this suggest about the utility (futility?) of such cross-cultural comparisons?

7

Review of Laws Having Racially Disparate Impacts

Adrien Katherine Wing

Race discrimination is a global phenomenon. Sometimes, the behavior is intentional. In the U.S. context, the Fourteenth Amendment has been interpreted to protect against such activity. In many other circumstances, there is a racially discriminatory impact, that is, the behavior was not intentional. In the United States, the Civil Rights Act covers this type of discrimination. Other countries have grappled with how to handle racially disparate impact as well. The main case selection in this chapter, *City Council of Pretoria v. Walker,* illustrates how South Africa is handling the concept. That country is emerging from a recent history of de jure segregation against a black majority by the white minority. South Africa has a new Constitutional Court that is interpreting a new post-apartheid constitution with a detailed equality clause that covers both intentional *and* unintentional behavior. The *Walker* case implicates issues of race, class, housing segregation, and "reverse discrimination" in interesting ways, and raises the question of how the U.S. Supreme Court would handle a similar case. The notes discuss the experience of the U.S., Brazil, Canada, Europe, and international law.

City Council of Pretoria v. Walker

South African Constitutional Court
1998 (3) BCLR 257 (CC) (S. Afr.); 1998 SACLR LEXIS 27 (S. Afr.)

Judgment by: Langa Deputy President

Factual Background

[1] The applicant is the City Council of Pretoria (the council). It sued the respondent, Mr. Walker, in the Pretoria Magistrate's Court for payment

of an amount of R4 753,84 being arrear charges for services rendered by the council during the period July 1995 to 23 April 1996. The respondent did not deny that he owed the amount claimed. He contended instead that he was entitled to withhold payment by reason of the fact that the council's conduct constituted a violation of his constitutional right to equality as enshrined in section 8 of the interim Constitution.

[2] The respondent's defence was not upheld by the magistrate and he was ordered to pay the amount claimed as well as costs. On appeal, the Transvaal High Court (the High Court) set aside the magistrate's order and substituted for it an order of absolution from the instance with costs. The council applied for leave to appeal to this Court against the High Court's judgment and order....

[4] The council was established by the consolidation, on 8 December 1994, of a number of municipalities into one. These included, among others, the two black townships of Atteridgeville and Mamelodi and the formerly white municipality which was known as the Pretoria City Council. It will be convenient to refer to this last area as "old Pretoria." The respondent is a resident of Constantia Park, a suburb in old Pretoria. It is common knowledge that the population of Mamelodi and Atteridgeville is black and that of old Pretoria overwhelmingly white and the case was argued on that basis.

[5] The facts which provide the background for the issues raised in this matter may be summarised as follows: electricity and water charges in the council's area were levied on a differential basis. The residents of old Pretoria, including the respondent, were levied on a tariff based on actual consumption measured by means of meters installed on each property. This had been the position long before the amalgamation. Residents of Mamelodi and Atteridgeville, in the absence of meters, were levied on the basis of a uniform rate for every household. This system, generally referred to as a flat rate, also predated the amalgamation.

[6] The respondent's objections to the council's conduct were based on the following grounds: (a) the flat rate in Mamelodi and Atteridgeville was lower than the metered rate and this therefore meant that the residents of old Pretoria subsidised those of the two townships; (b) the differentiation in the tariffs continued even after meters had been installed on some properties in Mamelodi and Atteridgeville; (c) only residents of old Pretoria were singled out by the council for legal action to recover arrears whilst a policy of non-enforcement was being followed in respect of Mamelodi and Atteridgeville. The respondent also complained that the council did not take the residents of old Pretoria into its confidence when the target dates for the implementation of a consumption-based tariff were not met. Instead, misleading information was given to old Pretoria residents, leaving them under the impression that the metered rate was being uniformly applied at a time when it was not. With regard to the objections, the respondent's complaint was that the council's conduct amounted

to unfair discrimination and was therefore a breach of section 8 of the interim Constitution. In its judgment on appeal, the High Court held that the actions of the council amounted to discrimination based on race; that the council had not, under section 8(4) of the interim Constitution, established that such discrimination was not unfair; and that accordingly such actions were unconstitutional as being inconsistent with section 8(2) of the interim Constitution....

Background to the Dispute

[19] Atteridgeville and Mamelodi are no different from other poverty-stricken black townships in South Africa; there are glaring disparities between the two townships on the one hand, and old Pretoria on the other, in property values, delivery of services and infrastructure. At the time of the amalgamation electrical installations in the townships were generally broken or damaged and there was no regulation which obliged the residents of Atteridgeville and Mamelodi to pay for services....

[21] On 9 December 1994 the council decided, as a temporary measure, not to apply the consumption-based tariff in Mamelodi and Atteridgeville but to operate on the basis of a flat rate. The consumption-based tariff was in operation elsewhere in the council area, including Constantia Park. The decision of the council in relation to Mamelodi and Atteridgeville was actually forced on it because there were no meters to record the individual consumption of water and electricity in these areas. Rather optimistically as it turned out, the council set itself a programme to install the 38 000 meters needed by June 1995. The idea was that once the meters had been installed, the residents in the two townships would also be subject to the same metered rates as was the case in old Pretoria. The actual installation of meters however only commenced in June 1995 and was completed in April 1996. On 1 July 1995 the council announced a consumption-based tariff for its whole area. At that time, meters had already been installed on some of the properties in the townships. The consumption-based tariff was not, however, applied to those properties; they continued instead to be charged according to the flat rate. Mr Eicker, a senior official of the council who was responsible for credit control, said in evidence that this was the result of a decision taken by council officials to continue charging the flat rate to domestic premises in Atteridgeville and Mamelodi until all the meters that were required in the two townships had been installed. According to Mr Eicker to do otherwise might have been counter-productive and might have resulted in violent resistance and vandalism. The delay in imposing a consumption-based tariff throughout the council area attracted criticism from some residents of old Pretoria....

Differentiation and Discrimination

[25] Section 8, in so far as it is relevant, provides as follows:

(1) Every person shall have the right to equality before the law and to equal protection of the law.
(2) No person shall be unfairly discriminated against, directly or indirectly, and, without derogating from the generality of this provision, on one or more of the following grounds in particular: race, gender, sex, ethnic or social origin, colour, sexual orientation, age, disability, religion, conscience, belief, culture or language.
(3)(a) This section shall not preclude measures designed to achieve the adequate protection and advancement of persons or groups or categories of persons disadvantaged by unfair discrimination, in order to enable their full and equal enjoyment of all rights and freedom.
(4) Prima facie proof of discrimination on any of the grounds specified in subsection (2) shall be presumed to be sufficient proof of unfair discrimination as contemplated in that subsection, until the contrary is established.

[26] The question whether there has been a breach of section 8 of the interim Constitution has to be assessed against the background set out in the preceding paragraphs. That assessment cannot be undertaken in a vacuum but should be based both on the wording of the section and in the constitutional and historical context of the developments in South Africa. What is clear is that not all differentiation amounts to discrimination as envisaged in section 8. It remains to be determined whether the differentiation in this case constitutes a violation of the right protected by section 8.

[27] In written argument on behalf of the respondent, it was argued that there was no rational connection between the discriminatory measures taken by the council and a legitimate governmental purpose "...which is proffered to validate it." In particular, respondent contended that the conduct of the council could not be said to have been authorised by section 8(3)(a) of the interim Constitution inasmuch as the discriminatory measures had not been "designed to achieve the adequate protection and advancement of persons or groups or categories of persons disadvantaged by unfair discrimination..." The council's attitude on the other hand was that the differentiation was rationally connected to the legitimate objective of dealing with the period of transition by phasing in the required changes in order to achieve equality between the residents of the different areas. The issue of a rational connection is of course relevant to the question whether the actions of the council breached respondent's section 8(1) right.

I am satisfied that the differentiation in the present case was rationally connected to legitimate governmental objectives. Not only were the measures of a temporary nature but they were designed to provide continuity in the rendering of services by the council while phasing in equality in terms of facilities and resources, during a difficult period of transition. This is however not the end of the enquiry as differentiation that does not constitute a violation of section 8(1) may nonetheless constitute unfair discrimination for the purposes of section 8(2)." When the matter was argued before us, counsel for the respondent concentrated his attack on what was alleged to be unfair discrimination in terms of section 8(2). This raises the question whether the differentiation complained of constitutes discrimination and if it does, whether that discrimination is unfair....

[29] In *Harksen* we held that the enquiry as to whether differentiation amounts to unfair discrimination is a two-stage one.

> Firstly, does the differentiation amount to "discrimination"? If it is on a specified ground, then discrimination will have been established. If it is not on a specified ground, then whether or not there is discrimination will depend upon whether, objectively, the ground is based on attributes and characteristics which have the potential to impair the fundamental human dignity of persons as human beings or to affect them adversely in a comparably serious manner.
>
> (b)(ii) If the differentiation amounts to "discrimination," does it amount to "unfair discrimination"? If it has been found to have been on a specified ground, then unfairness will be presumed. If on an unspecified ground, unfairness will have to be established by the complainant. The test of unfairness focuses primarily on the impact of the discrimination on the complainant and others in his or her situation.

[30] Section 8(2) prohibits unfair discrimination which takes place "directly or indirectly." This is the first occasion on which this Court has had to consider the difference between direct and indirect discrimination.

[31] The inclusion of both direct and indirect discrimination within the ambit of the prohibition imposed by section 8(2) evinces a concern for the consequences rather than the form of conduct. It recognises that conduct which may appear to be neutral and non-discriminatory may nonetheless result in discrimination, and if it does, that it falls within the purview of section 8(2).

[32] The emphasis which this Court has placed on the impact of discrimination in deciding whether or not section 8(2) has been infringed is consistent with this concern. It is not necessary in the present case to formulate a precise definition of indirect discrimination. It is sufficient for the purposes of this judgment to say that this conduct which differentiated between the treatment of residents of townships which were historically black areas and whose residents are still overwhelmingly black, and residents in municipalities which were historically white areas and whose residents are still overwhelmingly white constituted indirect discrimination on the grounds of race. The fact that the differential treatment was made applicable to geographical areas rather than to persons of a particular race may mean that the discrimination was not direct, but it does not in my view alter the fact that in the circumstances of the present case it constituted discrimination, albeit indirect, on the grounds of race. It would be artificial to make a comparison

between an area known to be overwhelmingly a "black area" and another known to be overwhelmingly a "white area," on the grounds of geography alone. The effect of apartheid laws was that race and geography were inextricably linked and the application of a geographical standard, although seemingly neutral, may in fact be racially discriminatory. In this case, its impact was clearly one which differentiated in substance between black residents and white residents. The fact that there may have been a few black residents in old Pretoria does not detract from this.

[33] I have had the opportunity of reading the judgment of Sachs J in which the view is expressed that the differentiation in the present case was based on "objectively determinable characteristics of different geographical areas, and not on race." I cannot subscribe to this view or to the proposition that this is a case in which, because of our history, a non-discriminatory policy has impacted fortuitously on one section of our community rather than another. There may be such cases, but in my view this is not one of them. The impact of the policy that was adopted by the council officials was to require the (white) residents of old Pretoria to comply with the legal tariff and to pay the charges made in terms of that tariff on pain of having their services suspended or legal action taken against them, whilst the (black) residents of Atteridgeville and Mamelodi were not held to the tariff, were called upon to pay only a flat rate which was lower than the tariff, and were not subjected to having their services suspended or legal action taken against them. To ignore the racial impact of the differentiation is to place form above substance....

[36] It was argued on behalf of the council that if on an evaluation of the facts of the present case discrimination was established, such discrimination was not "unfair." As already indicated, I am satisfied that the conduct of the council does amount to discrimination. Since, as I have already found, the differentiation was on one of the grounds specified in section 8(2), the council bears the burden of rebutting the presumption of "unfair discrimination."

Has the Presumption of Unfair Discrimination Been Rebutted?

[37] The enquiry into whether the presumption of unfair discrimination has been rebutted involves an examination of the impact of the discrimination on the respondent....

[39] With regard to the question whether intention has any relevance in the determination of unfairness, it is to be noted that intention to discriminate is [not] an essential element of unfair discrimination. The Chapter on Fundamental Rights in the interim Constitution is different to the Bill of Rights of the United States in that it contains not only an equal protection

clause in the form of section 8(1) but also an anti-discrimination clause, section 8(2)....

[44] This does not mean that absence of an intention to discriminate is irrelevant to the enquiry. The section prohibits "unfair" discrimination. The requirement of unfairness limits the application of the section and permits consideration to be given to the purpose of the conduct or action at the level of the enquiry into unfairness....

The Position of the Respondent in Society

[47] The respondent belongs to a group that has not been disadvantaged by the racial policies and practices of the past. In an economic sense, his group is neither disadvantaged nor vulnerable, having been benefited rather than adversely affected by discrimination in the past. In this case for instance, the respondent did not plead poverty as his reason for not paying the amount owing by him calculated on a consumption-based rate.

[48] The respondent does however belong to a racial minority which could, in a political sense, be regarded as vulnerable. It is precisely individuals who are members of such minorities who are vulnerable to discriminatory treatment and who, in a very special sense, must look to the Bill of Rights for protection. When that happens a Court has a clear duty to come to the assistance of the person affected. Courts should however always be astute to distinguish between genuine attempts to promote and protect equality on the one hand and actions calculated to protect pockets of privilege at a price which amounts to the perpetuation of inequality....

[53] The council's decision to confine the flat rate to Atteridgeville and Mamelodi and to continue charging the metered rate in old Pretoria and in businesses in Atteridgeville and Mamelodi that were equipped with meters was dictated by the circumstances with which it was confronted. In the circumstances the adoption of a flat rate as an interim arrangement while meters were being installed in the residential areas of the two townships was the only practical solution to the problem....

[68] I am satisfied that the operation of the flat rate and its continued application on properties where meters had been installed in Mamelodi and Atteridgeville, as well as the cross-subsidisation which may have resulted from any delay in implementing a metered tariff, did not impact adversely on the respondent in any material way. There was no invasion of the respondent's dignity nor was he affected in a manner comparably serious to an invasion of his dignity....

Selective Enforcement

[73] Whilst there can be no objection to a council taking into account the financial position of debtors in deciding whether to allow them extended

credit, or whether to sue them or not, such differentiation must be based on a policy that is rational and coherent....

[79] The picture that emerges from Mr Eicker's evidence is not of a rational and coherent plan adopted openly by the council or its officials to recover arrear and current charges from ratepayers in Atteridgeville and Mamelodi. It is instead a picture of confusion and uncertainty with officials being pulled in different directions by different pressure groups; of the truth being concealed and false information being disseminated; and of decisions being taken by officials without council approval to charge on a basis inconsistent with the tariff and not to enforce council resolutions dealing with the recovery of arrear charges....

[81] No members of a racial group should be made to feel that they are not deserving of equal "concern, respect and consideration" and that the law is likely to be used against them more harshly than others who belong to other race groups. That is the grievance that the respondent has and it is a grievance that the council officials foresaw when they adopted their policy. The conduct of the council officials seen as a whole over the period from June 1995 to the time of the trial in May 1996 was on the face of it discriminatory. The impact of such a policy on the respondent and other persons similarly placed, viewed objectively in the light of the evidence on record, would in my view have affected them in a manner which is at least comparably serious to an invasion of their dignity. This was exacerbated by the fact that they had been misled and misinformed by the council. In the circumstances it must be held that the presumption has not been rebutted and that the course of conduct of which the respondent complains in this respect, amounted to unfair discrimination within the meaning of section 8(2) of the interim Constitution....

Appropriate Relief

[96] I have found that the selective institution of legal proceedings by the council amounts to a breach of respondent's constitutional right not to be unfairly discriminated against. It has not been shown that respondent could not have availed himself of other, more practical remedies which would have been effective in getting the council to cease its objectionable conduct, thus eradicating the reason for the complaint. Instead of withholding amounts lawfully owing by him to the council, the respondent could, for instance, have applied to an appropriate court for a declaration of rights or a mandamus in order to vindicate the breach of his section 8 right.

[97] In the result I find that the course followed by the respondent in this case was inappropriate, to the extent that his reliance on the breach of the section 8 right is not a defence to the council's claim. I accordingly find that the order of the High Court of absolution from the instance with costs is not appropriate relief in this matter. The council must therefore succeed

in the appeal to the extent that the order of absolution from the instance cannot stand.

(Chaskalson P, Ackermann, Goldstone, Kriegler, Madala, Mokgoro, and O'Regan JJ concurred in the judgment of Langa DP)

Notes and Questions

1. Some of the framers of the South African Interim Constitution studied the 200-year-old American experience very carefully and realized that they were writing a constitution for a different era and a different society. For example, the *Postscript of the Interim Constitution* opens with the following words:

   > This Constitution provides a historic bridge between the past of a deeply divided society characterised by strife, conflict, untold suffering and injustice, and a future founded on the recognition of human rights, democracy and peaceful co-existence and development opportunities for all South Africans, irrespective of colour, race, class, belief or sex.

   For a discussion of the process leading up to the adoption of the Interim Constitution, see Adrien K. Wing, Communitarianism v. Individualism: *Constitutionalism in Namibia & South Africa*, 11 Wis. Int'l L.J. 295 (1993).

2. What test does the Court lay out? Should discrimination of all types, or only unfair discrimination, be outlawed? What do you think of the *Harksen* test to show unfair discrimination? In paragraph 27, what do you think of use of a rational relation instead of a strict scrutiny standard for race cases? Does it affect your analysis that in the South African context, the major group that had traditionally been discriminated against was the black *majority*?

   Was this a case of reverse discrimination against whites or was it an attempt to protect a pocket of privilege, as the court suggests in paragraph 48? According to Michelman, "redistributive social programs all must emanate from a nonwhite, political-majority-we for the benefit of a racially identifiable us at the apparent expense of a racially identifiable them." Frank I. Michelman, *Reasonable Umbrage: Race and Constitutional Antidiscrimination Law in the United States and South Africa*, 117 Harv. L. Rev. 1378, 1397 (2004). Do you think the Court is sufficiently solicitous of the needs of the whites living in Old Pretoria? As a result of the Court's opinion, what does Mr. Walker end up obtaining?

   Could an argument be made that the Court was *too* concerned with white minority rights given the history of white privilege? Do you agree with Justice Sachs' concurrence, that there was no race discrimination involved, whether direct or indirect, but merely geographic realities? Justice Sachs says:

   > [103] I find it jurisprudentially incongruous to regard the complainant as a victim of unfair discrimination as a result of such a process. He was disturbed in no way in his enjoyment of residence in a neighbourhood which had been made affluent by state-enforced advantage in the past. The group with which he identified himself continued to get the benefit of regular municipal services at all material times. He was not called upon to do any more than to pay what he owed for services he had always received. He was not being singled out or targeted in any way, neither because of his race nor even because he lived in a comfortable neighbourhood. In my view, although treated differently, he was not discriminated against in any manner whatsoever; alternatively, if the council's conduct can correctly be classed as discriminatory against him, it was by no means unfair.

Moreover, Justice Sachs notes that the *Harksen* case on which the Court relies for the test came out differently.

> [105] In *Harksen v Lane NO and Others* it was accepted that, even though the great majority of solvent spouses targeted by the insolvency law might well have been women, this did not raise questions of indirect discrimination against women.

See generally Harksen v. Lane NO 1997 (11) BCLR 1489 (CC) (S. Afr.), 1997 SACLR LEXIS 20 (S. Afr.).

The majority in *Harksen* concluded that there was a violation of the dignity of innocent spouses. Note the Court's emphasis in *Walker* on *dignity*. Does that concept have any legal meaning in the U.S. system? If the Court had found that unfair discrimination occurred based on a ground not listed under Art 8(2), that is, geography, how could it have developed the dignity analysis in more detail? For a discussion of South African race and gender discrimination as "spirit injury," *see* Adrien K. Wing, *Critical Race Feminist Conceptualization of Violence: South African and Palestinian Women*, 60 ALB. L. REV. 943 (1997).

Would it have satisfied the Court if the Council had prosecuted some whites *and* some blacks in default on their power bills?

Would your answers to any of the questions raised be affected by looking at the racial and gender demographics of the Court? Knowing more about their personal backgrounds or political ideologies? *See* Penelope E. Andrews, *The South African Judicial Appointments Process*, 44 OSGOODE HALL L.J. 565 (2006).

3. The Court has considered claims of indirect discrimination on grounds other than race. For example, in *Democratic Party v. Minister of Home Affairs* 1999 (3) SA 254 (CC) (S. Afr.), neutral provisions of the Electoral Act 73 of 98 required voters to identify themselves. A survey found that the people lacking the appropriate documents were either young, white, or rural people. The Court rejected the indirect discrimination claim on the grounds of either race, age, or residence. No evidence showed that these voters had been registered in smaller numbers. Even if this were the case, it could have been due to voter education efforts. What would be the result in the United States? For a discussion of the discrimination black women faced at the time of the Interim Constitution, *see* Adrien K. Wing & Eunice de Carvalho, *Black South African Women: Towards Equal Rights*, 8 HAR. HUM. RTS. J. 57 (1995). *See also* THE CONSTITUTION OF SOUTH AFRICA FROM A GENDER PERSPECTIVE (Sandy Liebenberg ed., 1995). For a discussion of how the Constitution has addressed poverty, *see* Penelope E. Andrews, *The South African Constitution as a Mechanism for Redressing Poverty*, *in* DEMOCRATIC REFORM IN AFRICA: TAKING STOCK OF ITS IMPACT ON GOVERNANCE AND POVERTY ALLEVIATION 57 (Muna Ndulo ed., 2006).

4. Additional readings: For more discussion of *Walker* and other cases, *see* IAIN CURRIE & JOHAN DE WAAL, THE BILL OF RIGHTS HANDBOOK 260–264 (5th ed. 2005); Janet Kentridge, *Equality*, *in* CONSTITUTIONAL LAW OF SOUTH AFRICA 14–55 to 14–66 (M. Chaskelson et al. eds., 1999); M. CHEADLE ET AL., SOUTH AFRICAN CONSTITUTIONAL LAW: THE BILL OF RIGHTS (2002); ZIYAD MOTALA & CYRIL RAMAPHOSA, CONSTITUTIONAL LAW 252–302 (2002).

THE U.S. APPROACH

1. In the United States, disparate impact or effect alone does not give rise to an equal protection claim under the Constitution. There must be evidence

of intent to discriminate. *See Washington v. Davis*, 426 U.S. 229 (1976) (upholding a law in spite of its racially disproportionate impact due to a lack of racially discriminatory purpose). According to Michelman, [I]t is this feature above all others that, in the eyes of domestic critics, has given our constitutional antidiscrimination discourse the stamp of a "perpetrator perspective"—one that locates the objection to racial differentiation in the wrongness of the act—as opposed to a "victim perspective" that locates it in the evil of the consequences. Frank I. Michelman, *Reasonable Umbrage: Race and Constitutional Antidiscrimination Law in the United States and South Africa*, 117 HARV. L. REV. 1378, 1391 (2004). Do you agree with Professor Michelman?

2. The disparate impact doctrine *is* used in Title VI and Title VII of the Civil Rights Act cases. Courts have seemed to reject the disparate impact doctrine in Title VI cases and accept it more often in Title VII cases. *See* Dan McCaughey, *The Death of Disparate Impact Under Title VI: Alexander v. Sandoval and Its Effects on Private Challenges to High-Stakes Testing Programs*, 84 B.U.L. REV. 247 (2003); Richard A. Primus, *Equal Protection and Disparate Impact: Round Three*, 117 HARV. L. REV. 493 (2003) (considering whether impact tests are unconstitutional); Jamie Darin Prenkert, *Bizarro Statutory Stare Decisis*, 28 BERKELEY J. EMP. & LAB. L. 217 (2007) (reviewing the success rates of disparate impact claims).
   Should the United States abandon the current discriminatory intent constitutional standard in favor of discriminatory impact, thus synthesizing constitutional and statutory standards? *See* Charles Abernathy, *Legal Realism and the Failure of the "Effects" Test for Discrimination*, 94 GEO. L.J. 267, 318 (2006), arguing that the effects test has failed in Title VI cases. "The overwhelming refusal to enforce an effects test—by judges from across the political spectrum—suggests that what happened with Title VI would have also happened for constitutional law." For more discussion of the effects test, *see* CHARLES F. ABERNATHY, CIVIL RIGHTS AND CONSTITUTIONAL LITIGATION 588–609 (3d ed. 2000).
   How would a case with facts similar to *Walker* be decided under current U.S. constitutional and statutory law standards? For a discussion in the primary and secondary school context, *see Parents Involved in Community Schools v. Seattle School District No. 1*, 127 S.Ct. 2738, 2788 (2007) (Kennedy, J., concurring).
3. The 1996 South African Constitution, which replaced the interim one, has an extensive list of grounds covered by the equality clause and applies the concept of indirect discrimination to them as well: Art 9(3) says

> the State may not unfairly discriminate directly or indirectly against anyone on one or more grounds, including race, gender, sex, pregnancy, marital status, ethnic or social origin, colour, sexual orientation, age, disability, religion, conscience, belief, culture, language or birth.

For more discussion of these identities, *see* the Introduction to ADRIEN WING, GLOBAL CRITICAL RACE FEMINISM: AN INTERNATIONAL READER 1 (2000).

How likely do you think such a clause could evolve in a U.S. context? How likely is it that even gender will be added to the U.S. Constitution in the near future? Note that many countries may have such language in their constitutions, but that the actual treatment of women and minorities and other groups may be better in the United States under various statutory schemes. Should the battle even be waged on the constitutional level? Are we better off with Title VII or laws like the Americans with Disabilities Act or state and municipal ordinances that may ban discrimination against other groups such as homosexuals?

THE EXPERIENCE OF OTHER COUNTRIES

1. Canada. In Canada, the disparate impact doctrine is called the adverse effects doctrine. There is Canadian case law that expressly provides for equal protection based on the adverse effects doctrine. *See Symes v. Canada* [1993], 110 D.L.R. (4th) 470, 552 (S.C.) (Can.); [1993] 4 S.C.R. 695, 755 (Can.); Joseph A. Seiner, *Disentangling Disparate Impact and Disparate Treatment: Adapting the Canadian Approach*, 25 YALE L. & POL'Y REV. 95 (2006) (observing that the Canadian Supreme Court has recently merged intent and effects tests in employment law).
2. Brazil. In Brazil, the doctrine has developed as well. *See* Benjamin Hensler, *Nao Vale a Pena (Not Worth the Trouble?) Afro-Brazilian Workers and Brazilian Anti-Discrimination Law*, 30 HASTINGS INT'L & COMP. L. REV. 267, 268 (2007):

> In September 2005, Brazilian public prosecutors filed a series of lawsuits that would have been nearly unimaginable in the country even a few years before. The suits, brought in Brasilia as civil complaints in the federal labor courts, charged five of the country's leading banks with violating the Brazilian constitution by discriminating against Afro-Brazilian employees and job applicants in hiring, promotion and compensation. The allegations were based on statistical evidence indicating significant disparities in occupational status and compensation of Afro-Brazilian employees relative to their white colleagues at the banks. The suits also asserted that the banks discriminated in hiring, based on under-representation of Afro-Brazilians in the banks' workforce when compared to their share of the local labor market. Up until the mid-1990s public prosecutors considered protection of minority rights at the bottom of their list of law enforcement priorities. Brazilian courts held that liability for racial discrimination could only be established through direct evidence of a defendant's prejudicial motive.

3. Europe. In Europe, national standards based on individual constitutions are giving way to European Union (EU) legislation. *See* Raphael Won-Pil

Suh & Richard Bales, *German and European Employment Discrimination Policy*, 8 Or. Rev. Int'l L. 263 (2006):

> The European Court of Justice (ECJ) created the doctrine of disparate impact on the basis of Article 119 of the Treaty of the European Community. An employment criterion has a disparate impact when the criterion is facially neutral in respect to sex, but has a discriminatory impact on either one of the sexes, because it requires characteristics that refer either to the male or female sex. Discriminatory intent is not required.
>
> U.S. constitutional law assesses gender discrimination with a different constitutional standard than it does race discrimination. The other jurisdictions mentioned in this chapter do not use a different standard. Do you think such a harmonization would be possible or desirable in the U.S. context?

Europe has applied the indirect effects notion to a broader array of "races" than the United States. *See* Bob Hepple, *The European Legacy of Brown v. Board of Education*, 2006 U. Ill. L. Rev. 605 (2006):

> The issue whether, and to what extent, Article 14 of the ECHR [the equality clause of the European Convention on Human Rights] extends to indirect discrimination is central to the highly important Ostrava Schools case, recently declared admissible by the European Court of Human Rights (the Strasbourg Court). The applicants are school children who are Czech citizens of the Roma ethnic group. Voluminous and compelling evidence has been presented showing that they have been wrongly and disproportionately placed in special schools for the mentally handicapped, which offer markedly inferior education and reduced educational and employment opportunities. According to the Council of Europe's Commissioner for Human Rights,
>
> The young members of the Roma/Gypsy community are drastically overrepresented in "special" schools and classes for children suffering from slight mental disability. Some figures produced indicate that 70% of all Roma/Gypsy children present in Czech territory are placed in these schools; while children from this community make up less than 5% of primary age pupils; they reportedly form 50% of the special school enrolment.

The question that has been declared admissible is whether the concept of indirect discrimination should be applied to the interpretation of Article 14 in the context of de facto racial segregation in schools, without the need to prove racist motives. Will the Strasbourg Court adopt the restrictive interpretation that the U.S. Supreme Court placed on the equal protection clause, or will it follow the precedents of the European Court of Justice which do not require proof of intent? There are good reasons for the Strasbourg Court to go beyond the American equal protection precedents and to interpret Article 14 of the Convention consistent with EU law, so creating a unified European jurisprudence concerned with the impact of facially neutral practices having disproportionate effects.

In November 2007, the Grand Chamber (the Appellate division) held that there had been a violation of Article 14 by a vote of thirteen to four.

> 194. Where it has been shown that the legislation produces such a discriminatory effect, the Grand Chamber considers that, as with cases concerning employment, or the provision of services, it is not necessary in cases in the educational sphere…to prove any discriminatory intent on the part of the relevant authorities.

Case of *D.H. and Others v. The Czech Republic*, App. No. 57325/00, Grand Chamber Eur. Ct. H.R. 13 Nov. 2007.

Would the Czech Roma be entitled to strict scrutiny under the U.S. equal protection clause? For a discussion of the treatment under EU law of indirect discrimination with respect to gender, *see infra* chapter 10, Review of Laws Having a Disparate Impact Based on Gender.

5. Additional reading. For further reading, *see* NEIL GOTUNDA, A CRITIQUE OF OUR CONSTITUTION IS COLORBLIND, IN CRITICAL RACE THEORY: KEY WRITINGS THAT FORMED THE MOVEMENT 257 (Kimberle Crenshaw et al. eds., 1995); Charles Lawrence III, *The Id, the Ego, and Equal Protection: Reckoning with Unconscious Racism*, 39 STAN. L. REV. 317 (1987); Penelope E. Andrews, *Evaluating the Progress of Women's Rights on the Fifth Anniversary of the South African Constitution*, 26 VT. L. REV. 829 (2002); THE POST-APARTHEID CONSTITUTIONS: PERSPECTIVES ON SOUTH AFRICA'S BASIC LAW (Penelope E. Andrews & Stephen Ellman eds., 2001); Eileen Kaufman, *Woman and Law: A Comparative Analysis of the United States and Indian Supreme Courts' Equality Jurisprudence*, 34 GA. J. INT'L & COMP. L. 557 (2006); Christopher D. Totten, *Constitutional Precommitments to Gender Affirmative Action in the European Union, Germany, Canada and the United States: A Comparative Approach*, 21 BERKELEY J. INT'L L. 27 (2003).

INTERNATIONAL LAW

International conventions also include the concept of disparate impact. See the International Convention on the Elimination of Race Discrimination:

> The term racial discrimination shall mean any distinction, exclusion, restriction or preference based on race, colour, descent or national or ethnic origin which has the purpose or effect of nullifying or impairing the recognition, enjoyment or exercise, on n equal footing, of human rights and fundamental freedoms in the political, economic, social, cultural or any field of public life. ICERD, GA Res. 2106 a (XX), 660 U.N.T.S. 195 (1969), available at www.unhchr.ch.

8

Affirmative Action and Benign Discrimination

Ashutosh Bhagwat

In many nations the government and the private sector provide preferences—in the allocation of benefits such as university admissions, employment, and contracts—to specific groups who have been subject to past discrimination, or who are for some other reason specially disadvantaged in the relevant society. The "preferred" groups might be defined by gender, race, ethnicity, national origin, religion, caste, language, or any number of other, sometimes overlapping factors. Such policies assume a variety of names. For example, in the United States, they are generically referred to as "affirmative action," in South Africa as "Black Economic Empowerment," and in India as "reservations." While different in particulars, each policy allocates benefits partially or absolutely based on membership in a favored group. Such policies are controversial because membership in the favored group is typically determined by a characteristic, such as race, gender, or caste, that is otherwise a forbidden ground for discrimination. As a consequence, preferential policies themselves have been subject to constitutional challenge in a number of countries.

In the United States, the Supreme Court has struggled with the constitutionality of governmental preferences based on race since its 1978 decision in *Regents of the University of California v. Bakke*, 438 U.S. 265 (1978). In recent years, a majority of the Supreme Court has coalesced around an approach to racial preferences that is highly skeptical, holding in *City of Richmond v. J.A. Croson Co.*, 488 U.S. 469 (1989) and *Adarand Constructors, Inc. v. Pena*, 515 U.S. 200 (1995), that all race-based governmental policies, whether favoring whites or racial minorities, must be subject to the highest, "strict" standard of scrutiny when challenged under the Equal Protection Clause of the Fourteenth Amendment (or in the case of federal policies, under the "equal protection component" of the Fifth Amendment's Due Process Clause). Under strict scrutiny, racial preferences are upheld only if they are narrowly tailored to further a compelling governmental interest.

More recently, however, some uncertainty has arisen regarding precisely the level of constitutional skepticism that should be accorded to official racial preferences in the United States. In *Grutter v. Bollinger*, 539 U.S. 306 (2003), the Supreme Court upheld the University of Michigan Law School's policy of using race as a factor in admissions, as a means of achieving a racially diverse student body. While the *Grutter* Court invoked strict scrutiny as required by precedent, it applied that standard in a relatively deferential fashion, an approach in tension with previous applications of strict scrutiny. Even more recently, in *Parents Involved in Community Schools v. Seattle School District No. 1 et al.*, 127 S. Ct. 2738 (2007), the Court in a highly splintered decision struck down the policies of two local school districts assigning students to schools based on race, in order to achieve racial integration within their schools. In the wake of the *Seattle School District* case, it is safe to say that the constitutional treatment of governmental racial preference policies remains very much in flux in the United States.

Many countries other than the United States have also struggled to reconcile group-based preferences with the equality or antidiscrimination provisions of their constitutions. This chapter examines preference policies and constitutional decisions in a number of such countries. We begin with, and focus primarily on, the Republic of South Africa, which provides an interesting comparison, and contrast, to the United States.

SOUTH AFRICA

South Africa has a complex history characterized by egregious racial discrimination, as well as a highly racially diverse population. South Africa's population today is approximately 80% black, 9% white, 9% "coloured" (i.e., mixed race), and 2–3% Asian (primarily of Indian origin). Until South Africa's 1994 democratic revolution, the country's policies of strict racial apartheid left South Africa's black majority politically disenfranchised, and extremely disadvantaged economically as well. In addition to strict racial segregation and white domination of politics, apartheid-era policies systematically denied black South Africans a modern education, and so the possibility of economic advancement. Apartheid came to an end in 1994, when South Africa's first multiracial elections were held. In December 1996 the new Constitution of the Republic of South Africa came into effect.

One of the new, post-apartheid South African government's priorities has been to alleviate the inequalities that pervade modern South African life. While the 1994 revolution ended the political disenfranchisement of non-white South Africans, it did little to ease the extraordinary economic inequalities that were the legacy of apartheid, as well as the domination of the higher levels of government (aside from elected leaders) by whites. Since 1994 the various levels of the South African government have pursued extensive programs of race- and gender-based preferences designed to alleviate those inequalities. Such preferences have been implemented in government hiring and contracting, and have also been extended to the private sector as well, through requirements imposed on companies doing business with the government, and those requiring government licenses. The preference policies are designed to both increase the number of high-level black employees in all sectors of the economy, and to increase black ownership of South African capital (the word "black" in this context is defined to include Coloureds and Indians as well as Blacks).

The provision of the South African Constitution most obviously relevant to the constitutionality of such measures is Section 9, which reads as follows:

> 9. Equality
> 1. Everyone is equal before the law and has the right to equal protection and benefit of the law.
> 2. Equality includes the full and equal enjoyment of all rights and freedoms. To promote the achievement of equality, legislative and other measures designed to protect or advance persons, or categories of persons, disadvantaged by unfair discrimination may be taken.
> 3. The state may not unfairly discriminate directly or indirectly against anyone on one or more grounds, including race, gender, sex, pregnancy, marital status, ethnic or social origin, colour, sexual orientation, age, disability, religion, conscience, belief, culture, language and birth.
> 4. No person may unfairly discriminate directly or indirectly against anyone on one or more grounds in terms of subsection (3). National legislation must be enacted to prevent or prohibit unfair discrimination.
> 5. Discrimination on one or more of the grounds listed in subsection (3) is unfair unless it is established that the discrimination is fair.

See http://www.info.gov.za/documents/constitution/index.htm (last visited August 11, 2008)

Unlike the Constitution of the United States, the South African Constitution not only includes a guarantee of "equal protection," but also permits preferential legislation.

Minister of Finance and Another v. Van Heerden

Constitutional Court of South Africa
2004 (11) BCLR 1125 (CC)

Judgment by Moseneke, J.

[Soon after South Africa's new Parliament was elected in 1994 through the nation's first multiracial elections, it established a new pension fund for its members. The rules of the fund provided for higher state contributions for members of Parliament first elected in 1994, as opposed to members who had been members of the previous, Apartheid-era Parliament and who therefore were eligible for pensions under a previous government pension fund. For obvious reasons, the membership in the "disadvantaged" group, defined as "Category C" in the pension plan, was highly racially skewed, being composed of 2 Blacks, 11 Indians, 28 Coloureds, and 105 Whites. Frederik Jacobus van Heerden, a member of the Category C group, challenged the pension plan, claiming it violated the equality provisions of the new South African Constitution.]

Equality and Unfair Discrimination

The achievement of equality goes to the bedrock of our constitutional architecture. The Constitution commands us to strive for a society built on the democratic values of human dignity, the achievement of equality, the advancement of human rights and freedom. Thus the achievement of equality is not only a guaranteed and justiciable right in our Bill of Rights but also a core and foundational value; a standard which must inform all law and against which all law must be tested for constitutional consonance.

For good reason, the achievement of equality preoccupies our constitutional thinking. When our Constitution took root a decade ago our society was deeply divided, vastly unequal and uncaring of human worth. Many of these stark social and economic disparities will persist for long to come. In effect the commitment of the Preamble is to restore and protect the equal worth of everyone; to heal the divisions of the past and to establish a caring and socially just society. In explicit terms, the Constitution commits our society to "improve the quality of life of all citizens and free the potential of each person."

The jurisprudence of this Court makes plain that the proper reach of the equality right must be determined by reference to our history and the underlying values of the Constitution. As we have seen a major constitutional object is the creation of a non-racial and non-sexist egalitarian society underpinned by human dignity, the rule of law, a democratic ethos and human rights. From there emerges a conception of equality that goes beyond mere formal equality and mere non-discrimination which requires identical treatment, whatever the starting point or impact.

Restitutionary Measures

A comprehensive understanding of the Constitution's conception of equality requires a harmonious reading of the provisions of section 9. Section 9(1) proclaims that everyone is equal before the law and has the right to equal protection and benefit of the law. On the other hand, section 9(3) proscribes unfair discrimination by the State against anyone on any ground including those specified. Section 9(5) renders discrimination on one or more of the listed grounds unfair unless its fairness is established. However, section 9(2) provides for the achievement of full and equal enjoyment of all rights and freedoms and authorises legislative and other measures designed to protect or advance persons or categories of persons disadvantaged by unfair discrimination. Restitutionary measures, sometimes referred to as "affirmative action," may be taken to promote the achievement of equality.

The measures must be "designed" to protect or advance persons disadvantaged by unfair discrimination in order to advance the achievement of equality.

Section 9(1) provides: "Everyone is equal before the law and has the right to equal protection and benefit of the law." Of course, the phrase "equal protection of the laws" also appears in the 14th Amendment of the US Constitution. The American jurisprudence has, generally speaking, rendered a particularly limited and formal account of the reach of the equal protection right.... Our equality jurisprudence differs substantively from the US approach to equality. Our respective histories, social context and constitutional design differ markedly.... We must therefore exercise great caution not to import, through this route, inapt foreign equality jurisprudence which may inflict on our nascent equality jurisprudence American notions of "suspect categories of State action" and of "strict scrutiny."

Thus, our constitutional understanding of equality includes what Ackermann J in *National Coalition for Gay and Lesbian Equality and Another v. Minister of Justice and Another* calls "remedial or restitutionary equality" [citation omitted]. Such measures are not in themselves a deviation from, or invasive of, the right to equality guaranteed by the Constitution. They are not "reverse discrimination" or "positive discrimination" as argued by the claimant in this case. They are integral to the reach of our equality protection. In other words, the provisions of section 9(1) and section 9(2) are complementary; both contribute to the constitutional goal of achieving equality to ensure "full and equal enjoyment of all rights". A disjunctive or oppositional reading of the two subsections would frustrate the foundational equality objective of the Constitution and its broader social justice imperatives.

Equality before the law protection in section 9(1) and measures to promote equality in section 9(2) are both necessary and mutually reinforcing but may sometimes serve distinguishable purposes, which I need not discuss now. However, what is clear is that our Constitution and in particular section 9 thereof, read as a whole, embraces for good reason a substantive conception of equality inclusive of measures to redress existing inequality. Absent a positive commitment progressively to eradicate socially constructed barriers to equality and to root out systematic or institutionalised under-privilege, the constitutional promise of equality before the law and its equal protection and benefit must, in the context of our country, ring hollow.

Onus of Proof and Section 9(2)

It seems to me plain that if restitutionary measures, even based on any of the grounds of discrimination listed in section 9(3), pass muster under section 9(2), they cannot be presumed to be unfairly discriminatory. To hold otherwise would mean that the scheme of section 9 is internally inconsistent or that the provisions of section 9(2) are a mere interpretative aid or even surplusage. I cannot accept that our Constitution at once authorises measures aimed at redress of past inequality and disadvantage but also labels them as presumptively unfair.

Requirements of Section 9(2)

When a measure is challenged as violating the equality provision, its defender may meet the claim by showing that the measure is contemplated by section 9(2) in that it promotes the achievement of equality and is designed to protect and advance persons disadvantaged by unfair discrimination. It seems to me that to determine whether a measure falls within section 9(2) the enquiry is threefold. The first yardstick relates to whether the measure targets persons or categories of persons who have been disadvantaged by unfair discrimination; the second is whether the measure is designed to protect or advance such persons or categories of persons; and the third requirement is whether the measure promotes the achievement of equality.

[Justice Moseneke concludes that the first two requirements are met.]

The third and last requirement is that the measure "promotes the achievement of equality." Determining whether a measure will in the long run promote the achievement of equality requires an appreciation of the effect of the measure in the context of our broader society. It must be accepted that the achievement of this goal may often come at a price for those who were previously advantaged. Action needs to be taken to advance the position of those who have suffered unfair discrimination in the past.

However, it is also clear that the long-term goal of our society is a non-racial, non-sexist society in which each person will be recognised and treated as a human being of equal worth and dignity. In particular, a measure should not constitute an abuse of power or impose such substantial and undue harm on those excluded from its benefits that our long-term constitutional goal would be threatened.

[Justice Moseneke concludes that the distinctions drawn in the new pension fund are reasonable, and do not violate the equality provisions of the Constitution.]

[Chaskalson, C.J., Langa, D.C.J., Madala, O'Regan, Sachs, Van der Westhuizen, and Yacoob, JJ. concurred in the judgment of Moseneke, J.]

By Mokgoro, J.

Introduction

I have read the judgment prepared by my colleague Moseneke J.... I also agree with his conclusion that the impugned measure does not violate section 9 of the Constitution, but am unable to agree with the route taken to arrive at this conclusion. Whereas Moseneke J concludes that section 9(2) of the Constitution applies to this case, I am of the view that the facts of this case are to be decided in terms of section 9(3) of the Constitution.

Equality and Unfair Discrimination

The role of the right to equality in our new dispensation cannot be overstated. Apartheid was not merely a system that entrenched political power and socioeconomic privilege in the hands of a minority nor did it only deprive the majority of the right to self actualisation and to control their own destinies. It targeted them for oppression and suppression. Not only did apartheid degrade its victims, it also systematically dehumanised them, striking at the core of their human dignity. The disparate impact of the system is today still deeply entrenched.

Restitutionary Measures

[Justice Mokgoro concluded that the pension fund distinctions did not qualify as a restitutionary measure under Section 9(2) because the favored group in the scheme are not "in the overwhelming majority designated in terms of race [or] political affiliation."]

The Scheme of the Equality Clause

The main judgment has made it clear that section 9(2) is part of a unified view of the right to equality in section 9. I support that view. A measure enacted in terms of section 9(2) is not an exception to our notion of equality; it is an integral part of it. From this must follow that section 9 must be viewed as a whole and any matter which engages the issue of equality engages the whole section.

In the present matter, the Minister has relied on facts in support of his contention that the measure falls under section 9(2). These facts in my view also support a finding that the discrimination in this case is fair. As I have found above, the measure does not meet the requirements of section 9(2). However, as I make clear below, it is my view that the measure does not constitute unfair discrimination.

Various factors are therefore relevant to an analysis of unfair discrimination. Of importance is the position of the complainants in society and whether they have suffered in the past from patterns of disadvantage. So too, whether the discrimination in the case under consideration is on a specified ground. The nature of the provision or power and the purpose sought to be achieved by it is also important. The question to be asked is whether the provision is aimed at an important societal goal. Unlike under section 9(2), other factors to emphasise include the extent to which the discrimination has affected the rights or interests of the complainants and whether the discrimination is of a serious nature and impairs the fundamental dignity of the complainants.

Assuming in favour of the respondent that the discrimination is based on race or political affiliation attracts the presumption that the measure unfairly discriminates. Even so, I am of the view that the measure is fair. The main judgment points out that the actuarial evidence before this Court shows that the respondent and the majority of his group "remain a privileged class of public pension beneficiaries notwithstanding the challenged remedial measures." This suggests that the consequences of the measure do not impact unduly on the interests of the respondent.

Moseneke J correctly points out that the measures do not impact negatively on the dignity of the complainants. The scheme does not have an impact on their dignity, because it does not negatively impact on the complainants' sense of self-worth. Furthermore, the respondent conceded in argument that the only loss suffered was pecuniary in nature. His motivation for contesting the measure was indeed to earn more.

Another factor of importance is whether the measure advances an important societal goal or whether it is aimed at impairing the complainant. It is clear that the current measure advances an important societal goal. It is aimed at creating equity between new MPs and those members of the current Parliament who, because of the fact that they were also members of the tri-cameral Parliament, are members of the [prior fund]....

[Sachs and Skweyiya, JJ. concurred in the judgment of Mokgoro, J.]

[Opinion by Ngcobo, J., joined by Sachs, J., omitted.]

By Sachs, J.

Paradoxical as it may appear, I concur in the judgment of Moseneke J on the one hand, and the respective judgments of Ngcobo and Mokgoro JJ, on the other, even though they disagree on one major issue and arrive at the same outcome by apparently different constitutional routes. In my view it is no accident that even though they started at different points and invoked different provisions they arrived at the same result. Though the formal articulation was different the basic constitutional rationale was the same. I agree with this basic rationale. I would go further and say that the core constitutional vision that underlies their separate judgments suggests that the technical frontier that divides them should be removed, allowing their overlap and commonalities to be revealed rather than to be obscured. If this is done, as I believe the Constitution requires us to do, then the apparent paradox of endorsing seemingly contradictory judgments is dissolved. Thus, I endorse the essential rationale of all the judgments, and explain why I believe that the Constitution obliges us to join together what the judgments put asunder.

The main difficulty concerning equality in this case is not how to choose between the need to take affirmative action to remedy the massive inequalities that disfigure our society, on the one hand, and the duty on the State not to discriminate unfairly against anyone on the grounds of race, on the other. It is how, in our specific historical and constitutional context, to harmonise the fairness inherent in remedial measures with the fairness expressly required of the State when it adopts measures that discriminate between different sections of the population. I agree with Mokgoro J that the main focus of section 9(2) of the Constitution is on the group advanced and the mechanism used to advance it, while the primary focus under section 9(3) is on the group of persons discriminated against. I do not however regard sections 9(2) and 9(3) as being competitive, or even as representing alternative approaches to achieving equality. Rather, I see them as cumulative, interrelated and indivisible. The necessary reconciliation between the different interests of those positively and negatively affected by affirmative action should, I believe, be done in a manner that takes simultaneous and due account both of the severe degree of structured inequality with which we still live, and of the constitutional goal of achieving an egalitarian society based on non-racism and non-sexism.

In this context, redress is not simply an option, it is an imperative. Without major transformation we cannot heal the divisions of the past and establish a society based on democratic values, social justice and fundamental human rights. At the same time it is important to ensure that the process of achieving equity is conducted in such a way that the baby of non-racialism is not thrown out with the bath-water of remedial action. Thus while I concur fully with Moseneke J that it would be illogical to permit a presumption of unfairness derived from section 9(3) (read with section 9(5)), to undermine and vitiate affirmative action programmes clearly authorised by section 9(2), by the same token I believe it would be illogical to say that unfair discrimination by the State is permissible provided that it takes place under section 9(2).

The illogic [sic] can best be cured if the frontier between sections 9(2) and 9(3) is dismantled rather than fortified. If the emphasis is on establishing an egalitarian continuum rather than defining cut-off points it becomes possible to avoid categorical or definitional skirmishing over precisely what is meant by persons or categories of persons disadvantaged by discrimination.

[Section 9(2)] functions in a manner that gives a clear constitutional pronouncement on issues which have divided legal thinking throughout the world in relation to problems concerning equal protection under the law. The whole thrust of section 9(2) is to ensure that equality be looked at from a contextual and substantive point of view, and not a purely formal one. As this Court has frequently stated, our Constitution rejects the notion of purely formal equality, which would require the same treatment for all who find themselves in similar situations. Formal equality is based on a status quo-oriented conservative approach which is particularly suited to countries where a great degree of actual equality or substantive equality has already been achieved. It looks at social situations in a neutral, colour-blind and gender-blind way and requires compelling justification for any legal classification that takes account of race or gender. The substantive approach, on the other hand, requires that the test for constitutionality is not whether the measure concerned treats all affected by it in identical fashion. Rather it focuses on whether it serves to advance or retard the equal enjoyment in practice of the rights and freedoms that are promised by the Constitution but have not already been achieved. It roots itself in a transformative constitutional philosophy which acknowledges that there are patterns of systemic advantage and disadvantage based on race and gender that need expressly to be faced up to and overcome if equality is to be achieved. In this respect, the context in which the measure operates, the structures of advantage and disadvantage it deals with, the impact it has on those affected by it and its overall effect in helping to achieve a society based on equality, non-racialism and non-sexism, become the important signifiers.

Even if section 9(2) had not existed, I believe that section 9 should have been interpreted so as to promote substantive equality and race-conscious remedial action. Other legal opinions might have been different. Section 9(2) was clearly inserted to put the matter beyond doubt. The need for such an express and firm constitutional pronouncement becomes understandable in the light of the enormous public controversies and divisions of judicial opinion on the subject in other countries. Such divisions had become particularly pronounced in the United States.

[Justice Sachs quotes from the majority opinion, and then extensively from Justice Marshall's dissenting opinion in *City of Richmond v. J.A. Croson Co.*]

Our Constitution pre-empted any judicial uncertainty on the matter by unambiguously directing courts to follow the line of reasoning that Marshall J relied on and that the majority of the US Supreme Court rejected. In South Africa we are far from having eradicated the vestiges of racial discrimination. I have no doubt that our Constitution requires that a matter such as the present be based on principles of substantive not formal equality.... Where I differ from my colleagues is in preferring to treat sections 9(2) and 9(3) as overlapping and indivisible rather than discreet.

Notes and Questions

1. In *Minister of Finance and Another v. Van Heerden*, the South African Constitutional Court takes a very different approach to questions of "equality" and "affirmative action" than have recent majorities on the U.S. Supreme Court. This different approach appears to be rooted in different understandings of the term "equality." The South African Justices emphasize that the Constitution of South Africa adopts a restitutionary, remedial approach to equality, and commits South Africa to the achievement of "actual," "substantive" equality rather than merely "formal" equality. What is the difference between "substantive" and "formal" equality? How is one to determine when "substantive" equality has been achieved, in a diverse society such as South Africa's?

2. What are the roots of the different visions of equality articulated in the United States and South Africa? Is it the fact that in Section 9(2), the South African Constitution, unlike the Constitution of the United States, explicitly authorizes

remedial measures? Does that mean that if Section 9(2) did not exist, a more formal reading of the equality concept stated in Section 9 would be required? Note that the language of Section 9(1) is quite similar to the language of the Fourteenth Amendment to the U.S. Constitution. Given that, can it be said that the constitutional text mandates *either* the South African or the United States' approach to equality?

3. If text does not provide a full answer, what about history? Is it true, as the South African Justices argue, that the history of South Africa makes a reading of equality permitting remedial preferences "imperative"? In light of its legacy of slavery and racial segregation, is the history of the United States sufficiently different from South Africa's to require or permit a different understanding? If the answer cannot be found in history, what about legal culture? What is it about the legal culture of the United States that seems to push toward a formal understanding of equality?

OTHER EXPERIENCES

India

Like South Africa and the United States, India is a vibrant, highly diverse democracy. India also has a long history of discrimination. Traditional Hindu society was divided into "castes," defined by hereditary occupation. The four primary castes were Brahmins (priests), Kshatriyas (warriors), Vaishyas (merchants), and Sudras (laborers), each subdivided into innumerable subcastes. Below, or perhaps outside of, this system were a group colloquially known as "untouchables," people outside the caste system to whom were delegated the most menial and religiously "impure" jobs. Untouchables, now known as Harijans, or Dalits, or "Scheduled Castes," came to constitute a large, socially outcaste minority, which suffered and continues to suffer enormous discrimination.

When India gained its independence from the British Empire in 1947, and soon thereafter adopted a Republican Constitution, untouchability was officially abolished. The new Constitution also contained numerous equality guarantees, including art. 14 (protecting "equality" and "equal protection"), art. 15 (prohibiting discrimination on the grounds of "religion, race, caste, sex, or place of birth"), and art. 16 (specifically prohibiting discrimination with respect to government employment). After a Supreme Court decision in 1951 holding that art. 16 prohibited preferential hiring policies in favor of former untouchables, the Constitution was promptly amended to add art. 16(4), which reads as follows:

> Nothing in this article shall prevent the State from making any provision for the reservation of appointments or posts in favour of any backward class of citizens which, in the opinion of the State, is not adequately represented in the services under the State.

Acting on the authority of art. 16(4), Indian governments at both the state and federal levels have enacted extensive "reservations" in public employment and university admissions, and indeed, for seats in Parliament, in favor of "Scheduled Castes" ("SCs") and "Scheduled Tribes" ("STs")—tribal people who were also outside the traditional caste system. Reservations in favor of SCs and STs tend to be 22.5% of available slots, reflecting their share of the population.

In the early 1990s, the reservations system began to be extended beyond the SC and ST groups, to what are called "Other Backward Classes" ("OBCs"), generally Sudras. This group might constitute as much as 52.5% of the entire population. Thus potentially, 75% of the population is entitled to preferences. Reservations for OBCs were targeted to be 27%, bringing total reservations to 49.5% (for reasons to be discussed). OBC reservations have proven highly controversial, eliciting massive protests including self-immolations.

The Indian system of reservations has triggered extensive constitutional litigation, as a result of which the Indian courts, including the Supreme Court of India, have been heavily engaged in implementing reservations. The Supreme Court has oscillated over the years between viewing art. 16(4) as a narrow exception, in derogation of general equality, and viewing art. 16(4) as an essential element of the equality principle in the Indian Constitution. In recent years, the latter view, as exemplified by the decisions in *State of Kerala v. Thomas*, A.I.R. 1976 S.C. 490, and *Indra Sawhney v. Union of India*, 80 A.I.R. 1993 S.C. 477, appears to have prevailed. Indeed, in *Thomas* the Supreme Court upheld a preference for members of SCs and STs in matters of promotion, even though the policy did *not* fall within the purview of art. 16(4) because it was not a "reservation." The modern approach of the Supreme Court appears to be that while art. 16(4), unlike the general equality provisions, does not create a "fundamental right," it is an important statement of equality principles. Courts must reconcile the different parts of art. 16 by balancing the need for reservations against the burden placed on individuals and the general needs of society. *Ajit Singh & Others v. State of Punjab & Others*, [2000] 1 L.R.I. 858. Using this balancing approach, the Supreme Court has held that reservations cannot constitute more than 50% of available slots (hence the 49.5% figures above), and in *Indra Sawhney*, that while caste may be used as a tool to identify "social backwardness," the government must create rules to ensure that privileged members of disfavored groups do not have access to reservations.

To what extent is the Indian experience similar to, or different from, that in the United States? Given the much longer history of discrimination in India (the caste system's roots are thousands of years old), is there a stronger justification for preferences in India? Given the large numbers of potential beneficiaries, is the justification weaker? Unlike in the United States, and (perhaps) South Africa, the Indian system relies heavily on numerical quotas. The U.S. Supreme Court, on the other hand, has expressed considerable hostility to quotas. What explains this difference? Which approach makes sense? Many commentators have pointed to the Indian example as a valuable one for the United States to study, primarily because the Indian system of reservations is generally more structured, and more nuanced, than affirmative action in the United States. That, in turn, seems at least in part due to the greater involvement of the Indian judiciary in setting guidelines on how, as opposed to whether, preferences can be implemented. Should the American judiciary become more active in this area? Would such activism be consistent with the constitutional role of at least the federal judiciary?

Malaysia

Malaysia is another postcolonial country with a racially diverse population. Malays and other indigenous groups—called "Bumiputeras"—constitute approximately 69% of the population, ethnic Chinese constitute 24%, and ethnic Indians 7%. After independence from Great Britain in 1957, the Malaysian economy came quickly to be dominated by ethnic Chinese and (to a lesser extent) ethnic Indians. Resentment at this pattern triggered racial riots in 1969. In response, in 1970 the government announced its "New Economic Policy," or "NEP," which implemented widespread, economy-wide preferences for Bumiputeras. In the period since 1970, Malaysia has had one of the fastest growing economies in the world, reducing poverty for all sectors of the population. In addition, the NEP has had modest success in improving the relative position of Malays vis-à-vis the Chinese minority, though not all of the NEP's goals have been achieved. Because the Malaysian Constitution makes it seditious to question the preferential policies of the NEP, there has been little public debate or constitutional litigation about the NEP's preferential policies. Given the radically different legal and political culture of Malaysia, to what extent is the Malaysian experience relevant to the United States?

Europe

Racial preferences in Europe are rare. However, some European countries, notably in Scandinavia, have adopted wide-ranging gender-based preferences, as a means of combating the underrepresentation of women in business and government. Norway, in particular, has been aggressive in this area. The major Norwegian political parties have, by voluntary agreement, consistently ensured that a substantial percentage of their candidates are women, and Norway is in the process of enforcing a law requiring that at least 40% of the Board of Directors of all public companies listed on the Oslo Stock Exchange are women. Even in Norway, however, legal problems have arisen. In *EFTA Surveillance Authority v. Norway*, [2003] 1 C.M.L.R. 23, the European Free Trade Association (EFTA) Court held that a Norwegian program setting aside certain academic positions at the University of Oslo for women violated the European Economic Area Agreement, an international treaty containing certain binding, civil rights obligations, including "the principle of equal treatment for men and women." After surveying decisions of the European Court of Justice in this area, the EFTA Court concluded that while gender-based preferences are not inherently inconsistent with the equality principle, the inflexibility of the Norwegian program, which completely prevented male applicants from competing for the set-aside positions, required its invalidation. In its hostility to set-asides, the EFTA decision has obvious similarities to recent decisions by the U.S. Supreme Court. Why is it that quotas and set-asides seem to elicit particular judicial disapproval? If the objective of a preferential policy is to increase female (or minority) representation, why is a system of open competition with "plus factors" to be preferred to set-asides?

CONCLUDING THOUGHTS: DEMOCRACY AND PREFERENCES

1. One obvious contrast between the U.S. Constitution and the Constitutions of South Africa and India is the fact that the U.S. Constitution does not contain an explicit authorization for racial preferences. In the case of India, that authorization was added through constitutional amendment, in response to a judicial decision invalidating a preference program. To what extent are the difficulties that U.S. courts faced in analyzing racial preferences a product of that lack of constitutional specificity? Would the United States benefit from a constitutional amendment addressing this question? Of course, most constitutions are easier to amend than the U.S. Constitution. To what extent are the complexities of U.S. constitutional law in this area (and many others) a product of the extraordinarily onerous amendment process established by Article V of the U.S. Constitution?
2. Another difference between racial preferences in the United States and elsewhere has to do with the nature of the beneficiary group. In the United States, racial preferences are explicitly targeted to racial minorities, and have sometimes been defended on the grounds that there is less cause for constitutional concern when an electoral majority chooses to burden itself. In South Africa and Malaysia, and perhaps even in India since the introduction of reservations for OBCs, the beneficiary group constitutes a majority of voters. When do racial preferences in favor of electoral majorities stop being "restitutionary" in nature, and become simple racial spoils? To what extent should these considerations influence constitutional analysis of racial preferences? Should judges in those countries be *more*, not *less* skeptical of racial preferences than in the United States? Or are there special factors at work in each of those countries, which justify majority preferences?

9

Discrimination on the Basis of Sexual Orientation

Nan D. Hunter

One of the most intellectually compelling aspects of sexual orientation law is that it is a rapidly growing field, one which is very much a work in progress in a world of global law. No nation's courts have fully resolved the constitutional legitimacy of government policies that adversely affect lesbian, gay, bisexual, and transgender (LGBT) persons. These evolving issues make up the first category within civil rights law for which the move from the margins to the center of constitutional concerns has occurred during the era of globalization. The result is a dynamic transnational legal environment, in which courts in multiple nations, in roughly the same time period, are applying contemporary notions of equality, privacy, and dignity to a newly visible and active social minority.

In many countries, the trajectory of legal reforms followed that of LGBT rights advocates in the United States: first, a decriminalization of same-sex sexual conduct; second, protection from discrimination in employment, housing, and other aspects of civil society; and third, recognition of equal status for LGBT partners and parents on such issues as custody, visitation, adoption of children, and equal marriage rights. *See* Kees Waaldijk, *Small Change: How the Road to Same-Sex Marriage Got Paved in the Netherlands, in* Legal Recognition of Same-Sex Partnerships (Robert Wintemute & Mads Andenaes eds., 2001). Decriminalization was the prerequisite for further reform because courts and legislatures in jurisdictions with sodomy laws reasoned that if government could criminalize the conduct that defined the group, then surely it could take the less draconian step of preferring heterosexual over LGBT persons in a wide variety of civil contexts. *See, e.g., Padula v. Webster*, 822 F.2d 97, 103 (D.C. Cir. 1987) (upholding dismissal of lesbian FBI agent).

Decriminalization efforts began almost simultaneously in the United States and England, with the issuance of formal reports from high-status national law reform commissions. In 1955, the American Law Institute published the Model Penal Code, which implicitly decriminalized sodomy by omitting it; and in 1957, the Wolfenden Commission in Britain recommended abolishing penalties for sex between adult men (sex between women was not criminal). Parliament followed this recommendation in 1967, but the American process required state-level reform, which was much slower.

By 1986, 26 states had dropped criminal penalties for sodomy (mostly by legislative repeal). That year the campaign suffered a major setback when the U.S. Supreme Court ruled that criminal laws against homosexual sex were constitutionally permissible. *Bowers v. Hardwick*, 478 U.S. 186 (1986). American advocates began seeking to gain protection under state constitutions, and succeeded in several state supreme courts as well as in a number of legislative repeal efforts. In 2003, the Supreme Court overruled *Hardwick* in *Lawrence v. Texas*, 539 U.S. 558 (2003), which invalidated what were by then only thirteen state criminal laws that remained on the books.

In a number of noncommon law countries, criminal prohibitions of sodomy ended much earlier, beginning with France in 1791, and including Belgium in 1795, the Netherlands in 1811, Brazil in 1830, Turkey in 1858, Mexico in 1871, Argentina in 1886, and Italy in 1890. Daniel Ottosson, *LGBT World Legal Wrap Up Survey* 3 (International Lesbian and Gay Ass'n 2006) (available at http://www.stonewall.org.uk/documents/world_legal_wrap_up_survey_november2006.pdf). These legislative acts occurred before homosexuality was a visible social identity and before there was a gay community as such. (Prosecutions on other grounds, such as indecency, continued in many places after sodomy laws were repealed, however.)

Decriminalization became a civil rights issue starting with the American and British reforms in the early 1960s, at the point when gay people had begun to self-identify and invoke civil rights and human rights principles. Debates over whether or how government should regulate consensual adult gay sexual behavior spread to other nations that still had criminal laws. Legislatures repealed laws against same-sex sexual conduct in countries including Canada (1969), Germany (1968 in what was then East Germany and 1969 in what was then West Germany), Norway (1972), Spain (1979), Israel (1988), Japan (1989), and China (1993). In Australia, with a federal system similar to that of the United States, state-by-state decriminalization began in 1975 and ended in 1997. *Id.*

Litigation challenges to sodomy laws began in the 1980s in courts around the world. Courts invalidated such laws in Northern Ireland, *Dudgeon v. United Kingdom*, 45 Eur. Ct. H.R. (ser. A) (1981); Ireland, *Norris v. Ireland*, 142 Eur. Ct. H.R. (ser. A) (1988); Cyprus, *Modinos v. Cyprus*, 259 Eur. Ct. H.R. (ser. A) (1993); Columbia, *Sentencia No. C-098/96* (Corte Constitutional, 1996); Ecuador, Constitutional Tribunal, Ecuador, *Sentencia No. 111-97-TC* in Registro Oficial (Official Registry), Supp. No. 203, Nov. 27, 1997; and South Africa, in the 1998 decision you read below. The South African decision draws on the principles used in several other national courts, but adds concepts such as dignity, derived from its own constitutional text. (See additional description of the cases in the Notes and Questions *infra*.)

This body of non-U.S. judicial reasoning was brought home to the U.S. Supreme Court by a comparative law amicus brief filed in *Lawrence v. Texas*, which argued that "it would be folly to ignore foreign practice and precedent at a time when courts across the world are increasingly caught up in a process of cross-fertilization among legal systems." *See* Brief Amici Curiae of Mary Robinson et al., 2003 WL 164151 at *29. The Court cited the brief and several of the foreign cases, stating, "The right the petitioners seek in this case has been accepted as an integral part of human freedom in many other countries. There has been no showing that in this country the governmental interest in circumscribing personal choice is somehow more legitimate or urgent." *Lawrence*, 538 U.S. at 577.

The National Coalition for Gay and Lesbian Equality v. The Minister of Justice

Constitutional Court of South Africa
1999 (1) SA 6 (CC) (S. Afr.), *available at* http://www.constitutionalcourt.org.za/Archimages/2076.PDF

Ackermann, J.:

...Section 9 of the 1996 Constitution stipulates:

(1) Everyone is equal before the law and has the right to equal protection and benefit of the law.
(2) Equality includes the full and equal enjoyment of all rights and freedoms. To promote the achievement of equality, legislative and other measures designed to protect or advance persons, or categories of persons, disadvantaged by unfair discrimination may be taken.
(3) The state may not unfairly discriminate directly or indirectly against anyone on one or more grounds, including race, gender, sex, pregnancy, marital status, ethnic or social origin, colour, sexual orientation, age, disability, religion, conscience, belief, culture, language and birth.
(4) No person may unfairly discriminate directly or indirectly against anyone on one or more grounds in terms of subsection (3). National legislation must be enacted to prevent unfair discrimination.
(5) Discrimination on one or more of the grounds listed in subsection (3) is unfair unless it is established that the discrimination is fair.

...The offence of sodomy...was defined...as "unlawful and intentional sexual intercourse per anum between human males," consent not depriving the act of unlawfulness, "and thus both parties commit the crime." Neither anal nor oral sex in private between a consenting adult male and a consenting adult female was punishable by the criminal law. Nor was any sexual act, in private, between consenting adult females so punishable....

In...*Harksen* [*Harksen v. Lane NO and Others* 1997 (11) BCLR 1489 (CC) (S. Afr.)] a multi-stage enquiry was postulated as being necessary when an attack of constitutional invalidity was based on [the correlative section] of the interim Constitution [to section 9]. In *Harksen* the approach was summarised as follows:...

(a) Does the provision differentiate between people or categories of people? If so, does the differentiation bear a rational connection to a legitimate government purpose? If it does not then there is a violation.... Even if it does bear a rational connection, it might nevertheless amount to discrimination.

(b) Does the differentiation amount to unfair discrimination? This requires a two stage analysis:

(i) Firstly, does the differentiation amount to "discrimination"? If it is on a specified ground, then discrimination will have been established. If it is not on a specified ground, then whether or not there is discrimination will depend upon whether, objectively, the ground is based on attributes and characteristics which have the potential to impair the fundamental human dignity of persons as human beings or to affect them adversely in a comparably serious manner.

(ii) If the differentiation amounts to "discrimination," does it amount to "unfair discrimination"? If it has been found to have been on a specified ground, then unfairness will be presumed. If on an unspecified ground, unfairness will have to be established by the complainant. The test of unfairness focuses primarily on the impact of the discrimination on the complainant and others in his or her situation.

If, at the end of this stage of the enquiry, the differentiation is found not to be unfair, then there will be no violation....

This does not mean, however, that in all cases the rational connection inquiry of stage (a) must inevitably precede stage (b). The stage (a) rational connection inquiry would be clearly unnecessary in a case in which a court holds that the discrimination is unfair and unjustifiable. I proceed with the enquiry as to whether the differentiation on the ground of sexual orientation constitutes unfair discrimination. Being a ground listed in section 9(3) it is presumed, in terms of section 9(5), that the differentiation constitutes unfair discrimination "unless it is established that the discrimination is fair."...

Although, in the final analysis, it is the impact of the discrimination on the complainant or the members of the affected group that is the determining factor regarding the unfairness of the discrimination, the approach to be adopted... is comprehensive and nuanced. [From] *Harksen*...:

> In order to determine whether the discriminatory provision has impacted on complainants unfairly, various factors must be considered. These would include:
>
> (a) the position of the complainants in society and whether they have suffered in the past from patterns of disadvantage, whether the discrimination in the case under consideration is on a specified ground or not;
>
> (b) the nature of the provision or power and the purpose sought to be achieved by it. If its purpose is manifestly not directed, in the first instance, at impairing the complainants in the manner indicated above, but is aimed at achieving a worthy and important societal goal, such as, for example, the furthering of equality for all, this purpose may, depending on the facts of the particular case, have a significant bearing on the question whether complainants have in fact suffered the impairment in question....

(c) with due regard to (a) and (b) above, and any other relevant factors, the extent to which the discrimination has affected the rights or interests of complainants and whether it has led to an impairment of their fundamental human dignity or constitutes an impairment of a comparably serious nature.

These factors, assessed objectively, will assist in giving 'precision and elaboration' to the constitutional test of unfairness. They do not constitute a closed list. Others may emerge as our equality jurisprudence continues to develop....

[Here:]

(a) The discrimination is on a specified ground. Gay men are a permanent minority in society and have suffered in the past from patterns of disadvantage. The impact is severe, affecting the dignity, personhood and identity of gay men at a deep level. It occurs at many levels and in many ways and is often difficult to eradicate.

(b) The nature of the power and its purpose is to criminalise private conduct of consenting adults which causes no harm to anyone else. It has no other purpose than to criminalise conduct which fails to conform with the moral or religious views of a section of society.

(c) The discrimination has, for the reasons already mentioned, gravely affected the rights and interests of gay men and deeply impaired their fundamental dignity.

The above analysis confirms that the discrimination is unfair. There is nothing which can be placed in the other balance of the scale. The inevitable conclusion is that the discrimination in question is unfair and therefore in breach of section 9 of the 1996 Constitution....

Thus far I have considered only the...inconsistency with the right to equality. This was the primary basis on which the case was argued. In my view, however, the common-law crime of sodomy also constitutes an infringement of the right to dignity which is enshrined in section 10 of our Constitution. [Section 10 provides "Everyone has inherent dignity and the right to have their dignity respected and protected."]...

Dignity is a difficult concept to capture in precise terms. At its least, it is clear that the constitutional protection of dignity requires us to acknowledge the value and worth of all individuals as members of our society. The common-law prohibition on sodomy...punishes a form of sexual conduct which is identified by our broader society with homosexuals. Its symbolic effect is to state that in the eyes of our legal system all gay men are criminals. The stigma thus attached to a significant proportion of our population is manifest. But the harm imposed by the criminal law is far more than symbolic. As a result of the criminal offence, gay men are at risk of arrest, prosecution and conviction of the offence of sodomy simply because they seek to engage in sexual conduct which is part of their experience of being human. Just as apartheid legislation rendered the lives of couples of different racial groups perpetually at risk, the sodomy offence builds insecurity and vulnerability into the daily lives of gay men. There can be no doubt that the existence of a law which punishes a form of sexual expression for gay men degrades and devalues gay men in our broader society. As such it is a palpable invasion of their dignity and a breach of section 10 of the Constitution....

Sachs, J. [concurring]:

Only in the most technical sense is this a case about who may penetrate whom where. At a practical and symbolical level it is about the status, moral citizenship and sense of self-worth of a significant section of the community. At a more general and conceptual level, it concerns the nature of the open, democratic and pluralistic society contemplated by the Constitution. In expressing my concurrence with the comprehensive and forceful judgment of Ackermann J, I feel it necessary to add some complementary observations on the broader matters. I will present my remarks...in the context of responding to three issues which emerged in the course of argument. The first concerns the relationship between equality and privacy, the second the connection between equality and dignity, and the third the question of the meaning of the right to be different in the open and democratic society contemplated by the Constitution.

Equality and Privacy

It is important to start the analysis by asking what is really being punished by the anti-sodomy laws. Is it an act, or is it a person? Outside of regulatory control, conduct that deviates from some publicly established norm is usually...punishable [only] when it is violent, dishonest, treacherous or in some other way disturbing of the public peace or provocative of injury. In the case of male homosexuality however, the perceived deviance is punished simply because it is deviant. It is repressed for its perceived symbolism rather than because of its proven harm. If proof were necessary, it is established by the fact that consensual anal penetration of a female is not criminalised. Thus, it is not the act of sodomy that is denounced by the law, but the so-called sodomite who performs it; not any proven social damage, but the threat that same-sex passion in itself is seen as representing to heterosexual hegemony.

The effect is that all homosexual desire is tainted, and the whole gay and lesbian community is marked with deviance and perversity. When everything associated with homosexuality is treated as bent, queer, repugnant or comical, the equality interest is directly engaged. People are subject to extensive prejudice because of what they are or what they are perceived to be, not because of what they do. The result is that a significant group of the population is, because of its sexual non-conformity, persecuted, marginalised and turned in on itself. I have no doubt that when the drafters of the Bill of Rights decided expressly to include sexual orientation in their list of grounds of discrimination that were presumptively unfair, they had precisely these considerations in mind. There could be few stronger cases than the present for invoking the protective concern and regard offered by the Constitution.

Against this background it is understandable that the applicants should urge this Court to base its invalidation of the anti-sodomy laws on the ground that they violated the equality provisions in the Bill of Rights. Less acceptable however, is the manner in which applicants treated the right to privacy, presenting it in their written argument as a poor second prize to be offered and received only in the event of the Court declining to invalidate the laws because of a breach of equality. Their argument may be summarised as follows: privacy analysis is inadequate because it suggests that homosexuality is shameful and therefore should only be protected if it is limited to the private bedroom; it tends to limit the promotion of gay rights to the decriminalisation of consensual adult sex, instead of contemplating a more comprehensive normative framework that addresses discrimination generally against gays; and it assumes a dual structure—public and private—that does not capture the complexity of lived life, in which public and private lives determine each other, with the mobile lines between them being constantly amenable to repressive definition.

These concerns are undoubtedly valid. Yet, I consider that they arise from a set of assumptions that are flawed as to how equality and privacy rights interrelate and about the manner in which privacy rights should truly be understood; in the first place, the approach adopted by the applicants subjects equality and privacy rights to inappropriate sequential ordering, while secondly, it undervalues the scope and significance of privacy rights. The cumulative result is both to weaken rather than strengthen applicants' quest for human rights, and to put the general development of human rights jurisprudence on a false track.

...The fact is that both from the point of view of the persons affected, as well as from that of society as a whole, equality and privacy cannot be separated, because they are both violated simultaneously by anti-sodomy laws. In the present matter, such laws deny equal respect for difference, which lies at the heart of equality, and become the basis for the invasion of privacy. At the same time, the negation by the state of different forms of intimate personal behaviour becomes the foundation for the repudiation of equality. Human rights are better approached and defended in an integrated rather than a disparate fashion. The rights must fit the people, not the people the rights. This requires looking at rights and their violations from a persons-centred rather than a formula-based position, and analysing them contextually rather than abstractly.

One consequence of an approach based on context and impact would be the acknowledgement that grounds of unfair discrimination can intersect, so that the evaluation of discriminatory impact is done not according to one ground of discrimination or another, but on a combination of both, that is, globally and contextually, not separately and abstractly. The objective is to determine in a qualitative rather than a quantitative way if the group concerned is subjected to scarring of a sufficiently serious nature as to merit constitutional intervention. [Two examples are] unmarried mothers, or homosexual parents, where nuanced rather than categorical approaches would be appropriate. Alternatively, a context rather than category-based approach might suggest that overlapping vulnerability is capable of producing overlapping discrimination. A notorious example would be African widows, who historically have suffered discrimination as blacks, as Africans, as women, as African women, as widows and usually, as older people, intensified by the fact that they are frequently amongst the lowest paid workers.

Conversely, a single situation can give rise to multiple, overlapping and mutually reinforcing violations of constitutional rights. The case before us is in point. The group in question is discriminated against because of the one characteristic of sexual orientation. The measures that assail their personhood are clustered around this particular personal trait. Yet the impact of these laws on the group is of such a nature that a number of different protected rights are simultaneously infringed. In these circumstances it would be as artificial in law as it would be in life to treat the categories as alternative rather than interactive. In some contexts, rights collide and an appropriate balancing is required. In others, such as the present, they inter-relate and give extra dimension to the extent and impact of the infringement. Thus, the violation of equality by the anti-sodomy laws is all the more egregious because it touches the deep, invisible and intimate side of people's lives. The Bill of Rights tells us how we should analyse this interaction: in technical terms, the gross interference with privacy will bear strongly on the unfairness of the discrimination, while the discriminatory manner in which groups are targeted for invasions of privacy will destroy any possibility of justification for such invasions.

The depreciated value given in argument to invalidation on the grounds of privacy, treating it as a poor relation of equality, was a result of adopting an impoverished version of the concept of privacy itself....

There is no good reason why the concept of privacy should, as was suggested, be restricted simply to sealing off from state control what happens in the bedroom, with the doleful sub-text that you may behave as bizarrely or shamefully as you like, on the understanding that you do so in private. It has become a judicial cliché to say that privacy protects people, not places. Blackmun J in *Bowers, Attorney General of Georgia v. Hardwick et al.* made it clear that the much-quoted "right to be left alone" should be seen not simply as a negative right to occupy a private space free from government intrusion, but as a right to get on with your life, express your personality and make fundamental decisions about your intimate relationships without penalisation.... [P]rivacy [must] be regarded as suggesting at least some responsibility on the state to promote conditions in which personal self-realisation can take place....

At the same time, there is no reason why the concept of privacy should be extended to give blanket libertarian permission for people to do anything they like provided that what they do is sexual and done in private. In this respect, the assumptions about privacy rights are too broad. There are very few democratic societies, if any, which do not penalise persons for engaging in inter-generational, intra-familial, and cross-species sex, whether in public or in private....

Equality and Dignity

...[T]he motif which links and unites equality and privacy, and which, indeed, runs right through the protections offered by the Bill of Rights, is dignity. This Court has on a number of occasions emphasised the centrality of the concept of dignity and self-worth to the idea of equality. In an interesting argument, the Centre for Applied Legal Studies (the Centre) has mounted a frontal challenge to this approach, arguing that the equality clause is intended to advance equality, not dignity, and that the dignity provisions in the Bill of Rights should take care of protecting dignity. This was part of an invitation to the Court to re-visit its whole approach to equality jurisprudence, shifting from what the Centre called the defensive posture of reliance on unlawful discrimination under section 9(3) to what it claimed to be an affirmative position of promoting equality under the broad provisions of section 9(1). The constitutional vocation of section 9(1), it argued, had been reduced from that of the guarantor of substantive equality to that of a gatekeeper for claims of violation of dignity.

Ackermann J has, I believe, dealt convincingly with the assertion that the Court has failed to promote substantive as opposed to formal equality. Indeed, his judgment is itself a good example of a refusal to follow a formal equality test, which could have based invalidity simply on the different treatment accorded by the law to anal intercourse according to whether the partner was male or female. Instead, the judgment has with appropriate sensitivity for the way anti-gay prejudice has impinged on the dignity of members of the gay community, focussed on the manner in which the anti-sodomy laws have reinforced systemic disadvantage both of a practical and a spiritual nature. Furthermore, it has done so not by adopting the viewpoint of the so-called reasonable lawmaker who accepts as objective all the prejudices of heterosexual society as incorporated into the laws in question, but by responding to the request of the applicants to look at the matter from the perspective of those whose lives and sense of self-worth are affected by the measures. I would like to endorse, and I believe, strengthen this argument by referring to reasons of principle and strategy why, when developing equality jurisprudence, the Court should continue to maintain its focus on the defined antidiscrimination principles of sections 9(3), (4) and (5), which contain respect for human dignity at their core.

...There are, I believe, additional considerations [beyond those stated in the majority opinion] supporting a structured focus on non-discrimination as the heart of implementable equality guarantees: institutional aptness, functional effectiveness, technical discipline, historical congruency, compatibility with international practice and conceptual sensitivity.

By developing its equality jurisprudence around the concept of unfair discrimination this Court engages in a structured discourse centred on respect for human rights and non-discrimination. It reduces the danger of over-intrusive judicial intervention in matters of broad social policy, while emphasising the Court's special responsibility for protecting fundamental rights in an affirmative manner. It also diminishes the possibility of the Court being inundated by unmeritorious claims, and best enables the Court to focus on its special vocation, to use the techniques for which it has a special aptitude, and to defend the interests for which it has a particular responsibility. Finally, it places the Court's jurisprudence in the context of evolving human rights concepts throughout the world, and of our country's own special history.

Contrary to the Centre's argument, the violation of dignity and self-worth under the equality provisions can be distinguished from a violation of dignity under section 10 of the Bill of Rights. The former is based on the impact that the measure has on a person because of membership of an historically vulnerable group that is identified and subjected to disadvantage by virtue of certain closely held personal characteristics of its members; it is the inequality of treatment that leads to and is proved by the indignity. The violation of dignity under section 10, on the other hand, contemplates a much wider range of situations. It offers protection to persons in their multiple identities and capacities. This could be to individuals being disrespectfully treated, such as somebody being stopped at a roadblock. It also could be to members of groups subject to systemic disadvantage, such as farm workers in certain areas, or prisoners in certain prisons, such groups not being identified because of closely held characteristics, but because of the situation they find themselves in. These would be cases of indignity of treatment leading to inequality, rather than of inequality relating to closely held group characteristics producing indignity.

Once again, it is my view that the equality principle and the dignity principle should not be seen as competitive but rather as complementary. Inequality is established not simply through group-based differential treatment, but through differentiation which perpetuates disadvantage and leads to the scarring of the sense of dignity and self-worth associated with membership of the group. Conversely, an invasion of dignity is more easily established when there is an inequality of power and status between the violator and the victim.

One of the great gains achieved by following a situation-sensitive human rights approach is that analysis focuses not on abstract categories, but on the lives as lived and the injuries as experienced by different groups in our society. The manner in which discrimination is experienced on grounds of race or sex or religion or disability varies considerably—there is difference in difference. The commonality that unites them all is the injury to dignity imposed upon people as a consequence of their belonging to certain groups.

Dignity in the context of equality has to be understood in this light. The focus on dignity results in emphasis being placed simultaneously on context, impact and the point of view of the affected persons. Such focus is in fact the guarantor of substantive as opposed to formal equality.

As Marshall J reminds us,

> the lessons of history and experience are surely the best guide as to when, and with respect to what interests, society is likely to stigmatise individuals as members of an inferior caste or view them as not belonging to the community. Because prejudice spawns prejudice, and stereotypes produce limitations that confirm the stereotype on which they are based, a history of unequal treatment requires sensitivity to the prospect that its vestiges endure. (quoting *City of Cleburne v. Cleburne Living Center*, 473 US 432, 473 (1985) (concurring))

At the heart of equality jurisprudence is the rescuing of people from a caste-like status and putting an end to their being treated as lesser human beings because they belong to a particular group. The indignity and subordinate status may flow from institutionally imposed exclusion from the mainstream of society or else from powerlessness within the mainstream; they may also be derived from the location of difference as a problematic form of deviance in the disadvantaged group itself, as happens in the case of the disabled. In the case of gays it comes from compulsion to deny a closely held personal characteristic. To penalise people for being what they are is profoundly disrespectful of the human personality and violatory of equality....

The Treatment of Difference in an Open Society

...[I]n my view the implications of this judgment extend well beyond the gay and lesbian community. It is no exaggeration to say that the success of the whole constitutional endeavour in South Africa will depend in large measure on how successfully sameness and difference are reconciled, an issue central to the present matter.

The present case shows well that equality should not be confused with uniformity; in fact, uniformity can be the enemy of equality. Equality means equal concern and respect across difference. It does not pre-suppose the elimination or suppression of difference. Respect for human rights requires the affirmation of self, not the denial of self. Equality therefore does not imply a levelling or homogenisation of behaviour but an acknowledgment and acceptance of difference. At the very least, it affirms that difference should not be the basis for exclusion, marginalisation, stigma and punishment. At best, it celebrates the vitality that difference brings to any society....

The acknowledgment and acceptance of difference is particularly important in our country where group membership has been the basis of express advantage and disadvantage. The development of an active rather than a purely formal sense of enjoying a common citizenship depends on recognising and accepting people as they are.... What the Constitution requires is that the law and public institutions acknowledge the variability of human beings and affirm the equal respect and concern that should be shown to all as they are. At the very least, what is statistically normal ceases to be the basis for establishing what is legally normative. More broadly speaking, the scope of what is constitutionally normal is expanded to include the widest range of perspectives and to acknowledge, accommodate and accept the largest spread of difference. What becomes normal in an open society, then, is not an imposed and standardised form of behaviour that refuses to acknowledge difference, but the acceptance of the principle of difference itself, which accepts the variability of human behaviour....

A state that recognises difference does not mean a state without morality or one without a point of view. It does not banish concepts of right and wrong, nor envisage a world without good and evil. It is impartial in its dealings with people and groups, but is not neutral in its value system. The Constitution certainly does not debar the state from enforcing morality. Indeed, the Bill of Rights is nothing if not a document founded on deep political morality. What is central to the character and functioning of the state, however, is that the dictates of the morality which it enforces, and the limits to which it may go, are to be found in the text and spirit of the Constitution itself....

In my view, the decision of this Court should be seen as part of a growing acceptance of difference in an increasingly open and pluralistic South Africa. It leads me to hope that the emancipatory effects of the elimination of institutionalised prejudice against gays and lesbians will encourage amongst the heterosexual population a greater sensitivity to the variability of the human kind....

Notes and Questions

1. *Doctrinal convergence.* Just as the U.S. Supreme Court could have decided *Lawrence v. Texas*, 539 U.S. 558 (2003), on either substantive due process or equal protection grounds, the South African Constitutional Court had a variety of doctrinal paths open to it in ruling on the constitutionality of sodomy law. In *Lawrence*, the Court chose due process as the foundation for its holding; in *NCGLE*, the court opted for equality and dignity. Does the difference matter? Note that both courts inflected the doctrinal analysis supporting the holding with language suggestive of broader themes; for example, the rhetoric of *Lawrence* evokes equality concerns, even though the ruling is based on other grounds. How might the meanings of these seemingly generic categories for human rights concepts—privacy, equality, and dignity—differ depending on the political and constitutional cultures? To what extent would Justice Sachs' analysis of the relationship among the categories apply in the United States?

2. *The role of legislatures.* In 1981, a challenge to the Northern Ireland sodomy law was brought before the European Court of Human Rights, predicated on Article 8 of the European Convention on Human Rights, providing for "the right to respect for...private and family life..." *Dudgeon v. United Kingdom*, 45 Eur. Ct. H.R. (1981). The court invalidated the law, but noted that

> [T]he Government drew attention to what they described as profound differences of attitude and public opinion between Northern Ireland and Great Britain in relation to questions of morality. Northern Irish society was said to be more conservative and to place greater emphasis on religious factors, as was illustrated by more restrictive laws even in the field of heterosexual conduct....
>
> [T]he Court acknowledges that such differences do exist to a certain extent and are a relevant factor.... [I]n assessing the requirements of the protection of morals in Northern Ireland, the contested measures must be seen in the context of Northern Irish society.
>
> ...Where there are disparate cultural communities residing within the same State, it may well be that different requirements, both moral and social, will face the governing authorities.
>
> As the Government correctly submitted, it follows that the moral climate in Northern Ireland in sexual matters, in particular as evidenced by the opposition to the proposed legislative change, is one of the matters which the national authorities may legitimately take into account in exercising their discretion. There is, the Court accepts, a strong body of opposition stemming from a genuine and sincere conviction shared by a large number of responsible members of the Northern Irish community that a change in the law would be seriously damaging to the moral fabric of society....
>
> Notwithstanding the margin of appreciation left to the national authorities, it is for the Court to make the final evaluation as to whether the reasons it has found to be relevant were sufficient in the circumstances, in particular whether the interference complained of was proportionate to the social need claimed for it.... [The court noted that there had been no enforcement of the statute "in recent years" against adults engaged in private consensual conduct, nor had there been public demand for enforcement.]

In 1988, the government of Ireland defended its sodomy law against an Article 8 challenge by invoking this portion of *Dudgeon*, but the court again struck down the statute. *Norris v. Ireland*, 142 Eur. Ct. H.R. (1988). How does the principle of "proportionate to the social need claimed for [the statute]" compare to the standards used by U.S. courts for deference to the legislature?

In a New Zealand marriage case, by contrast, legislative authority trumped judicial review. In *Quilter v. Attorney-General*, a lesbian couple challenged New Zealand's laws limiting marriage to opposite-sex couples. *Quilter v. Attorney-General* [1996] N.Z.F.L.R. 418 (H.C.). The High Court, after reviewing multiple statutes relating to marital benefits and rights, concluded that although the exclusion was inconsistent with the right to be free from discrimination, parliament had the authority under the New Zealand Bill of Rights to reasonably limit the equality right. The court found that it was the job of parliament to regulate social policy.

Marriage cases in Canada and South Africa have led to extensive interbranch engagement. In Canada, federal courts in eight of the ten provinces upheld challenges to the exclusion of same-sex couples from marriage, beginning with *Halpern v. Canada (Att'y Gen.)*, [2003] 65 O.R.3d 161 (Ont. C.A.). In *Halpern*, the Court of Appeal for Ontario found that the definition of marriage as between a man and a woman violated Section 15(1) [the guarantee of equality] of the Canadian Charter of Rights and Freedoms. The government did not appeal the ruling, but sent a formal inquiry to the Supreme Court of Canada, asking whether the national parliament had the authority to define marriage or whether that was solely a question of provincial law; whether clergy would be free not to perform marriages of same-sex couples; and whether a failure to include same-sex couples would violate the Charter. The Supreme Court answered that the national legislature had jurisdiction and that clergy could not be forced to perform marriages to which they objected, but the Court declined to answer the final question (*Reference re Same-Sex Marriage*, [2004] 3 S.C.R. 698 (SC) (Can.)). In July 2005, parliament passed the Civil Marriage Act, which legalized marriage between same-sex partners. In South Africa, the Constitutional Court found that the common law and the Marriage Act unconstitutionally excluded same-sex couples based on the rights of equality and dignity. However, the Court suspended its order for a year so that parliament could amend the law (*Minister of Home Affairs v. Fourie*, 2006 (1) SA 524 (CC) (S. Afr.)). Parliament passed new legislation on the day before the deadline expired.

In the four nations other than Canada and South Africa that have legalized marriage between same-sex couples (the Netherlands, Norway, Belgium, and Spain), legislative rather than judicial action drove the process for change.

3. *Originalism*. In *S. v. Banana*, the High Court of Harare in Zimbabwe invoked history to reject a claim that laws criminalizing sexual acts between males were unconstitutional under the prohibition on sex discrimination. *S. v. Banana*, 1998 (2) ZLR 533 (H). The court reasoned that because the laws predated the Constitution and because Zimbabwe's Constitution, unlike the Constitution of South Africa, did not explicitly prohibit sexual orientation discrimination, the framers did not intend to invalidate sodomy laws.

4. *Military service*. Most countries do not have an explicit policy on military service by gay and lesbian troops. Of the twenty-four countries that allow openly gay and lesbian troops to serve, only the United Kingdom changed its policy based on a judicial ruling. In *Smith and Grady v. United Kingdom*, 29 Eur. Ct. H.R. (1999), two members of the Royal Air Force challenged their discharges based on homosexuality. The European Court of Human Rights found that the policy of not allowing gays and lesbians to serve violated Article 8 of the European Convention on Human Rights (protection against interference in private life). Applying the *Dudgeon* standard that justification required pressing social need and proportionality, the Court of Human Rights rejected the government's argument that the special nature of military life, including attention to morale and military efficiency, made such policies necessary. *Accord, Lustig-Prean and Beckett v. United Kingdom*, 29 Eur. Ct. H.R. (1999) (same ruling as to Royal Navy).

5. *Transgender issues*. In addition to sexual orientation issues, non-U.S. courts have adjudicated rights in a series of cases brought by persons seeking to change, or who had changed, their gender. Until recently, the European Court of Human Rights, which has ruled in several such cases, deferred to national legislatures, recommending that they review scientific and medical advances and accordingly adjust their social policies. *See, e.g., X, Y, and Z v. United Kingdom*, 143 Eur. Ct. H.R. (1997) (upholding a decision barring a female-to-male transsexual from registering as father on a birth certificate given the complexity of transgender issues). However, in *Goodwin v. United Kingdom*, 35 Eur. Ct. H.R. (2002), the court determined that the United Kingdom was not reviewing its policies as the court had directed, and ruled that postoperative transsexuals had the right under Articles 8 and 12 of the Convention [protecting private life and the right of marriage] to change the gender on their birth certificates and to marry.

10

Review of Laws Having a Disparate Impact Based on Gender

Vicki C. Jackson[1]

The U.S. Constitution is one of the world's oldest. Its principal provisions were drafted by representative bodies in which women did not participate, and it was ratified through processes that, for the most part, also excluded women. *See also* Kathleen M. Sullivan, *Constitutionalizing Women's Equality*, 90 CALIF. L. REV. 735 (2002). ("The U.S. Constitution is the only major written constitution that includes a bill of rights but lacks a provision explicitly declaring the equality of the sexes," in contrast to those of France, Germany, India, Canada, and South Africa.)

A distinctive feature of U.S. constitutional law on gender (and race) equality is that the Constitution has been interpreted by the Court to bar only *intentional* forms of discrimination. By contrast, a distinctive feature of the case law of the European Court of Justice (ECJ)—applicable in the now twenty-seven Member States of the European Union (EU)—is its "indirect discrimination," disparate-impact doctrine interpreting the controlling Treaty requirement that men and women receive equal pay for equal work. Although this comparison will be the focus here, caution is required—one cannot draw broad conclusions about gender equality jurisprudence looking only at constitutional (or quasi-constitutional treaty) text, or only at one issue area. Jurisdictions with explicit constitutional commitments to gender equality continue to uphold overt gender classifications: Even in South Africa, whose new Constitution manifests pervasive commitments to equality (*compare Omar v. Government, RSA*, 2006 (2) BCLR 253 (CC) (S. Afr.) (affirming national government's power to protect against domestic violence and rejecting constitutional challenge to a statute requiring courts to issue protective orders) *with United States v. Morrison*, 529 U.S. 598 (2000) (holding a provision of the Violence Against Women Act beyond federal power), the Court upheld the president's decision to pardon imprisoned mothers of young children without pardoning similarly situated men. *President of*

---

[1] Thanks are due to Professors Andrea Biondi (Kings College, London), Sandra Fredman (Oxford University), and Daniel Halberstam (University of Michigan), and to Goran Selanec (S.J.D. candidate, University of Michigan), for their very helpful comments on earlier drafts. The author alone is responsible for any remaining errors; research was completed in 2007.

the Federal Republic v. Hugo, 1997 (6) BCLR 708 (CC) (S. Afr.). In Europe, although the ECJ struck a complete bar on women serving in the military (Case C-285/98, *Kreil v. Bundesrepublik Deutschland*, [2000] E.C.R. I-69), it upheld a limitation of compulsory military service to men (Case C-186/01, *Dory v. Bundesrepublik Deutschland*, [2003] E.C.R. I-2479), indicated that women could be excluded from police work in certain areas if their gender would attract more violence (Case C-222/84, *Johnston v. Chief Constable of the Royal Ulster Constabulary*, [1986] E.C.R. 1651) and that women could be excluded from the British Royal Marines where their presence was assertedly incompatible with requirements of combat "interoperability" (Case C-273/97, *Sirdar v. Army Board*, [1999] E.C.R. I-7403). Nonetheless, its disparate impact case law provides an interesting contrast.

In *Handels-og Kontorfunktionaerernes Forbund i Danmark v. Dansk Arbejdsgiverforening acting on behalf of Danfoss*, Case 109/88, [1989] ECR 3199 [*Danfoss*], the ECJ was asked to review several criteria claimed to justify pay differences between women and men doing similar work. It held, inter alia, that a criterion of "mobility... to reward the employees' adaptability to variable hours and varying places of work," could "work to the disadvantage of female employees, who, because of household and family duties for which they are frequently responsible, are not as able as men to organize their working time flexibility," *Danfoss* ¶¶ 18–21, and thus, arguably infringed the Equal Pay Directive and Treaty Article 119 (now 141), which "established the principle that men and women should receive equal pay for equal work...." Catherine Barnard, EC Employment Law 298 (3d ed. 2006). Consistent with earlier case law on paying part-time workers (more likely to be women) less than full-time workers, the Court indicated that the employer could try to "justify the remuneration of such adaptability by showing it is of importance for the performance of specific tasks entrusted to the employee" (*Danfoss*, ¶ 22).

By contrast, with respect to the "criterion of length of service," although recognizing that it "may involve less advantageous treatment of women than of men in so far as women have entered the labour market more recently than men," *Danfoss* nonetheless concluded that

> since length of service goes hand in hand with experience and since experience generally enables the employee to perform his duties better, the employer is free to reward it without having to establish the importance it has in the performance of specific tasks entrusted to the employee. ¶24.

In subsequent case law, questions arose whether, to the extent *Danfoss* stood for the proposition that service-length criteria for pay could not be challenged, it was still good law. In the case that follows, we excerpt first from the Advocate-General's opinion and then from the Court's judgment. The Advocate-General is a member of the Court, who sits with the judges during argument and may pose questions, but does not vote or participate in the deliberations of the judges who do. Before the Court rules, the

Advocate-General issues a nonbinding opinion as a recommendation to the voting members of the Court. *See* Cyril Ritter, *A New Look at the Role and Impact of Advocates-General – Collectively and Individually*, 12 COLUM. J. EUR. L. 751 (2006). Note how the Court's judgment differs from the Advocate-General's.

B.F. Cadman v. Health & Safety Executive Intervenor: Equal Opportunities Commission

Case C-17/05 [2006] E.C.R. I-09583[2] Opinion of Advocate General Poiares Maduro May 18, 2006

1. This reference for a preliminary ruling from the Court of Appeal (England and Wales) (Civil Division) concerns the development of the Community case law concerning equal pay. At the heart of the debate is the continuing applicability of the *Danfoss* judgment...

2. ...[E]quality between women and men...is a fundamental principle of EC law under Articles 2 EC and 3(2) EC and forms part of the foundations of the Community....

4. Although not expressly provided for in Article 141 EC, the notion of indirect sex discrimination was developed by the case law [(Case 96/80 Jenkins [1981] IRLR 228)] and then incorporated into legislation [referring to Council Directives].[3]...

III—Analysis...

23. Unlike direct discrimination, indirect discrimination arises from provisions which, on their face, apply equally to men and women. If a neutral provision in fact works to the disadvantage of women it can be deemed indirectly discriminatory..... Inherent in the concept of indirect discrimination is a requirement that there should be a substantive notion of equality....

24. There can be no justification for direct discrimination. However, in keeping with settled case-law...indirect discrimination can be justified.

25. In...indirect discrimination cases, Article 4 of Directive 97/80 sets out the rules concerning the allocation of the burden of proof as between

---

[2] The opinion of the Advocate General and the Judgment of the Grand Chamber in this case are also available at http://curia.europa.eu/en/.

[3] "EC" refers to the governing treaty instrument; "directives" are forms of legislation enacted pursuant to the treaty.

the employer and the employee. A complainant who makes an allegation of indirect discrimination must adduce proof that the contested provision actually produces a disparate impact on women.... The requirement for the employer or the legislature to produce justification for a practice or a policy that is neutral on its face will arise only if such proof is provided. Once such evidence has been produced, the employer or the legislature...will have to demonstrate that the measures concerned pursue a legitimate aim, are strictly necessary to achieve this legitimate aim and are proportionate....

29. The United Kingdom Government defended the view that length of service should in principle be considered as justified even if the employee shows that it has a disproportionate impact on women. The employer would have to provide specific justification only if the employee were first to show that the weight given to length of service was wholly disproportionate.

30. Ireland and the French Government took a more radical approach, suggesting that it followed from *Danfoss* that length of service should always be considered as a legitimate criterion for the determination of pay.

31. Mrs Cadman...submit[s] on the contrary that *Danfoss* should be interpreted to mean that "in a job in which experience enables a person to perform his duties better, length of service may be used appropriately as a reasonable proxy for the measure of the differential ability of staff to perform their duties." In [her] view, the employer is therefore always required to provide specific justification....

34. ...I see no reason why the employee should bear the burden of demonstrating that a wholly disproportionate weight is given to the length-of-service criterion instead of the employer having the burden of proving that the system is in fact proportionate.... The nature of this justification...is another matter. It is in this respect that the traditional arguments in favour of a seniority criterion may be relevant....

35. ...*Danfoss* was decided before the adoption of Directive 97/80...[when] it was open to courts to make a finding, as the Court may have done in *Danfoss*, that the use of seniority did not need to be justified by an employer. Following adoption of the Directive, a criterion having a disadvantageous impact on women could no longer be excluded from the scope of Article 4....

37. [I]f the interpretation advocated by the French Government and Ireland were adopted, this would run counter to the aim of Directive 97/80, which...is "to ensure that the measures taken by the Member States to implement the principle of equal treatment are made more effective." The principle of equal pay enshrined in Article 141 EC would thus be undermined as well....

47. [D]irective 97/80.... which is based on Article 141 EC, has harmonised and codified the...allocation of the burden of proof, so that the solution adopted by the Court in *Danfoss*, although it is understandable given the specific circumstances with which that case was concerned, cannot be

relied on in the present case.... [T]he answer to the first question raised by the Court of Appeal should be that, where the use by an employer of the criterion of length of service as a determinant of pay has a disparate impact as between relevant male and female employees, Article 141 EC, together with Article 2(2) and Article 4 of Directive 97/80, require the employer to justify recourse to that criterion....

48. ... [A] variety of possible justifications for measures which work to the disadvantage of women [have been advanced]. It will often be left to the national court to determine whether the measures adopted for the purpose of pursuing a legitimate aim are proportionate in view of the justification advanced by the employer.

49. Contrary to the contention of [France] and Ireland,... *Danfoss* cannot be read as conferring a blanket justification on all pay systems based on length of service. But, contrary to what Mrs Cadman and the EOC... argu[e], a complaint of indirect discrimination by an employee cannot trigger a requirement for the employer to justify the pay awarded to one employee as compared with others. Acceptance of that argument would entail a risk of an intolerable burden being imposed on employers.... [T]he burden of proof borne by the employer can be satisfied if the criterion adopted for its pay system is justified....

50. [T]he United Kingdom Government's representative submitted that there are... many reasons why an employer might decide to use a pay system based on seniority. An experienced worker will usually be more productive at work, since he or she will be more familiar with the employer's business and with its clients. Stability of the workforce also allows the employer to reduce training costs and avoid a costly recruitment process. There is therefore an obvious business incentive for the employer to reward length of service.

51. In its oral submission the French Government further explained why a public employer has a legitimate reason for rewarding long-serving employees. In the French public service, seniority is not linked with the type of work performed but is justified by the relationship of the civil servant to the administration. A pay system based on seniority ensures the independence and neutrality of civil servants.

52. Although the legitimacy of the criterion of seniority is not questioned..., the question does arise as to the extent to which the employer's economic interests have to accommodate the employees' interest in the equal-pay principle being respected.... [A]lthough it is legitimate for employers to remunerate length of service and/or loyalty,... there are situations where a pay system, though neutral in its conception, works to the disadvantage of women....

53. As the United Kingdom Government has acknowledged, a pay system with automatic pay increases depending solely on length of service has a negative impact on female workers, since women generally enter the

workforce later and interrupt their service more frequently for reasons associated with maternity and caring responsibilities.

54. The United Kingdom Government argues that, in *Danfoss*, the Court accorded special status to length of service, since "the employer was entitled to prove justification by resort to a generalisation rather than by specific proof." Ireland broadly supports the same view. This would mean...that, since length of service can be considered a proxy for better performance, recourse to length of service in a pay system will always be compatible with Article 141 EC.

55 & 56. [T]his assumption....does not satisfy the proportionality test set out in Article 2(2) of Directive 97/80 defining the notion of indirect discrimination...[and requiring] evidence demonstrating that the criticised criterion "is appropriate and necessary and can be justified by objective factors unrelated to sex."

57. If it were accepted that a general justification, such as the fact that length of service enables an employee to perform his or her duties better, was sufficient to justify a pay system disadvantaging women from the perspective of Article 141 EC, virtually no scope would remain for an employee to challenge a pay system on this ground.

58. Moreover, no judicial scrutiny would be possible in such circumstances....[T]he proportionality test imposed by Article 2(2) requires the employer to demonstrate that the pay system adopted, even where it is based on a legitimate aim, is conceived so as to minimise its disparate impact on women. This requires...a review of...how length of service is taken into account and how it is balanced in the pay system with other criteria (such as merit) which are less disadvantageous to women....

60. ...[F]or the purposes of Article 141 EC, together with Article 2(2) and Article 4 of Directive 97/80, it is not sufficient to demonstrate that a criterion based on length of service can, in general, pursue a legitimate aim (rewarding experience and loyalty). Such a criterion must be proportionate to that aim, account being taken of any disadvantageous impact it may have on women....

62. Advocates General Darmon and La Pergola both expressed doubts as to whether the taking into account of experience should be accepted as a general...rule. The Court has also rejected such an approach....[I]n *Nimz* [addressing a comparison between part-time and full-time employees], the Court held that: "although experience goes hand in hand with length of service, and experience enables the worker in principle to improve performance of the tasks allotted to him, the objectivity of such criterion depends on all the circumstances in a particular case, and in particular on the nature of the work performed and the experience gained from the performance of that work upon completion of a certain number of working hours."...

63. In view of the foregoing..., the standard of proof which the employer must discharge in order to show that recourse to a length-of-service criterion

does not lead to indirect discrimination can be summarised as follows. First,...it should be clear how much weight is placed, in the determination of pay, on length of service—conceived either as a way of measuring experience or as a means of rewarding loyalty—as compared with other criteria such as merit and qualifications. In addition, the employer should explain why experience will be valuable for a specific job, and why it is rewarded proportionally. In this respect, while an analysis will have to be carried out by the national court, there can be no doubt, for example, that experience will be more valuable—and therefore legitimately rewarded—in the case of posts involving responsibility and management tasks than in the case of repetitive tasks, in respect of which the length-of-service criterion can account for only a small proportion of pay. This criterion may be of particular relevance in the training phase but become less relevant once the employee has acquired sufficient command of his or her job. Finally, the way length of service is accounted for must also minimise the negative impact of the criterion on women....[A] system which excludes periods of maternity or paternity leave, although...prima facie neutral, would result in indirect discrimination against women.

64. The standard of proof required in cases involving indirect discrimination remains general in the sense that the employer will not need to justify why a specific employee is paid more than another, as long as the pay system has been consistently structured so as to take into account job specifications and the undertaking's business needs and so as to minimise the disparate impact it may have on women....

65. In Mrs Cadman's case, it will be for the national court to assess whether the HSE [Health & Safety Executive] has provided sufficient justification for the use of length of service [in determining pay]....

66. ...Where the use by an employer of the criterion of length of service as a determinant of pay has a disparate impact as between female and male employees, Article 141 EC, together with Articles 2(2), and Article 4 of Directive 97/80, require the employer to demonstrate [the business need for its use] and that the criterion is applied proportionately so as to minimise the disadvantageous impact it has on women. If the employer is unable to provide justification for the structure of the pay system, it will have to provide specific justification for the difference in pay levels as between the employee who has complained and other employees performing the same job....

[In later paragraphs of the opinion, the Advocate General agreed with Ireland and the United Kingdom that a holding that employers must justify recourse to length-of-service criteria when an employee shows that it "works to the disadvantage of women" should be given *prospective* effect only (in cases not already filed). He explained that although his "proposed interpretation of Article 141 EC...will continue to allow the use of length of service as a criterion in pay systems,...it may affect...the way length of service is taken into account and balanced with other relevant criteria." Further, and in light of *Danfoss,* "there was some uncertainty as to how to interpret Article 141 EC in relation to the use of length of service in a pay system;" a considerable percentage—in the United Kingdom, perhaps "36% of all employees are remunerated according to a pay system based on length of service;" and the parties had acted in "good faith."]

Court of Justice of the European Communities
Judgment of the Court (Grand Chamber)

October 3, 2006

Judgment

1. This reference for a preliminary ruling concerns the interpretation of Article 141 EC....

3. Article 141(1) and (2) EC provides:

> 1. Each Member State shall ensure that the principle of equal pay for male and female workers for equal work or work of equal value is applied.
> 2. For the purpose of this article, "pay" means the ordinary basic or minimum wage or salary and any other consideration...which the worker receives directly or indirectly, in respect of his employment, from his employer.
>
> Equal pay without discrimination based on sex means:
> (a) that pay for the same work at piece rates shall be calculated on the basis of the same unit of measurement;
> (b) that pay for work at time rates shall be the same for the same job.

4. Article 1 of Council Directive 75/117/EEC of 10 February 1975 on...the principle of equal pay for men and women...provides

> The principle of equal pay for men and women outlined in Article [141 EC], hereinafter called "principle of equal pay," means, for the same work or for work to which equal value is attributed, the elimination of all discrimination on grounds of sex with regard to all aspects and conditions of remuneration.
>
> In particular, where a job classification system is used for determining pay, it must be based on the same criteria for both men and women and so drawn up as to exclude any discrimination on grounds of sex.
>
> ...

6. Article 2(2) of [Council] Directive 97/80 [on the burden of proof in sex discrimination cases] states:

> For purposes of the principle of equal treatment..., indirect discrimination shall exist where an apparently neutral provision, criterion or practice disadvantages a substantially higher proportion of the members of one sex unless that provision, criterion or practice is appropriate and necessary and can be justified by objective factors unrelated to sex.

7. Under Article 4(1) of Directive 97/80, Member States 'shall take such measures as are necessary...to ensure that, when persons who consider

themselves wronged...establish...facts from which it may be presumed that there has been direct or indirect discrimination, it shall be for the respondent to prove that there has been no breach of the principle of equal treatment.'

...

9. Article 2(2) of Council Directive 76/207/EEC of 9 February 1976 on the implementation of the principle of equal treatment for men and women...as amended...provides [the following definition]:

> indirect discrimination: where an apparently neutral provision, criterion or practice would put persons of one sex at a particular disadvantage compared with persons of the other sex, unless that provision, criterion or practice is objectively justified by a legitimate aim, and the means of achieving that aim are appropriate and necessary...

10. Under Article 3(1) of Directive 76/207:

> Application of the principle of equal treatment means that there shall be no direct or indirect discrimination on the grounds of sex in the public or private sectors...in relation to:...
>
> (c) employment and working conditions, including...pay...

13. Mrs Cadman is employed by the HSE. Since she has been working for that body the pay system has been altered several times. Before 1992 the system was incremental[;]...each employee received an annual increase until he reached the top of the pay scale for his grade. In 1992, the HSE introduced a performance-related element so that the amount of the annual increment was adjusted to reflect the employee's individual performance. Under this system high performing employees could reach the top of the scale more quickly. Following the introduction in 1995 of a long term pay agreement, annual pay increases were set in accordance with the award of points called "equity shares" linked to the employee's performance. That change had the effect of decreasing the rate at which pay differentials narrowed between longer-serving and shorter-serving employees on the same grade. Finally, in 2000, the system was altered again to enable employees lower down the pay bands to be paid larger annual increases and, therefore, to progress more quickly through the pay band.

14. In June 2001, Mrs Cadman lodged an application before the employment tribunal based on the Equal Pay Act. At the date of her claim, she had been engaged as a band 2 inspector, a managerial post, for nearly five years. She took as comparators four male colleagues who were also band 2 inspectors.

15. Although they were in the same band as Mrs Cadman, those four persons were paid substantially more than her. In the financial year 2000/01 Mrs Cadman's annual salary was GBP 35,129, while the corresponding figures paid to her comparators were GBP 39,125, GBP 43,345, GBP 43,119 and GBP 44,183.

16. It is common ground that at the date of the claim lodged at the employment tribunal the four male comparators had longer service than Mrs Cadman, acquired in part in more junior posts....

[An employment tribunal held for Mrs. Cadman, finding that her contract should be modified to bring her pay in line with her four "comparators." The Employment Appeal Tribunal reversed, however, holding, inter alia, that under *Danfoss*, "where unequal pay arose because of the use of length of service as a criterion, no special justification was required." On Mrs. Cadman's appeal, the Court of Appeal indicated that the pay differentials at issue resulted from a structure for pay increases that "reflects and rewards length of service."]

21. Since women in pay band 2 and generally in the relevant part of the HSE's workforce have on average shorter service than men, the use of length of service as a determinant of pay has a disproportionate impact on women.

22. The Court of Appeal states that evidence submitted by the Equal Opportunities Commission, and accepted by all the parties to the dispute, shows that in the United Kingdom and throughout the European Union the length of service of female workers, taken as a whole, is less than that of male workers. The use of length of service as a determinant of pay plays an important part in the continuing, albeit slowly narrowing, gap between female and male workers.

23. In that regard, the Court of Appeal is uncertain whether the case-law of the Court has departed from the finding in *Danfoss* that "the employer does not have to provide special justification for recourse to the criterion of length of service." Recent cases...arguably represent second thoughts on the part of the Court of Justice....

25. In those circumstances, the Court of Appeal (England and Wales) (Civil Division) decided to stay its proceedings and to refer the following questions to the Court for a preliminary ruling:

(1) Where the use by an employer of the criterion of length of service as a determinant of pay has a disparate impact as between relevant male and female employees, does Article 141 EC require the employer to provide special justification for recourse to that criterion? If the answer depends on the circumstances, what are those circumstances?
(2) Would the answer to the preceding question be different if the employer applies the criterion of length of service on an individual basis to employees so that an assessment is made as to the extent to which greater length of service justifies a greater level of pay?
(3) Is there any relevant distinction to be drawn between the use of the criterion of length of service in the case of part-time workers and the use of that criterion in the case of full-time workers?

26. By its first and second questions,...the national court asks essentially whether, and if so in what circumstances, Article 141 EC requires an employer to provide justification for recourse to the criterion of length

of service as a determinant of pay where use of that criterion leads to disparities in pay between the men and women to be included in the comparison....

27. Article 141(1) EC lays down the principle that equal work or work of equal value must be remunerated in the same way, whether it is performed by a man or a woman....

28. As the Court held in case 43/75 Defrenne [1976] ECR 455, paragraph 12, that principle, which is a particular expression of the general principle of equality which prohibits comparable situations from being treated differently unless the difference is objectively justified, forms part of the foundations of the Community....

29. Furthermore, it must be recalled that the general rule laid down in the first paragraph of Article 1 of Directive 75/117, which is principally designed to facilitate the practical application of the principle of equal pay outlined in Article 141(1) EC, in no way alters the content or scope of that principle.... That rule provides for the elimination of all discrimination on grounds of sex with regard to all aspects and conditions of remuneration for the same work or for work to which equal value is attributed....

30. The scope of Article 141(1) EC covers not only direct but also indirect discrimination (see... *Jenkins*, paragraphs 14 and 15, and case C-285/02 Elsner-Lakeberg [2004] ECR I-5861, paragraph 12).

31. It is apparent from settled case law that Article 141 EC, like its predecessor Article 119 of the EEC Treaty..., must be interpreted as meaning that whenever there is evidence of discrimination, it is for the employer to prove that the practice at issue is justified by objective factors unrelated to any discrimination based on sex (see, to that effect, inter alia, *Danfoss*, paragraphs 22 and 23...).

32. The justification given must be based on a legitimate objective. The means chosen to achieve that objective must be appropriate and necessary for that purpose (see, to that effect, case 170/84 Bilka [1986]ECR 1607, paragraph 37)....

33. In paragraphs 24 and 25 of the judgment in *Danfoss*, the Court, after stating that it is not to be excluded that recourse to the criterion of length of service may involve less advantageous treatment of women than of men, held that the employer does not have to provide special justification for recourse to that criterion.

34. By adopting that position, the Court acknowledged that rewarding... experience acquired which enables the worker to perform his duties better constitutes a legitimate objective of pay policy.

35. As a general rule, recourse to the criterion of length of service is appropriate to attain that objective. Length of service goes hand in hand with experience, and experience generally enables the worker to perform his duties better.

36. The employer is therefore free to reward length of service without having to establish the importance it has in the performance of specific tasks entrusted to the employee.

37. In the same judgment, the Court did not, however, exclude the possibility that there may be situations in which recourse to the criterion of length of service must be justified by the employer in detail.

38. That is so, in particular, where the worker provides evidence capable of giving rise to serious doubts as to whether recourse to the criterion of length of service is, in the circumstances, appropriate to attain the abovementioned objective. It is in such circumstances for the employer to prove that that which is true as a general rule, namely that length of service goes hand in hand with experience and that experience enables the worker to perform his duties better, is also true as regards the job in question.

39. It should be added that where a job classification system based on an evaluation of the work to be carried out is used in determining pay, it is not necessary for the justification for recourse to a certain criterion to relate on an individual basis to the situation of the workers concerned. Therefore, if the objective pursued by recourse to the criterion of length of service is to recognise experience acquired, there is no need to show in the context of such a system that an individual worker has acquired experience during the relevant period which has enabled him to perform his duties better. By contrast, the nature of the work to be carried out must be considered objectively....

40. It follows from all of the foregoing considerations, that the answer to the first and second questions referred must be that Article 141 EC is to be interpreted as meaning that, where recourse to the criterion of length of service as a determinant of pay leads to disparities in pay, in respect of equal work or work of equal value, between the men and women to be included in the comparison:

- since, as a general rule, recourse to the criterion of length of service is appropriate to attain the legitimate objective of rewarding experience acquired which enables the worker to perform his duties better, the employer does not have to establish specifically that recourse to that criterion is appropriate to attain that objective as regards a particular job, unless the worker provides evidence capable of raising serious doubts in that regard;
- where a job classification system based on an evaluation of the work to be carried out is used in determining pay, there is no need to show that an individual worker has acquired experience during the relevant period which has enabled him to perform his duties better....

43. Since this judgment contains only a clarification of the case law in this field, there is no need to limit its temporal effects....

Notes and Questions

1. *Holding*: What, precisely did the ECJ hold? According to a same-day press release by Cadman's attorneys:

   > Before the ECJ's ruling in this case, the principle that length of service is a valid criterion in a pay system was generally accepted. But in this case, the ECJ was persuaded that because length of service is a criterion which weighs disproportionately against women, who are more likely to have taken a career break than men, there will be some circumstances in which its use requires justification.
   >
   > The case is likely to have a significant impact on closing pay disparities within the civil service and throughout the public and private sectors, wherever long service-based pay schemes exist. (Russell, Jones & Walker, Solicitors, Changing the law on equal pay—test cases, October 3, 2006, *Cadman v. Health & Safety Executive*, available at http://www.rjw.co.uk/library/case-studies/changing-the-law-on-equal-pay-test-cases (visited September 21, 2007))

   But cf. Gender Equality: No Justification Needed for Length of Service Criteria, Eur. Rep. (61610), Oct. 5, 2006 (describing *Cadman* as rejecting the Advocate General's position while accepting the U.K. position that length-of-service criteria "only require justification where the employee can prove that it is totally disproportionate"). Cadman's application is now being litigated in several pending challenges to seniority-based pay systems in Britain. *See* Mindy Kay Bricker, *EU Pay Case Opens Legal Door on Wage Gap*, Women's E-News (Jan. 15, 2007) (quoting counsel for Cadman saying that a door previously closed by *Danfoss* "is at least ajar or opened partly."). How does *Cadman*'s holding on the burden of proof compare with Directive 97/80, on which the Advocate-General relied?

2. *Precedent*: Predecessors to *Cadman* include Case 96/80, *Jenkins v. Kingsgate*, [1981] E.C.R. 911, where the ECJ opened the possibility that paying lower hourly rates for part-time work than for full-time work (when a larger percentage of women worked part-time) could violate Article 119 of the EC Treaty, and Case 170/84, *Bilka-Kaufhaus v. Von hartz*, [1986] E.C.R. 1607, extending *Jenkins* to supplemental pension schemes available only to those with specified years of full-time employment. Does the course of decisions suggest the implicit workings of principles of precedent? Of changing legal and social commitments to gender equality as a substantive matter? Could one tell which of these explanations was more persuasive?

3. *Proportionality*: Note that under the Advocate-General's approach, even if there were a legitimate reason for relying on length of service in setting pay that results in a disparate impact, a further inquiry as to the *proportionality* of that interest as against the harm to women's equality must be considered. Does U.S. law have any similar doctrine? What are the benefits, and drawbacks, of considering *proportionality* as an element of analyzing the constitutionality of facially neutral criteria?

4. *Supranational treaty or constitution?* Space does not permit full exploration of the important (and contentious) questions whether, or in what sense, EU treaties are "constitutional." Arguably, they are entrenched, since the people of any one Member State cannot modify or amend EU law on their own and treaty modifications generally require unanimous consent. Further, under the ECJ's established case law, it has interpretive authority over the meaning of EU law—which has direct effect and is supreme over the domestic law of Member States. (How

might the "supranational" character of the ECJ—for example, having one judge nominated from each of the twenty-seven different Member States of the EU—influence its judgments? Explain differences between the Advocate-General's opinion and the Court's?)

5. *"Directives" and the treaty?* Efforts to characterize ECJ case law as "constitutional" in character may be further complicated by the relationships of "directives" to treaty instruments. "Directives" are a form of EU legislation, proposed by a Commission (with some involvement by an elected Parliament) and adopted by a Council on which each Member State is represented. Many directives used to require adoption by unanimous agreement in the Council; now most directives may be adopted (or modified) through qualified majority voting in the Council. Although the ECJ has generally treated the Equal Pay Directive as an elaboration of the requirements of Treaty art. 141 itself, questions have arisen in other contexts (e.g., the old Equal Treatment Directive) whether ECJ rulings should be understood as interpretations of fundamental treaty norms or as interpretations of more particular directives.

6. *Constitutions and statutes*: Although even the foreseeable, substantial disparate impact on women of, for example, a veterans' preference law, does not violate U.S. *constitutional* equality norms, *see Personnel Administrator of Massachusetts v. Feeney*, 442 U.S. 256 (1979), *statutory* law has been interpreted since 1971 to prohibit many employment practices with a disparate impact based on race or gender, unless the employer can justify the practice with a legitimate business need. *See Griggs v. Duke Power Co.*, 401 U.S. 424 (1971). (*Griggs* may have influenced development of ECJ case law—in noteworthy references to non-European law, Advocate General opinions in *Jenkins* and *Bilka* cited *Griggs*.) Most U.S. gender equality law is statutory and can (in theory) be changed by Congress and/or state governments. In the EU, gender equality law is—arguably—quasi-constitutional insofar as it implements a Treaty provision that cannot be changed except in accordance with the procedures for Treaty amendment.

   (a) Is this difference overdrawn? Could Title VII (the most prominent U.S. antidiscrimination statute in employment law) be regarded as a form of "superstatute," embodying such deeply entrenched norms as to be almost as unlikely as the Constitution to be changed in fundamental respect? *Cf.* William N. Eskridge, Jr. & John Ferejohn, *Super-Statutes*, 50 DUKE L.J. 1215(2001). Should a court's role in interpretation vary based on such differences?

   (b) What are the relationships between statutory and constitutional rights, or, more generally, between different institutional sources of norms? In the EU, the ECJ has arguably led the way on some issues, *see, e.g.*, Annick Masselot, *The State of Gender Equality Law in the European Union*, 13 EUR. L.J. 152, 155, 164 (2007) (describing the 1990 *Dekker* case on pregnancy as direct sex discrimination), but not others. In the United States, the Equal Pay Act (1963) provided an *exception* from its ban on gender-based wage discrimination for those payments "made pursuant to (i) a seniority system; (ii) a merit system; (iii) a system which measures earnings by quantity or quality of production...." Provisions insulating seniority systems from challenge were carried forward in Title VII. *See* 42 U.S.C. §2000e-2(h). To what extent might such statutory provisions influence (or reflect underlying values that influence) constitutional interpretation in cases like *Feeney*?

7. *Constitutions and legal culture:* Even in Title VII cases, U.S. courts have been reluctant to consider comparisons between part-time and full-time workers. *See* Joan C. Williams & Elizabeth S. Westfall, *Deconstructing the Maternal Wall: Strategies for Vindicating the Civil Rights of "Carers" in the Workplace,* 13 DUKE J. GENDER L. & POL'Y 31, 37 (2006) (discussing a lone district court case holding that the Equal Pay Act and Title VII do "not categorically preclude a part-time plaintiff from establishing a prima facie pay discrimination claim by designating a full-time comparator") (internal citation omitted). Other U.S. courts, they write, do not allow part-timers to "use full-timers as comparators, regardless of their 'actual tasks, duties, and responsibilities'," thus "creat[ing] enormous loopholes in the Equal Pay Act and Title VII," potentially allowing employers "to avoid [the statutory] strictures by simply employing women in jobs with slightly reduced-hour schedules and paying them at a lower rate than their male counterparts," thereby "subverting [statutory] purpose." *Id.* at 39 (internal citation omitted). Do the statutory exclusions of seniority systems, and the reluctance of U.S. courts to compare part-time and full-time workers, suggest that even under a "disparate impact" approach, the constitutionality of such practices would be upheld as "justified"? Consider also the significance of litigation approaches in understanding substantive differences in "constitutional" gender equality law. The U.S. women's movement used constitutional test cases based on "sameness" models of equality to challenge legislative classifications based on gender, whether they disadvantaged men or women. *See, e.g., Weinberger v. Weisenfeld,* 420 U.S. 636 (1975); *Frontiero v. Richardson,* 411 U.S. 677 (1973). Did that approach reflect broader constitutional currents? Contribute to an emphasis on "formal" equality? Are there factors in Europe more conducive to a focus on substantive, rather than formal equality? Consider, for example, the widespread ratification in Europe of the International Covenant on Economic, Social and Cultural Rights (not yet ratified by the United States). Even if differences are in part understood through distinctive histories and cultural forces, does this imply anything about the normative value of the different approaches for women in Europe and the United States?

8. *Positive conceptions of the state:* Is there a link between the EU's embrace of substantive equality (i.e., an effects test) and other European constitutional commitments to "positive" or "social welfare" obligations of government—for example, in Italy's Constitution art. 3 (1948) (asserting the "duty" of the state "to remove... obstacles of an economic and social nature" that prevent the "full development" of individuals)? *See* Chapters Five and Sixteen. To what extent is the European Court's approach informed by a developing understanding that it is the affirmative mission of the EU to eliminate gender-based differences as a substantive matter? *See, e.g.,* Treaty of Amsterdam (1997), art. 2 ("The Community shall have as its task... to promote... equality between men and women"); art. 3(2): ("In all the activities referred to in this Article the Community shall aim to eliminate inequalities and to promote equality, between men and women...."); *cf. id.,* art. 141(4) (providing that the equal treatment principle shall not prevent Member State "measures providing for specific advantages in order to make it easier for the under-represented sex to pursue a vocational activity or to prevent or compensate for disadvantages in their professional careers.")

9. Professor Sullivan argues that drafting a constitution today to express commitments to women's equality

> would require choosing: (1) between a general provision favoring equality or a specific provision favoring sex equality, (2) between limiting classifications based on sex or protecting the class of women, (3) between reaching only state discrimination or reaching private discrimination as well, (4) between protecting women from discrimination or also guaranteeing affirmative rights to the material preconditions for equality, and (5) between setting forth only judicially enforceable or also broadly aspirational equality norms. (Sullivan, *supra*, at 747)

Might some of these choices arise for interpreters, as well as drafters? Consider how the European treaty-based law of gender equality compares to the U.S. constitutional law of gender equality on items (1)–(4).

11

Free Speech and the Incitement of Violence or Unlawful Behavior: Statutes Directed at Speech

Steven G. Gey

Virtually all modern legal systems that are based on a written constitution have some type of formal protection for freedom of speech and the press. Many of these constitutional provisions are phrased broadly and can easily be interpreted to protect aggressive advocacy. The key question is often not whether the relevant constitutional provisions protect incitement but rather, what level of proof does the government have to muster before punishing someone who engages in speech that could incite unlawful behavior? When attempting to ascertain a particular legal system's degree of legal protection for speech that takes the form of incitement, it is helpful to take into account three common considerations.

The first is the context in which the speech occurs. The issue of context turns on the likelihood and immediacy of the harm that the government believes will flow from the speech in question. In other words, does the government's fear of an unlikely and distant harm provide a sufficient reason to suppress speech? A subsidiary question deals with the nature of the harm that the government is allowed to protect against. Is the government allowed to suppress speech in order to protect against minor or insignificant harms, or must the government assert that the speech in question will lead to a serious harm? Also, must the nature of the harm take the form of a physical threat to other citizens or property, or may the harm be abstract or ideological? Can the government suppress speech that incites peaceful civil disobedience to protest government policies? Finally, must the harm that is being incited be political in nature? In other words, does the legal system in question permit the government to prevent speakers from inciting disfavored social or sexual practices or other forms of immoral behavior?

The second consideration has to do with the clarity and explicitness of the speech being suppressed. Can the government suppress speech that is so ambiguous or subtle that it does not clearly advocate or urge others to engage in immediate unlawful action? Governments will have a much freer hand in suppressing the speech of legitimate political opponents if the government's agents are allowed to freely interpret ambiguous speech as dangerous to the civil order, but subtle and ambiguous speech is often the most dangerous kind. Do courts have the authority to override the interpretation of ambiguous speech offered by police officers and government officials, or must the courts defer to the government with regard to the existence and meaning of implicit messages embedded in the speech?

The third and final consideration in assessing legal protection of incitement is the intent of the speaker. Is the speaker's intent a factor in the prosecution of a particular instance of speech? Can the government prosecute an example of speech based solely on what the audience might believe the speaker was advocating, without regard to whether the speaker actually intended to communicate the impermissible message? May the courts override the government's judgment about the speaker's intent?

Cases raising these issues come to the attention of the courts in many ways. Sometimes criminal prosecutions are brought under statutes that are specifically political in nature, as in the case excerpted in this chapter, *Zana v. Turkey*. Another way in which these issues are sometimes raised is in conjunction with civil actions such as immigration proceedings, as in the recent Canadian decision expelling the holocaust denier Ernst Zündel and the British decision denying entry to the Nation of Islam leader Louis Farrakhan, both of which are discussed below. These actions raise the question whether the government is truly concerned about breach of the peace or incitement, or rather is trying to suppress ideas that the government finds ideologically unpalatable. When reading the materials below, consider whether a government operating under a legal system that protects freedom of speech should ever be allowed to classify certain sets of ideas or beliefs as out-of-bounds for public discussion.

Zana v. Turkey

European Court of Human Rights
(1997) 27 Eur. H.R. Rep. 667

Procedure

1. The case was referred to the Court by the European Commission of Human Rights ("the Commission") on 28 May 1996 and by the Turkish Government ("the Government") on 29 July 1996, within the three-month period laid down by Article 32 § 1 and Article 47 of the Convention for the Protection of Human Rights and Fundamental Freedoms ("the Convention"). It originated in an application (no. 18954/91) against the Republic of Turkey lodged with the Commission under Article 25 by a Turkish national, Mr Mehdi Zana, on 30 September 1991...

As to the Facts

I. Circumstances of the Case

9. Mr Mehdi Zana, a Turkish citizen born in 1940, is a former mayor of Diyarbakır, where he currently lives.

A. The situation in the south-east of Turkey

10. Since approximately 1985, serious disturbances have raged in the south-east of Turkey between the security forces and the members of the PKK (Workers' Party of Kurdistan). This confrontation has so far, according to the Government, claimed the lives of 4,036 civilians and 3,884 members of the security forces.

11. At the time of the Court's consideration of the case, ten of the eleven provinces of south-east Turkey had since 1987 been subjected to emergency rule.

B. The applicant's statement to journalists

12. In August 1987, while serving several sentences in Diyarbakır military prison, the applicant made the following remarks in an interview with journalists:

> I support the PKK national liberation movement; on the other hand, I am not in favour of massacres. Anyone can make mistakes, and the PKK kill women and children by mistake...

That statement was published in the national daily newspaper *Cumhuriyet* on 30 August 1987....

C. The criminal proceedings

17. By means of an indictment dated 19 November 1987, the Diyarbakır military prosecutor's office instituted proceedings in the Diyarbakır Military Court against Mr Zana (among others) under Article 312 of the Criminal Code. The applicant was charged with supporting the activities of an armed organisation, the PKK, whose aim was to break up Turkey's national territory....

D. The judgment of the Diyarbakır National Security Court

25. The proceedings then continued before the Diyarbakır National Security Court [to which the case had been transferred], where the applicant was represented by his lawyers.

26. In a judgment of 26 March 1991 the Diyarbakır National Security Court sentenced the applicant to twelve months' imprisonment for having "defended an act punishable by law as a serious crime" and "endangering public safety." In accordance with the Act of 12 April 1991, he would have

to serve one-fifth of the sentence (two months and twelve days) in custody and four-fifths on parole.

27. The National Security Court held that the PKK qualified as an "armed organisation" under Article 168 of the Criminal Code, that its aim was to bring about the secession of part of Turkey's territory and that it committed acts of violence such as murder, kidnapping and armed robbery. The court also held that Mr Zana's statement to the journalists, the exact terms of which had been established during the judicial investigation, amounted to an offence under Article 312 of the Criminal Code.

II. Relevant Domestic Law

A. Substantive law

31. The relevant provisions of the Criminal Code at the material time provided:

> Article 168
>
> It shall be an offence punishable by at least fifteen years' imprisonment to form an armed gang or organisation or to assume control or special responsibility within such a gang or organisation with the intention of committing any of the offences referred to in Articles 125...
>
> It shall be an offence punishable by five to fifteen years' imprisonment to belong to such an organisation.
>
> Article 312
>
> It shall be an offence, punishable by six months' to two years' imprisonment and a "heavy" fine of 6,000 to 30,000 liras publicly to praise or defend an act punishable by law as a serious crime or to urge the people to disobey the law.
>
> It shall be an offence, punishable by one year's to three years' imprisonment and by a heavy fine of 9,000 to 36,000 liras, publicly to incite hatred or hostility between the different classes in society, thereby creating discrimination based on membership of a social class, race, religion, sect or region. Where such incitement endangers public safety, the sentence shall be increased by one-third to one-half.

III. Turkey's Declaration of 22 January 1990 under Article 46 of the Convention

33. On 22 January 1990 the Turkish Minister for Foreign Affairs deposited with the Secretary General of the Council of Europe the following declaration under Article 46 of the Convention:

> On behalf of the Government of the Republic of Turkey and acting in accordance with Article 46 of the European Convention for the Protection of Human Rights and Fundamental Freedoms, I hereby declare as follows:
>
> The Government of the Republic of Turkey acting in accordance with Article 46 of the European Convention for the Protection of Human Rights and

Fundamental Freedoms, hereby recognises as compulsory *ipso facto* and without special agreement the jurisdiction of the European Court of Human Rights in all matters concerning the interpretation and application of the Convention which relate to the exercise of jurisdiction within the meaning of Article 1 of the Convention, performed within the boundaries of the national territory of the Republic of Turkey, and provided further that such matters have previously been examined by the Commission within the power conferred upon it by Turkey....

Final Submissions to the Court

36. In their memorial the Government requested the Court

(a) to declare that it has no jurisdiction *ratione temporis* as regards the complaint under Article 10 of the Convention;

(b) to declare that domestic remedies have not been duly exhausted as regards the complaints under Article 6 of the Convention[.]...

As to the Law

I. Alleged Violation of Article 10 of the Convention

38. Mr Zana maintained that his conviction by the Diyarbakır National Security Court on account of his statement to journalists had infringed his right to freedom of expression. He relied on Article 10 of the Convention, which provides:

1. Everyone has the right to freedom of expression. This right shall include freedom to hold opinions and to receive and impart information and ideas without interference by public authority and regardless of frontiers. This Article shall not prevent States from requiring the licensing of broadcasting, television or cinema enterprises.

2. The exercise of these freedoms, since it carries with it duties and responsibilities, may be subject to such formalities, conditions, restrictions or penalties as are prescribed by law and are necessary in a democratic society, in the interests of national security, territorial integrity or public safety, for the prevention of disorder or crime, for the protection of health or morals, for the protection of the reputation or rights of others, for preventing the disclosure of information received in confidence, or for maintaining the authority and impartiality of the judiciary.

39. He also complained of an interference with his right to freedom of thought, guaranteed by Article 9 of the Convention.... [T]he Court considers that this complaint is bound up with the one made under Article 10....

B. Merits of the complaint

45. ....[T]he applicant's conviction and sentence by the Turkish courts for remarks made to journalists indisputably amounted to an "interference"

with his exercise of his freedom of expression. This point was, indeed, not contested.

46. The interference contravened Article 10 unless it was "prescribed by law", had one or more of the legitimate aims referred to in paragraph 2 of Article 10 and was "necessary in a democratic society" for achieving such an aim or aims.

1. "Prescribed by law"

47. The Court notes that the applicant's conviction and sentence were based on Articles 168 and 312 of the Turkish Criminal Code (see paragraph 31 above) and accordingly considers that the impugned interference was "prescribed by law". This point was likewise undisputed.

2. Legitimacy of the aims pursued

48. The Government maintained that the interference had pursued legitimate aims, namely the maintenance of national security and public safety, the preservation of territorial integrity and the prevention of crime. As the PKK was an illegal terrorist organisation, the application of Article 312 of the Turkish Criminal Code by the national courts in the case had had the aim of punishing any act calculated to afford support to that type of organisation.

49. In the Commission's view, such a statement from a person with some political standing—the applicant is a former mayor of Diyarbakır—could reasonably lead the national authorities to fear a stepping up of terrorist activities in the country. The authorities had therefore been entitled to consider that there was a threat to national security and public safety and that measures were necessary to preserve the country's territorial integrity and prevent crime.

50. The Court notes that in the interview he gave the journalists the applicant indicated that he supported "the PKK national liberation movement" and, as the Commission noted, the applicant's statement coincided with the murders of civilians by PKK militants.

That being so, it considers that at a time when serious disturbances were raging in south-east Turkey such a statement—coming from a political figure well known in the region—could have an impact such as to justify the national authorities' taking a measure designed to maintain national security and public safety. The interference complained of therefore pursued legitimate aims under Article 10 § 2.

3. Necessity of the interference

(a) General principles

51. The Court reiterates the fundamental principles which emerge from its judgments relating to Article 10:

(i) Freedom of expression constitutes one of the essential foundations of a democratic society and one of the basic conditions for its progress and for each individual's self-fulfilment. Subject to paragraph 2, it is applicable not only to "information" or "ideas" that are favourably received or regarded as inoffensive or as a matter of indifference, but also to those that offend, shock or disturb. Such are the demands of that pluralism, tolerance and broadmindedness without which there is no "democratic society." As set forth in Article 10, this freedom is subject to exceptions, which must, however, be construed strictly, and the need for any restrictions must be established convincingly.

(ii) The adjective "necessary," within the meaning of Article 10 § 2, implies the existence of a "pressing social need." The Contracting States have a certain margin of appreciation in assessing whether such a need exists, but it goes hand in hand with European supervision, embracing both the legislation and the decisions applying it, even those given by an independent court. The Court is therefore empowered to give the final ruling on whether a "restriction" is reconcilable with freedom of expression as protected by Article 10.

(iii) In exercising its supervisory jurisdiction, the Court must look at the impugned interference in the light of the case as a whole, including the content of the remarks held against the applicant and the context in which he made them. In particular, it must determine whether the interference in issue was "proportionate to the legitimate aims pursued" and whether the reasons adduced by the national authorities to justify it are "relevant and sufficient". In doing so, the Court has to satisfy itself that the national authorities applied standards which were in conformity with the principles embodied in Article 10 and, moreover, that they based themselves on an acceptable assessment of the relevant facts.

(b) Application of the above principles to the instant case

52. Mr Zana submitted that his conviction and sentence were wholly unjustified. An activist in the Kurdish cause since the 1960s, he had always spoken out against violence. In maintaining that he was supporting the PKK's armed struggle, the Government had, he argued, misinterpreted what he had said. In reality he had told the journalists that he supported the national liberation movement but was opposed to violence, and he had condemned the massacres of women and children. At all events, he was not a member of the PKK and had been imprisoned for belonging to the "Path of Freedom" organisation, which had always advocated non-violent action.

53. The Government, on the other hand, maintained that the applicant's conviction and sentence were perfectly justified under paragraph 2 of Article 10. They emphasised the seriousness of what the applicant had said at a time when the PKK had carried out a number of murderous attacks in south-east Turkey. In their submission, a State faced with a terrorist situation that threatened its territorial integrity had to have a wider margin of appreciation than it would have if the situation in question had consequences only for individuals.

54. The Commission accepted the Government's views for the most part and expressed the opinion that there had been no violation of Article 10.

55. The Court considers that the principles set out in paragraph 51 above also apply to measures taken by national authorities to maintain national security and public safety as part of the fight against terrorism. In this connection, it must, with due regard to the circumstances of each case and a State's margin of appreciation, ascertain whether a fair balance has been struck between the individual's fundamental right to freedom of expression and a democratic society's legitimate right to protect itself against the activities of terrorist organisations.

56. In the instant case the Court must consequently assess whether Mr Zana's conviction and sentence answered a "pressing social need" and whether they were "proportionate to the legitimate aims pursued". To that end, it considers it important to analyse the content of the applicant's remarks in the light of the situation prevailing in south-east Turkey at the time.

57. The Court takes as a basis the applicant's statement as published in the national daily newspaper *Cumhuriyet* on 30 August 1987, which the applicant did not contest in substance. The statement comprises two sentences. In the first of these the applicant expresses his support for the "PKK national liberation movement," while going on to say that he is not "in favour of massacres." In the second he says "Anyone can make mistakes, and the PKK kill women and children by mistake."

58. Those words could be interpreted in several ways but, at all events, they are both contradictory and ambiguous. They are contradictory because it would seem difficult simultaneously to support the PKK, a terrorist organisation which resorts to violence to achieve its ends, and to declare oneself opposed to massacres; they are ambiguous because whilst Mr Zana disapproves of the massacres of women and children, he at the same time describes them as "mistakes" that anybody could make.

59. The statement cannot, however, be looked at in isolation. It had a special significance in the circumstances of the case, as the applicant must have realised. As the Court noted earlier (see paragraph 50 above), the interview coincided with murderous attacks carried out by the PKK on civilians in south-east Turkey, where there was extreme tension at the material time.

60. In those circumstances the support given to the PKK—described as a "national liberation movement"—by the former mayor of Diyarbakır, the most important city in south-east Turkey, in an interview published in a major national daily newspaper, had to be regarded as likely to exacerbate an already explosive situation in that region.

61. The Court accordingly considers that the penalty imposed on the applicant could reasonably be regarded as answering a "pressing social need" and that the reasons adduced by the national authorities are "relevant and sufficient"; at all events, the applicant served only one-fifth of his sentence in prison.

62. Having regard to all these factors and to the margin of appreciation which national authorities have in such a case, the Court considers that the interference in issue was proportionate to the legitimate aims pursued. There has consequently been no breach of Article 10 of the Convention.

[The Court also held that the government had violated Mr. Zana's right to a fair trial under Article 6 of the Convention by denying him the right to attend portions of the trial and by extending his criminal proceedings over a period of several years.]

Partly Dissenting Opinion of Judge Van Dijk, joined by Judges Palm, Loizou, Mifsud Bonnici, Jambrek, Kūris, and Levits:

I do not find it possible to join the majority in concluding that there has not been a breach of Article 10 of the Convention.

In the judgment, the majority summarise the three fundamental principles which the Court has applied so far when determining whether interferences with freedom of expression were necessary in a democratic society. In my opinion, however, there are no solid grounds for concluding, as the majority do after applying those principles to the instant case, that here the interference was necessary, and in particular was proportionate to the aim of maintaining national security and public safety.

Even if one accepts—and in view of the circumstances prevailing in south-east Turkey at the relevant time I am prepared to do so—that the maintenance of national security and public safety constituted a legitimate aim for the purpose of taking measures in respect of the statement made by the applicant, his conviction and twelve-month prison sentence for making that statement cannot, in my opinion, be held to be proportionate to those aims, considering the content of the statement. If the Government were of the opinion that the statement constituted a threat to national security and public safety, they could have taken more effective and less intrusive measures to prevent or restrict such harm. The fact that the applicant had to serve only one-fifth of his sentence in prison does not suffice to convert me to a different view, since I would also find a sentence of two months' imprisonment disproportionate in the circumstances of the case.

I base my opinion mainly on the following considerations, which are largely to be found in the judgment also:

(i) Freedom of expression constitutes one of the essential foundations of a democratic society. Although relying on the situation in south-east Turkey at the moment when the applicant made his statement, the Government did not claim that the statement was not made in a democratic society and that it deserved less protection on that account.

(ii) Article 10 also applies to information or ideas that offend, shock or disturb. The mere fact that in his statement the applicant indicated support for a political organisation whose aims and means the Government reject and combat cannot, therefore, be a sufficient reason for prosecuting and sentencing him.

(iii) In assessing whether the interference was necessary, the Court must take into consideration the content of the remarks held against the applicant and the context in which he made them (see paragraph 51 of the judgment). In his statement the applicant expresses support for the PKK but at the same time dissociates himself to some extent from the violence used by the PKK. According to the applicant, he was misinterpreted by the Government and had in reality told the journalists that he was opposed to violence. He claimed that, as an activist in the Kurdish cause since the 1960s, he had always spoken out against violence and referred to having been imprisoned for belonging to the "Path of Freedom" organisation, which had always advocated non-violent action. This claim by the applicant as to the content of his statement and the personal background against which it had to be interpreted, was not dealt with by the Government or discussed by the majority in the judgment.

(iv) I have to grant the majority that the applicant's statement as recorded in *Cumhuriyet* is partly contradictory and ambiguous. However—and this is my main point of disagreement with the majority—the Court should have taken into consideration that the Turkish court which ultimately examined the charges against the applicant and convicted and sentenced him did not offer him any opportunity to explain what he had actually said and had meant to say and against what background the statement had to be interpreted. Indeed, when discussing the alleged violation of Article 6 §§ 1 and 3, the Court makes the following observation: "If the applicant had been present at the hearing, he would have had an opportunity, in particular, to say what his intention had been when he made his statement and in what circumstances the interview had taken place, to summon journalists as witnesses or to seek production of the recording." If the Court deems the fact that this opportunity was withheld from the applicant relevant to its examination under Article 6, why did it not also take that fact into consideration when looking at the content and context of the statement in order to determine the proportionality of the interference?

(v) Finally, the statement having been made by "the former mayor of Diyarbakır, the most important city in south-east Turkey," the Court should, in order to determine the possible effect the statement might have had in the "already explosive situation in that region," have expressly indicated what weight it attached to the fact that the interview was with a *former* mayor who, moreover, was in prison at the relevant time.

...Dissenting Opinion of Judge Thór Vilhjálmsson

In August 1987 the newspaper *Cumhuriyet*, which is published in Istanbul, printed the following remarks made by the applicant to journalists who visited him in prison in Diyarbakır in south-east Turkey:

> I support the PKK national liberation movement; on the other hand, I am not in favour of massacres. Anyone can make mistakes, and the PKK kill women and children by mistake...

The plain meaning of these words is that the applicant has the same opinion as the PKK on the question of the status of the territory where Kurds live in Turkey but he disapproves of the methods used by this organisation. I have to believe that this public statement is in breach of Turkish law. However, I do not see how these words, published in a newspaper in Istanbul, can be taken as a danger to national security or public safety or territorial integrity, let alone that they endorse criminal activities.

Accordingly, I am of the opinion that the restrictions and the penalty imposed did not pursue a legitimate aim and were not necessary in a democratic society. I have therefore found a violation of Article 10 of the Convention.

Notes and Questions

1. *Free speech and incitement under Article 10 of the European Convention for the Protection of Human Rights and Fundamental Freedoms.* As interpreted in *Zana*, Article 10 is relatively unprotective of radical political speech. There is little about the facts in *Zana* that would indicate any immediate threat that those reading Mr. Zana's comments in the newspaper would respond by engaging in acts of terror or other forms of illegal or revolutionary behavior. Likewise, one of the dissents points out that Mr. Zana's comments merely stated that he agreed with the general objectives of the PKK, not with their illegal activities. Indeed, he specifically said that he disagreed with the group's terroristic methods. The Turkish authorities nevertheless disregarded Mr. Zana's stated reservations, focused on his supportive statements, and interpreted the comments as potentially inciting violence. The court deferred to the Turkish authorities in interpreting Mr. Zana's statement, noting that in the volatile area where the PKK operated, those ambiguous comments "had to be regarded as likely to exacerbate an already explosive situation in that region." Finally, as one of the dissenting opinions again pointed out, the court seems to have determined that intent was irrelevant to the Article 10 issues, since intent was not mentioned by the majority with regard to the free speech claims in the case. The single most important factor in the court's Article 10 determination seems to have been the fact that Mr. Zana expressed publicly and prominently his support for a group that was incontestably engaged in a violent confrontation with the legal government of Turkey. It is unclear whether the court would have applied the same relatively lenient standards to the government in the absence of an ongoing and well-organized armed conflict within its borders.

2. *Turkish regulation of dissenting speech and the European Court of Human Rights.* The government of Turkey has appeared several times before the European Court of Human Rights in recent years to defend against Article 10 challenges to government actions allegedly infringing the rights of free speech, press, and association. As in the *Zana* case, many of these cases involve the government's interpretation of radical dissent as incitement of illegal activity. The Turkish government has not always fared as well in the European court, however, as it did in *Zana*. In *Ek v. Turkey*, (2002) 35 Eur. H.R. Rep. 41, for example, the European Court overturned two criminal convictions obtained under Turkish antiterrorism laws against a

Turkish human rights lawyer. One conviction was for signing a statement supporting the Kurds, and the other was for publishing a book that included an essay criticizing conditions in Turkish prisons. The European Court explained its decision overturning the convictions by reference to the "public's right to be informed of a different perspective," and distinguish *Zana* on that ground:

> The Court is naturally aware of the concern of the authorities about words or deeds which have the potential to exacerbate the security situation in the region, where since approximately 1985 serious disturbances have raged between the security forces and the members of the PKK involving a very heavy loss of life and the imposition of emergency rule in much of the region. [Citing *Zana*.] However, it would appear to the Court that the domestic authorities in the instant case failed to have sufficient regard to the public's right to be informed of a different perspective on the situation in south-east Turkey, irrespective of how unpalatable that perspective may be for them.

Id. at ¶89.

In another case, the European Court overturned three criminal convictions obtained under antiterrorism laws against a Kurdish member of the Turkish parliament *See Ibrahim Aksoy v. Turkey*, (2002) 34 Eur. H.R. Rep. 57. The convictions were for "spreading separatist propaganda," and were based on comments made in a speech, an article, and a booklet. The European Court held unanimously that the convictions violated Article 10 of the Convention. The key distinction in this case seems to have been that the writer specifically disavowed violence and illegal activity generally, even though he argued for fundamental changes in the structure of the Turkish state:

> On examination, the Court finds nothing in the impugned booklet which might be taken as a call to violence, uprising or any other form of rejection of democratic principles. There is, admittedly, the issue of self-determination for the Kurdish people. In the eyes of the Court, the fact that such a political goal is regarded as incompatible with the current principles and structures of the Turkish State does not make it contrary to the rules of democracy. It is of the essence of democracy that it should permit the proposal and discussion of diverse political projects, even those which call into question the current organisation of a State, provided that they do not seek to undermine democracy itself. In this regard, it should be noted that the author stresses on numerous occasions the need to achieve the political goal proposed while abiding by the rules of democracy, in a peaceful and equitable manner. In the sentence stating that "the Kurdish people's liberation struggle still continues," the booklet restricts itself to making a neutral observation and contains no incitement to the use of violence or departure from the rules of democracy.

Id. at ¶78. In this decision the European Court referred to *Zana* in briefly referencing "the sensitive nature of the security situation prevailing in southeastern Turkey," *id.* at ¶49, but made no effort to distinguish the holding of that case. *See also Sener v. Turkey*, (2003) 37 Eur. H.R. Rep. 34 (overturning as a violation of Article 10 an anti-terrorism conviction of a Turkish journalist who had published an article regarding Kurdish separatism); *Özgür Gündem v. Turkey*, (2001) 31 Eur. H.R. Rep. 49 (holding that the Turkish government had violated a pro-Kurdish newspaper's Article 10 rights by various forms of harassment, and noting that "[t]he Court is not persuaded that, even against the background of serious disturbances in the region, expressions which appear to support the idea of a separate Kurdish entity must be regarded as inevitably exacerbating the situation"). Note the very different level of oversight that the European Court chose to exercise in these cases as opposed to the extremely deferential approach toward government claims of terroristic incitement that is evident in *Zana*. Given the fact that the European Court seems to be applying the same general theory of the Article 10 right of free expression in each of these cases, what might explain the different outcomes?

In several other cases, freedom of expression in the electoral process itself has been the main issue in appeals brought against Turkey in the European Court. In *Refah Partisi (the Welfare Party) v. Turkey* (2003) 37 Eur. H.R. Rep. 1, for example, the Constitutional Court of Turkey disbanded the largest political party in the country and banned its leaders from holding similar offices in other political parties for five years. The justification for the Constitutional Court's action was that the party had become "a centre of activities contrary to the principle of secularism." (Under the Turkish Constitution secularism is explicitly named as a defining feature of the Turkish state.) In essence, the government charged that the party's electoral activities were inciting citizens to change the nature of the Turkish nation. The party challenged the government's action in the European Court as a violation of Article 11 of the Convention, which guarantees freedom of association. The European Court upheld the banning of the party, concluding that the ban "met a 'pressing social need' and [was] 'proportionate to the aims pursued.' It follows that Refah's dissolution may be regarded as 'necessary in a democratic society' within the meaning of Art.11." In contrast to its decision in *Refah Partisi*, the European Court had been less favorably disposed to attempts by the Turkish government to dissolve opposition political parties in previous cases. The European Court had previously rejected Turkish government efforts to ban the Communist Party, see *United Communist Party of Turkey v. Turkey*, (1998) 26 Eur. H.R. Rep. 121, and the Socialist Party, *see Socialist Party v. Turkey*, (1998) 27 Eur. H.R. Rep. 51. In both the Communist Party and Socialist Party cases, the government argued that the parties were closely connected to terroristic activities. The European Court rejected this claim, arguing that political parties were so important to democratic self-governance that only "convincing and compelling evidence" of a party's direct involvement in such activities could justify a total ban, a standard that Turkey was unable to meet in these two cases.

3. *Freedom of association, incitement, and the German Basic Law.* Turkey is not the only European country that has sought to outlaw radical political parties for inciting illegal activity or fomenting fundamental political change. The German government has also done so, in a domestic constitutional context that contains some of the weakest protections of free speech in Europe. The German Basic Law (*Grundgesetz*) contains several provisions guaranteeing freedom of speech and freedom of association. *See* Art. 5(1) CG ("Every person shall have the right freely to express and disseminate his opinions in speech, writing, and pictures and to inform himself without hindrance from generally accessible sources. Freedom of the press and freedom of reporting by means of broadcasts and films shall be guaranteed. There shall be no censorship."); Art. 9(1) CG ("All Germans shall have the right to form corporations and other associations."). In addition to these fairly commonplace provisions protecting free expression, however, the German Basic Law also contains some broad provisions allowing the government to limit individual expression when necessary to protect the common good. *See* Art. 18 CG ("Whoever abuses the freedom of expression, in particular the freedom of the press (paragraph (1) of Article 5), the freedom of teaching (paragraph (3) of Article 5), the freedom of assembly (Article 8), the freedom of association (Article 9), the privacy of correspondence, posts and telecommunications (Article 10), the rights of property (Article 14), or the right of asylum (Article 16a) in order to combat the free democratic basic order shall forfeit these basic rights."); Art. 21(2) CG ("Parties that, by reason of their aims or the behavior of their adherents, seek to undermine or abolish the free democratic basic order or to endanger the existence of the Federal Republic of Germany shall be unconstitutional."). Both provisions give the Federal Constitutional Court the authority to declare the forfeiture of rights by those who abuse them. The German court exercised the authority granted to it under these restrictive provisions during the 1950s, when it outlawed two political parties, one on the far left and the other on the far right. *See Socialist Reich Party*, 2 BVerfGE 1 (1952); *Communist Party*, 5 BVerfGE 85 (1956). Although the Federal Constitutional Court granted the government's request to ban both parties, it emphasized that something more than the mere abstract advocacy of revolution or fundamental political change was necessary to justify such an order.

   The German courts have become somewhat more tolerant of radical political activity in recent years. *See* Donald P. Kommers, The Constitutional Jurisprudence of the Federal Republic of Germany 236 (2d ed. 1997). The applicability of the Convention coupled with enforcement actions in the European Court of Human Rights may further moderate German efforts to quell activists and groups on the political fringes. In one case, for example, the European Court rejected a German effort to impose a political loyalty requirement on a member of a radical political party who was employed as a public school teacher. In *Vogt v. Germany*, (1996) 21 Eur. H.R. Rep. 205, the European court overturned the German government's decision to fire a teacher from a public school because the teacher was an active member of the German Communist Party (the *Deutsche Kommunistische Partei*, or DKP—a new party, which was not connected to the previous version of the Communist Party that was outlawed in 1956).

4. *"Indirect incitement" and recent British antiterrorism legislation.* In 2006, the British Parliament passed the Terrorism Act. This act includes provisions dealing with

the encouragement of terrorism and "indirect incitement." These provisions include

1. encouragement of Terrorism
   (1) This section applies to a statement that is likely to be understood by some or all of the members of the public to whom it is published as a direct or indirect encouragement or other inducement to them to the commission, preparation or instigation of acts of terrorism or Convention offences.
   (2) A person commits an offence if-
      (a) he publishes a statement to which this section applies or causes another to publish such a statement; and
      (b) at the time he publishes it or causes it to be published, he
         (i) intends members of the public to be directly or indirectly encouraged or otherwise induced by the statement to commit, prepare or instigate acts of terrorism or Convention offences; or
         (ii) is reckless as to whether members of the public will be directly or indirectly encouraged or otherwise induced by the statement to commit, prepare or instigate such acts or offences.
   (3) For the purposes of this section, the statements that are likely to be understood by members of the public as indirectly encouraging the commission or preparation of acts of terrorism or Convention offences include every statement which
      (a) glorifies the commission or preparation (whether in the past, in the future or generally) of such acts or offences; and
      (b) is a statement from which those members of the public could reasonably be expected to infer that what is being glorified is being glorified as conduct that should be emulated by them in existing circumstances.
   (4) For the purposes of this section the questions how a statement is likely to be understood and what members of the public could reasonably be expected to infer from it must be determined having regard both
      (a) to the contents of the statement as a whole; and
      (b) to the circumstances and manner of its publication.
   (5) It is irrelevant for the purposes of subsections (1) to (3)
      (a) whether anything mentioned in those subsections relates to the commission, preparation or instigation of one or more particular acts of terrorism or Convention offences, of acts of terrorism or Convention offences of a particular description or of acts of terrorism or Convention offences generally; and,
      (b) whether any person is in fact encouraged or induced by the statement to commit, prepare or instigate any such act or offence.

Note how broadly the new British statute defines the new crime of encouraging terrorism. Under the terms of the statute, a speaker can be convicted without ever explicitly inciting any illegal activity. According to the Act, indirect incitement is punished to the same extent as direct incitement. Indeed, under Section 3(a), merely praising someone who engages in a terrorist act is sufficient to bring a speaker within the scope of the statute. Likewise, a speaker can be convicted even though the terms of the speech were entirely general and related to no particular action or planned action. With respect to context, although the full circumstances and manner of the speech have to be taken into account in determining whether the statute has been violated, the government may prosecute a speaker without ever having to prove that any illegal activity or terrorist action ever resulted from the speech—or, for that matter, that anyone ever paid any attention to the speech. Thus, totally ineffectual speech may be treated exactly the same as speech leading directly to violent acts of terrorism. Finally, the speaker's intent is also irrelevant. Simple "recklessness" is sufficient to bring a speaker within the scope of the statute.

Does the new Terrorism Act in effect revive the previously discredited law of seditious libel, under which it was a criminal offense "to excite Her Majesty's subjects to attempt otherwise than by lawful means the alteration of any matter in Church or State by law established," or to say anything that might "raise discontent or disaffection amongst Her Majesty's subjects"? JAMES FITZJAMES STEPHEN, II A HISTORY OF THE CRIMINAL LAW OF ENGLAND 298 n.1 (1883). Enforcement of the law of seditious libel was heavily restricted in England by the end of the nineteenth century by the addition of requirements that the government prove that the speaker directly incited the audience to illegal conduct and that the speech had an immediate tendency to produce a breach of the peace. *Id.* at 299–300. These strict limits were deemed necessary because the unfettered application of the law of seditious libel effectively criminalized political dissent by providing the government with broad discretion to squelch speech simply because the speech instigated public discord that might be channeled in illegal directions. In any event, it remains to be seen whether the Terrorism Act 2006 will be used against speech containing only abstract advocacy that has no connection to any concrete events or actions. It also remains to be seen whether, if the government does use the Act against such abstract speech, this application will survive scrutiny under Article 10 of the European Convention for the Protection of Human Rights and Fundamental Freedoms. For a general discussion of the background of the Terrorism Act, its relationship to the history of British speech regulation, and the implications for free speech rights, *see* David G. Barnum, *Indirect Incitement and Freedom of Speech in Anglo-American Law*, 2006 E.H.R.L.R. 3, 258.

IDEAS AND IMMIGRATION LIMITATIONS

Legal discussions of the regulation of incitement usually occur in the criminal context, as in *Zana*. But governments also have sometimes used a noncitizen speaker's history of alleged incitement as the justification for excluding that person from the country altogether. One prominent example of this regulation of incitement involves the American leader of the Nation of Islam, Louis Farrakhan. In 1986 the British Secretary of State personally directed that Mr. Farrakhan should be excluded from the United Kingdom on the ground that his presence in the United Kingdom "was not conducive to the public good." Mr. Farrakhan requested reconsideration of this decision several years later, and a successor Secretary of State reaffirmed the exclusion order in the following letter:

> [The Secretary of State] has given close attention to the current tensions in the Middle East and to the potential impact on community relations in the United Kingdom. He has concluded that a visit to the United Kingdom by Mr Farrakhan, or the lifting of his exclusion generally, would at the present time pose an unwelcome and significant threat to community relations and in particular to relations between the Muslim and Jewish communities here and a potential threat to public order for that reason. Further, the Home Secretary remains concerned that the profile of Mr Farrakhan's visit...would create a risk of public disorder at those meetings.

Regina (Farrakhan) v. Secretary of State for the Home Department, 2002 Q.B. 1391, 1399 (CA). In the original exclusion order, the Secretary of State expressed the opinion that based on Mr. Farrakhan's public statements "he would be likely to cause racial disharmony and possibly commit the offence of inciting racial hatred" (*Id.* at 1402).

Mr. Farrakhan appealed the reaffirmation of the order excluding him from the United Kingdom. The Court of Appeal first held that a government decision refusing entry to an alien to prevent that person from expressing an opinion within the country was governed by Article 10 of the European Convention for the Protection of Human Rights and Fundamental Freedoms. The court noted that Article 10(2) recognizes that the prevention of disorder is one of the legitimate aims that can justify placing restrictions on freedom of expression. After noting that "the merits of this appeal are finely balanced," the court ruled that it had "come to the conclusion that the Secretary of State provided sufficient explanation for a decision that turned on his personal, informed, assessment of risk to demonstrate that his decision did not involve a disproportionate interference with freedom of expression" (*Id.* at 1419). In discussing its decision to reject Mr. Farrakhan's free speech claim, the court explained that the avoidance of incitement outweighed the speaker's interest in reaching his audience personally:

> The reality is that it was a particular forum which was denied to him rather than the freedom to express his views. Furthermore, no restriction was placed on his disseminating information or opinions within the United Kingdom by any means of communication other than his presence within the country. In making this observation we do not ignore the fact that freedom of expression extends to receiving as well as imparting views and information and that those within this country were not able to receive these from Mr. Farrakhan face to face. (*Id.* at 1418)

The British Secretary of State's claim that Mr. Farrakhan would incite disorder involved a fairly typical assessment of the practical consequences that an inflammatory speech or speaker will have at a particular time and place. In a recent immigration case in Canada, a judge went beyond assessing the likelihood that a speaker would incite immediate disorder, and based an exclusion order on a controversial speaker's more generalized threat to civic unity and public order.

The subject of the Canadian exclusion order was Ernst Zündel. Mr. Zündel is a German citizen who had lived in Canada from 1958 to 2000. Mr. Zündel is notorious for writing books praising Hitler and denying the existence of a Holocaust. The government's motion to exclude Mr. Zündel was based on provisions of the Canadian immigration laws that render foreign nationals inadmissible to Canada on security grounds if they are engaged in terrorism, a danger to the security of Canada, engaged in acts of violence that would or might endanger the lives or safety of persons in Canada, or belong to an organization that engages in such activity. The government's factual predicate for applying this provision was "that Mr. Zündel's status within the White Supremacist Movement (the Movement) is such that he is a leader and ideologue who inspires, influences, supports and directs adherents of the Movement to actuate his ideology" (*In the Matter of Ernst Zündel*, [2005] F.C.J. No. 314, at ¶5).

Although the court acknowledged that Mr. Zündel had never himself participated in acts of violence, it held that Zündel's long association with a wide variety of white supremacists and white supremacist groups was sufficient to justify his exclusion under Canadian immigration laws. According to the judge,

> if Mr. Zündel did not subscribe to the views expressed by all those people and organizations, then he should have clearly expressed, both publicly and privately, his total opposition to the kind of material, propaganda, violence and hatred promoted by those individuals and associations. I simply cannot accept the proposition that Mr. Zündel is a pacifist, while at the same time, he continues to maintain a close association and to support the above-mentioned extremists. (*Id.* at ¶45)

In short, the court based its decision to uphold the exclusion order on Mr. Zündel's ideological leadership of a disparate group of individuals, many of whom espoused violent ideologies:

> Mr. Zündel has associated, supported and directed members of the Movement who in one fashion or another have sought to propagate violent messages of hate and have advocated the destruction of governments and multicultural societies. Mr. Zündel's activities are not only a threat to Canada's national security but also a threat to the international community of nations. Mr. Zündel can channel the energy of members of the White Supremacist Movement from around the world, providing funding to them, bringing them together and providing them advice and direction. (*Id.* at ¶112)

After the court upheld the exclusion order, Mr. Zündel was deported to Germany, where he was later tried and convicted for violating provisions of the German criminal code prohibiting incitement of group hatred.

It is by no means certain that the courts of most countries would apply even weakened versions of domestic free speech law to immigration proceedings such as *Farrakhan* and *Zündel*. The British court in *Farrakhan* itself expressed deep reservations about the applicability of Article 10 free expression principles in exclusion cases.

> Article 10 requires the authorities of a state to permit those within its boundaries freely to express their views, even if these are deeply offensive to the majority of the community. It did not seem to us to follow that those authorities should be obliged to allow into the state a person bent on giving its citizens such offence. (*Regina (Farrakhan)*, 2002 Q.B. at 1409)

Despite its reservations, the court applied Article 10 principles in *Farrakhan* (in part because the Secretary of State conceded that Article 10 applied), and ultimately held that the protections of free expression embodied in Article 10 had not been violated.

Leaving aside the intricacies of the overlap between immigration law and constitutional or statutory protections of free speech, what do the *Farrakhan* and *Zündel* cases tell us about the nature of incitement and the extent to which free speech principles should protect inflammatory discourse? Should the government be allowed to punish incitement without any evidence that an immediate physical altercation will result from the speech? Should the government be allowed to punish as incitement abstract ideological advocacy, if that advocacy does not contain any entreaties to engage in illegal or violent conduct? In other words, to borrow from one of the U.S. Supreme Court's famous opinions on the subject, is "[t]he essential distinction...that those to whom the advocacy is addressed must be urged to do something, now or in the future, rather than merely to believe in something"? *See Yates v. United States*, 354 U.S. 298, 325 (1957). If governments are allowed to punish advocacy urging belief as well as immediate action, then perhaps the entire category of "incitement" will begin to lose its meaning, and will be subsumed into even deeper questions about whether the principles of free speech allow governments to legally identify "good" ideas and punish "bad" ones.

Notes and Questions

Comparing the American and European systems of free speech and the regulation of incitement. The American constitutional jurisprudence on political advocacy and incitement is both extensive and very protective of speakers. During the early part of the twentieth century, the Supreme Court interpreted the First Amendment protection of free speech very narrowly. Under this early interpretation, speech could be prosecuted even if it did not include direct incitements, *see Debs v. United States*, 249 U.S. 211 (1919), and juries were allowed to infer the likelihood of harm stemming from the speech with virtually no judicial oversight, *see Schenck v. United States*, 249 U.S. 47 (1919). During the late 1950s, the

Supreme Court moved away from this unprotective standard, and adopted an analysis that focused on whether the speech in question incited particular illegal actions (which remained unprotected) or merely advocated abstract ideas (which the Court deemed protected by the First Amendment). *See Yates v. United States*, 354 U.S. 298 (1957). By the late 1960s, the Court had gone even further, and adopted the standard that still governs the application of the First Amendment to political advocacy and incitement today. Under this standard, the government may only punish advocacy if that advocacy explicitly incites illegal conduct, is uttered in a context in which illegal action will immediately be instigated by the speech, and the speaker intended this illegal action to occur. *See Brandenburg v. Ohio*, 395 U.S. 444 (1969). Each of these requirements is very difficult for the government to satisfy. The Court has protected speakers against claims of incitement even when the speech in question contained overtly threatening language, *see NAACP v. Claiborne Hardware Co.*, 458 U.S. 886 (1982). The Court has also refused to find "immediate" harm even where the speech was uttered in relatively close proximity to violent activities that the speaker encouraged. *See Hess v. Indiana*, 414 U.S. 105 (1973). It is highly doubtful that anything like the British Terrorism Act 2006 could survive scrutiny under the First Amendment of the U.S. Constitution. Finally, the U.S. Supreme Court has also applied a very high level of protection to expressive association, including association through political parties and radical political groups. Essentially, the Court applies the same explicitness, immediacy, and specific intent standards that were developed in the verbal speech context to expressive associations. Thus, the Court has prohibited a state from barring the Communist Party access to the ballot. The Court held that although the Party advocated the abstract doctrine of violent overthrow of the government, it had stopped short of inciting anyone to immediately undertake acts of political violence. *Communist Party of Indiana v. Whitcomb*, 414 U.S. 441 (1974). Likewise, with regard to membership in radical organizations, the Court has held that the government may not prosecute an individual for membership in such an organization unless there is "clear proof that a defendant 'specifically intend[s] to accomplish [the aims of the organization] by resort to violence.'" *Scales v. United States*, 367 U.S. 203, 229 (1961) (quoting *Noto v. United States*, 367 U.S. 290, 299 (1961)).

12

Free Speech and the Incitement of Violence or Unlawful Behavior: Statutes Not Specifically Directed at Speech

Steven G. Gey

Issues of incitement or verbal instigation of breach of the peace are often raised in prosecutions under statutes that have nothing to do with dangerous ideas or political radicalism. These issues are often litigated under statutes relating generally to public decorum or breach of the peace, as in the Australian decision *Coleman v. Power*, which is excerpted below. Although the legal contexts in which these issues are raised differ widely from the speech-specific statutes discussed in the previous chapter, the basic principles of free speech (and the ways in which courts discuss these principles) are often strikingly similar in each context.

One of the questions raised by these cases is whether the prosecution of antisocial or offensive speech is just a cover for official suppression of the government's ideological adversaries. Many of the statutes used against disruptive speakers involve public order or public decorum mandates. Should legal regimes protecting freedom of speech recognize a legitimate governmental interest in protecting the public from gratuitously abusive or insulting language? If so, should political dissenters nevertheless receive broader protection from official attempts to regulate the style of a speaker's discourse? How would Mr. Coleman be viewed in this regard? Although his pamphlet complained of police corruption, he was not engaged in what would traditionally be considered political advocacy or political dissent. Viewed from this angle, these cases raise the question whether rules protecting free speech should treat generalized antiauthoritarianism in the same manner as more traditional political dissent.

Along the same lines, does the prosecution of antisocial speech under general statutes change the dynamic of risk tolerance that the protection of free speech imposes on governments? As noted in the previous chapter, most legal protections of free speech require governments to accept a certain political risk arising from the public expression of political dissidence. Should free speech rules require governments to accept the same risks when the speaker is not discussing politics overtly? One argument might be that political speakers are serving an important function in checking the excesses of government power, and therefore should be given more leeway than speakers who are not serving this important social function. On the other hand, speakers such as Mr. Coleman may be serving exactly the same checking function, albeit in a different way. It may be that there is no objective manner in which to decide when political speech stops and "other" speech begins. If so, then by default rogues such as Mr. Coleman will end up benefitting from the same presumption in favor of speech as political candidates and protesters.

Coleman v. Power

High Court of Australia
(2004) 220 C.L.R. 1

[Coleman was prosecuted for handing out leaflets in violation of Section 7 (1)(d) of the Vagrants Act, which makes it a criminal offense to use "any threatening, abusive, or insulting words to any person" in a public place. The following rendition of the facts is taken from Justice McHugh's opinion]:

In March 2000, the appellant, Patrick John Coleman, was handing out pamphlets in a mall in Townsville. The mall was a public place. One of the headings in the pamphlet was in capital letters and in bold type stated: "GET TO KNOW YOUR LOCAL CORRUPT TYPE COPS." Behind the appellant was a placard upon which were written the words: "Get to know your local corrupt type coppers; please take one." The second and third lines in the body of the pamphlet declared that the appellant was "going to name corrupt cops." One of the police officers named in the pamphlet was the first respondent, Brendan Jason Power. The second page of the pamphlet contained the following statement:

> Ah ha! Constable Brendan Power and his mates, this one was a beauty—sitting outside the mall police beat in protest at an unlawful arrest—with simple placards saying TOWNSVILLE COPS—A GOOD ARGUMENT FOR A BILL OF RIGHTS—AND DEAR MAYOR—BITE ME—AND TOWNSVILLE CITY COUNCIL THE ENEMY OF FREE SPEECH—the person was saying nothing just sitting there talking to an old lady then BAMMM arrested dragged inside and detained. Of course not happy with the kill, the cops—in eloquent prose having sung in unison in their statements that the person was running through the mall like a madman belting people over the head with a flag pole before the dirty hippie bastard assaulted and [sic] old lady and tried to trip her up with the flag while ... while ... he was having a conversation with her before the cops scared her off ... boys boys boys, I got witnesses so KISS MY ARSE YOU SLIMY LYING BASTARDS.

During the day, the appellant gave one of the pamphlets to Constable Carnes who told Constable Power about the contents of the pamphlet. As a result, Constable Power in the company of another constable approached the appellant and asked for a pamphlet. The appellant refused to give him one, saying, "No, you know what's in it." What happened thereafter was the subject of dispute between the police officers and the appellant as to whether he pushed Constable Power before or after his arrest.

According to Constable Power's evidence, when the appellant refused to give him a copy of the pamphlet he took out a "notice to appear" to give to the appellant, and told him to stop handing out the pamphlets or he would be arrested. The appellant then pushed him and yelled out: "This is Constable Brendan Power, a corrupt police officer." Constable Power then told the appellant he was under arrest. A bystander then asked why the appellant was being arrested and Constable Power answered: "Insulting language." The statement that Constable Power was a corrupt police officer formed the basis of [the Vagrancy Act] charge.

[The High Court of Australia reversed Mr. Coleman's conviction by a 4–3 vote. Representative opinions from both the majority (Justice Kirby) and the dissent (Chief Justice Gleeson) are excerpted below.]

[Opinion of Justice Kirby.]

The Implied Freedom of Communication

208. Unlike the basic laws of most nations, the Australian Constitution does not contain an express guarantee of freedom of expression, such as that included in the *Constitution of the United States* and now in the *Canadian Charter of Rights and Freedoms*. Nor has legislation providing such a guarantee been enacted at a federal or State level in Australia, as it has in New Zealand and more recently in the United Kingdom. In this respect, Australia's constitutional arrangements are peculiar and now virtually unique.

209. Following a series of earlier divided decisions of this Court in which an implication of the Australian Constitution protecting freedom of communication was upheld, against a standard held necessary to maintain the system of representative and responsible government prescribed by the Constitution, this Court in *Lange v Australian Broadcasting Corporation*, unanimously expressed a constitutional principle defensive of freedom of communication concerning governmental or political subjects. As a matter of authority, the rule in that unanimous decision should be upheld and applied. As a matter of constitutional principle and policy, it should not be watered down.

210. *Lange* establishes that two questions must be answered when deciding the validity of a law alleged to infringe the implied constitutional freedom of communication: (1) Does the law effectively burden freedom of communication about governmental or political matters, either in its terms, operation or effect? (2) If so, is the law reasonably appropriate and adapted (or, as I prefer to express it, proportional) so as to serve a legitimate end, the fulfillment of which is compatible with the maintenance of the system of government prescribed by the Constitution.

213. It follows that, once it is established that a law in the Australian Commonwealth purports to impose an effective burden upon freedom of

communication about governmental or political matters, such a law will be invalid unless it seeks to achieve its ends in a manner that is consistent with the system of representative government that the Constitution creates. In the case of dispute, it is ultimately this Court that decides the matter. It does so by the measure of the Constitution, not by what the Parliament or anyone else might reasonably be capable of thinking....

215. This appeal is the latest attempt to invoke the constitutional implication. The ultimate issue is therefore whether the implication applies and, if so, with what consequences for the State law that was in contest in these proceedings, namely s 7(1)(d) of the Act.

216. In some cases, that decision will result in invalidation of the provision in question. In other cases, where the offending section can be read down or severed, the validity of the law will be saved but its ambit and application will be reduced....

Interpretive Principles and the Meaning of the State Law

223. *The competing meanings of "insulting."* The interpretation of s 7(1)(d) of the Act entails consideration, principally, of the meaning of the word "insulting" in that section. What meaning should that word be given, if regard is had to textual, purposive, historical and contextual considerations? Do these ordinary modes of interpreting the contested statutory expression provide a clear meaning for "insulting"? In my opinion, they do not. Such sources afford support both for a wide or narrow construction of the word "insulting" in this context....

225. *Ambiguity and the preferable meaning*: In the light of my conclusion that the above factors are not ultimately determinative, so as to yield an incontestable meaning for the word "insulting" in the disputed provision of the Act, I turn to three norms of statutory construction (or interpretative principles) that aid in deciding the scope of s 7(1)(d) of the Act, applicable to this case. First, in the event of ambiguity, a construction of legislation should be preferred which avoids incompatibility with the Constitution. Secondly, a construction that would arguably diminish fundamental human rights (including as such rights are expressed in international law) should not normally be preferred if an alternative construction is equally available that involves no such diminution. Thirdly, courts should not impute to the legislature a purpose of limiting fundamental rights at common law. At least, they should not do so unless clear language is used. Such a purpose must be express and unambiguous.

226. Together, the principles convince me that "insulting" should not be given its widest meaning in the context of s 7(1)(d) of the Act. Specifically, the word should be read so that it does not infringe the implied constitutional freedom of political communication. Thus, words are not "insulting" within s 7(1)(d) of the Act if they appear in, or form part of, a communication

about government or political matters. It follows that the construction explained in the joint reasons should be preferred. Thus, "insulting" means words which are intended to provoke unlawful physical retaliation, or are reasonably likely to provoke unlawful physical retaliation....

237. If "insulting" were given the interpretation most clearly favoured in this appeal by [the dissenting Justices], the potential operation on political discourse of an unqualified offence of expressing insulting language in any public place would be intolerably over-wide. It would be difficult or impossible to characterise such a law as one achieving its ends in a manner that is consistent with the system of representative government envisioned by the Constitution.

238. Reading the description of civilised interchange about governmental and political matters in the reasons of [dissenting Justice Heydon], I had difficulty in recognising the Australian political system as I know it. His Honour's chronicle appears more like a description of an intellectual salon where civility always (or usually) prevails. It is not, with respect, an accurate description of the Australian governmental and political system in action.

239. One might wish for more rationality, less superficiality, diminished invective and increased logic and persuasion in political discourse. But those of that view must find another homeland. From its earliest history, Australian politics has regularly included insult and emotion, calumny and invective, in its armoury of persuasion. They are part and parcel of the struggle of ideas. Anyone in doubt should listen for an hour or two to the broadcasts that bring debates of the Federal Parliament to the living rooms of the nation. This is the way present and potential elected representatives have long campaigned in Australia for the votes of constituents and the support of their policies. It is unlikely to change. By protecting from legislative burdens governmental and political communications in Australia, the Constitution addresses the nation's representative government as it is practised. It does not protect only the whispered civilities of intellectual discourse. "Insulting" therefore requires a more limited interpretation in order for s 7(1)(d) to be read so as not to infringe the constitutional freedom defined in *Lange*.

240. *Interpretation: international law*: A restrictive reading of s 7(1)(d) is also supported by the principle of statutory construction that where words of a statute are susceptible to an interpretation that is consistent with international law, that construction should prevail over one that is not. International law provides for a freedom of expression, subject to stated exceptions. Relevantly, Art 19 of the International Covenant on Civil and Political Rights ("ICCPR") states:

> 19.2 Everyone shall have the right to freedom of expression; this right shall include freedom to seek, receive and impart information and ideas of all

kinds, regardless of frontiers, either orally, in writing or in print, in the form of art, or through any other media of his choice.

19.3 The exercise of the rights provided for in paragraph 2 of this article carries with it special duties and responsibilities. It may therefore be subject to certain restrictions, but these shall only be such as are provided by law and are necessary:

(a) For the respect of the rights or reputations of others;

(b) For the protection of national security or of public order (*ordre public*) or of public health or morals.

241. Australia is a party to the ICCPR. Moreover, it is a party to the First Optional Protocol that permits communications to be made to the United Nations Human Rights Committee where it is alleged that Australian law does not conform to the requirements of the ICCPR. This Court has accepted that these considerations inevitably bring to bear on the expression of Australian law the influence of the ICCPR and the principles there stated.

242. Expression characterised as political expression is clearly protected by Art 19 of the ICCPR. The widest possible meaning of "insulting," postulated for the operation of s 7(1)(d) of the Act, would travel far beyond the permissible exceptions to the freedom of expression set out in Art 19.3 of the ICCPR. Those exceptions are to be construed strictly and narrowly. The interpretation of "insulting" supported by the joint reasons would fall within the permitted exception contemplated by Art 19.3(b) of the ICCPR as one arguably necessary "for the protection … of public order." While the precise scope of public order is unclear at international law, it is evident that public order includes the following: "prescription for peace and good order," public "safety" and "prevention of disorder and crime." It is also clear that permissible limitations on Art 19 rights include "prohibitions on speech which may incite crime [or] violence." These considerations reinforce the conclusion to which the construction of the language of the Act would lead me.

243. *Criticism of interpretive principle*: There is, with respect, no substance in the criticism of the use of the foregoing principles of international human rights law to assist in the interpretation of contemporary Australian statutory provisions. My own use of these principles (where they are relevant) is frequent, consistent and of long standing. It preceded my service on this Court. It extends beyond the elaboration of the written law to the expression of the common law.

244. In time, the present resistance to the interpretive principle that I favour will pass. The principles of human rights and fundamental freedoms, expressed in the ICCPR, preceded their expression in that treaty. They long preceded Australia's adherence to it and to the First Optional Protocol. The words of Lord Diplock in *Garland v. British Rail Engineering Ltd* are obiter dicta. They are unnecessary to the decision in that case. I regard them as unduly narrow. In any event, they are concerned with a treaty obligation of a different and more limited kind, namely a specific

treaty adjusting the powers of states to European institutions (the European Economic Community Treaty) and a Council Directive. Even if the same approach to such a question would be taken by United Kingdom courts today (a matter that is debatable), it says nothing about the use of an international treaty stating comprehensive human rights and fundamental freedoms. These considerations derive from inherent human dignity. They do not derive, ultimately, from inter-governmental negotiations as to national rights inter se, where different and additional considerations apply. This is not to say that treaty provisions such as those expressed in the ICCPR are directly binding. They are not. They have not been enacted as part of Australian municipal law. But that does not prevent courts using the statement of human rights and fundamental freedoms set forth in the ICCPR in the way that I favour....

254. It follows that s 7(1)(d) can, and should be, construed so that it conforms to the *Lange* test as reformulated in this appeal. As so construed, "insulting" words in the context of the Act are those that go beyond words merely causing affront or hurt to personal feelings. They refer to words of an aggravated quality apt to a statute of the present type, to a requirement that the insulting words be expressed "to" the person insulted, and to a legislative setting concerned with public order. They are words intended, or reasonably likely, to provoke unlawful physical retaliation. They are words prone to arouse a physical response, or a risk thereof. They are not words uttered in the course of communication about governmental or political matters, however emotional, upsetting or affronting those words might be when used in such a context....

256. The Act, so interpreted, is confined to preventing and sanctioning public violence and provocation to such conduct. As such, it deals with extreme conduct or "fighting" words. It has always been a legitimate function of government to prevent and punish behaviour of such kind. Doing so in State law does not diminish, disproportionately, the federal system of representative and responsible government. On the contrary, it protects the social environment in which debate and civil discourse, however vigorous, emotional and insulting, can take place without threats of actual physical violence....

258. There was no prospect that the respondent police officers would be provoked to unlawful physical violence by the words used. At least the law would not impute that possibility to police officers who, like other public officials, are expected to be thick skinned and broad shouldered in the performance of their duties. Nor would others nearby be so provoked to unlawful violence or the risk thereof against the appellant by words of the kind that he uttered.

259. Some, who heard the appellant's words would dismiss them, and his conduct, as crazy and offensive. Others, in today's age, might suspect that there could be a grain of truth in them. But, all would just pass on. Arguably, if there is an element of *insult* in this case, it lies in the use of

police powers by and for the very subject of the appellant's allegations. The powers under the Act were entrusted to police officers by the Parliament of Queensland for the protection of the people of the State. They were not given to police officers to sanction, or suppress, the public expression of opinions about themselves or their colleagues or governmental and political issues of corruption of public officials.

260. History, and not only in other societies, teaches that attempts to suppress such opinions, even when wrong-headed and insulting, are usually counter-productive and often oppressive and ultimately unjustified. In Australia, we tolerate robust public expression of opinions because it is part of our freedom and inherent in the constitutional system of representative democracy. That system requires freedom of communication. It belongs as much to the obsessive, the emotional and the inarticulate as it does to the logical, the cerebral and the restrained.

261. This conclusion requires that the appellant's conviction of an offence against s 7(1)(d) of the Act be set aside.

[Opinion of Chief Justice Gleeson.]

...

2. The appellant was convicted of the offence of using insulting words to the first respondent in a public place. The primary issue in the appeal is whether he was rightly convicted. The appellant contends that the legislation creating the offence is invalid, as an unconstitutional restriction on freedom of speech.

3. The first step is to construe the statutory language creating the offence of using insulting words to a person in a public place. In that respect, both the legislative context and the statutory history are important. The *Vagrants, Gaming and Other Offences Act 1931* (Q) ("the Vagrants Act") created a number of what are sometimes called "public order offences." Legislation of this general kind is familiar in the United Kingdom, in all Australian jurisdictions, and in New Zealand. The immediate context of the expression "insulting words" is s 7 of the Vagrants Act, which provides:

> [§] 7 (1) Any person who, in any public place or so near to any public place that any person who might be therein, and whether any person is therein or not, could view or hear-
>
> (a) sings any obscene song or ballad;
> (b) writes or draws any indecent or obscene word, figure, or representation;
> (c) uses any profane, indecent, or obscene language;
> (d) uses any threatening, abusive, or insulting words to any person;
> (e) behaves in a riotous, violent, disorderly, indecent, offensive, threatening, or insulting manner;
>
> shall be liable to a penalty of $100 or to imprisonment for 6 months....

4. The words the subject of s 7(1)(d) must be used to, and not merely about, a person, and they must be used in a public place or in circumstances

where they could be heard from a public place. Section 7 protects various aspects of public order, ranging from decency to security.

5. There is no reason to doubt that "insulting" has the same meaning in par[a]s (d) and (e). Those two paragraphs deal separately with a subject that had previously been dealt with compendiously, that is to say, insulting words and behaviour. Section 7 of the Vagrants Act replaced s 6 of the *Vagrant Act 1851* (Q). That section prohibited the using of threatening, abusive or insulting words or behaviour in any public street, thoroughfare or place with intent to provoke a breach of the peace or whereby a breach of the peace may be occasioned. The omission of the element relating to a breach of the peace, in the 1931 Act, was plainly deliberate. Furthermore, the 1931 Act, in s 7(1)(e), expanded the kinds of behaviour that were prohibited. It continued to include threatening or insulting behaviour, but it also included, for example, disorderly, indecent, or offensive behaviour, which might involve no threat of a breach of the peace but which was nevertheless regarded by Parliament as contrary to good order....

9. It is open to Parliament to form the view that threatening, abusive or insulting speech and behaviour may in some circumstances constitute a serious interference with public order, even where there is no intention, and no realistic possibility, that the person threatened, abused or insulted, or some third person, might respond in such a manner that a breach of the peace will occur. A group of thugs who intimidate or humiliate someone in a public place may possess such an obvious capacity to overpower their victim, or any third person who comes to the aid of the victim, that a forceful response to their conduct is neither intended nor likely. Yet the conduct may seriously disturb public order, and affront community standards of tolerable behaviour. It requires little imagination to think of situations in which, by reason of the characteristics of those who engage in threatening, abusive or insulting behaviour, or the characteristics of those towards whom their conduct is aimed, or the circumstances in which the conduct occurs, there is no possibility of forceful retaliation. A mother who takes her children to play in a park might encounter threats, abuse or insults from some rowdy group. She may be quite unlikely to respond, physically or at all. She may be more likely simply to leave the park. There may be any number of reasons why people who are threatened, abused or insulted do not respond physically. It may be (as with police officers) that they themselves are responsible for keeping the peace. It may be that they are self-disciplined. It may be simply that they are afraid. Depending upon the circumstances, intervention by a third party may also be unlikely.

10. Violence is not always a likely, or even possible, response to conduct of the kind falling within the terms of s 7(1)(d) of the Vagrants Act. It may be an even less likely response to conduct falling within other parts of s 7. And if violence should occur, it is not necessarily unlawful. Depending upon the circumstances, a forceful response to threatening or insulting words or behaviour may be legitimate on the grounds of self-defence or provocation.

Furthermore, at common law, in an appropriate case a citizen in whose presence a breach of the peace is about to be committed has a right to use reasonable force to restrain the breach. I am unable to accept that, when it removed the element of intended or actual breach of the peace in 1931, the legislature nevertheless, by implication, confined the prohibition in s 7(1)(d) to cases where there was an intention to provoke, or a likelihood of provoking, unlawful physical retaliation. That seems to me to be inconsistent with the statutory language, the context, and the legislative history.

11. That having been said, the removal in 1931 of the requirement concerning a breach of the peace undoubtedly gave rise to a problem of confining the operation of the legislation within reasonable bounds.

12. Concepts of what is disorderly, or indecent, or offensive, vary with time and place, and may be affected by the circumstances in which the relevant conduct occurs. The same is true of insulting behaviour or speech. In the context of legislation imposing criminal sanctions for breaches of public order, which potentially impairs freedom of speech and expression, it would be wrong to attribute to Parliament an intention that any words or conduct that could wound a person's feelings should involve a criminal offence. At the same time, to return to an example given earlier, a group of thugs who, in a public place, threaten, abuse or insult a weak and vulnerable person may be unlikely to provoke any retaliation, but their conduct, nevertheless, may be of a kind that Parliament intended to prohibit.

13. There is a similar problem in applying the concept of offensive behaviour, which often arises in relation to conduct undertaken in the exercise of political expression and action. In *Ball v. McIntyre*, Kerr J considered the conduct of a student who demonstrated against the Vietnam War by hanging a placard on a statue in Canberra. He decided that the behaviour was not offensive within the meaning of the *Police Offences Ordinance* 1930-1961 (ACT) even though some people may be offended by it. He said:

> The word "offensive" in [the Ordinance] is to be found with the words "threatening, abusive and insulting," all words which, in relation to behaviour, carry with them the idea of behaviour likely to arouse significant emotional reaction.

He said that what was involved had to be behaviour that would produce, in the reasonable person, an emotional reaction (such as anger, resentment, disgust or outrage) beyond a reaction that was no more than the consequence of a difference of opinion on a political issue.

14. Section 7(1)(d) covers insulting words intended or likely to provoke a forceful response, whether lawful or unlawful; but it is not limited to that. However, the language in question must be not merely derogatory of the person to whom it is addressed; it must be of such a nature that the use of the language, in the place where it is spoken, to a person of that kind, is contrary to contemporary standards of public good order, and

goes beyond what, by those standards, is simply an exercise of freedom to express opinions on controversial issues.

15. It is impossible to state comprehensively and precisely the circumstances in which the use of defamatory language in a public place will involve such a disturbance of public order, or such an affront to contemporary standards of behaviour, as to constitute the offence of using insulting words to a person. An intention, or likelihood, of provoking violence may be one such circumstance. The deliberate inflicting of serious and public offence or humiliation may be another. Intimidation and bullying may constitute forms of disorder just as serious as the provocation of physical violence. But where there is no threat to the peace, and no victimisation, then the use of personally offensive language in the course of a public statement of opinions on political and governmental issues would not of itself contravene the statute. However, the degree of personal affront involved in the language, and the circumstances, may be significant.

16. The fact that the person to whom the words in question were used is a police officer may also be relevant, although not necessarily decisive. It may eliminate, for practical purposes, any likelihood of a breach of the peace. It may also negate a context of victimisation. As Glidewell LJ pointed out in *Director of Public Prosecutions v. Orum*, it will often happen that "words and behaviour with which police officers will be wearily familiar will have little emotional impact on them save that of boredom". But police officers are not required to be completely impervious to insult. A public accusation of corruption made about a police officer to his face, even in the context of a political protest or demonstration, is a form of conduct that a magistrate is entitled to regard as a serious contravention of public order by contemporary standards of behaviour. There was no challenge in the Court of Appeal, or, as I followed the argument, in this Court, to that aspect of the magistrate's decision.

17. Before leaving the question of the meaning of s 7 of the Vagrants Act, I should comment upon the proposition that the provisions of international treaties to which Australia is a party, and in particular the International Covenant on Civil and Political Rights ("ICCPR"), support a construction which confines s 7(1)(d) to the use of words in circumstances where there is an intention to provoke, or a likelihood of provoking, unlawful physical violence.

18. First, this is not an argument that was put by, or to, counsel during the course of the appeal. We are concerned with the interpretation of a State Act, enacted in 1931. The possibility that its meaning is affected (perhaps changed) by an international obligation undertaken by the Australian Government many years later raises questions of general importance.

19. The ICCPR was made in 1966, signed by Australia in 1972, and ratified in 1980. The First Optional Protocol came into force in Australia in 1991.... [It] is difficult to reconcile with the theory that the reason for

construing a statute in the light of Australia's international obligations... is that Parliament, prima facie, intends to give effect to Australia's obligations under international law. Of one thing we can be sure: the Queensland Parliament, in 1931, did not intend to give effect to Australia's obligations under the ICCPR....

22. [U]nless s 7 of the Vagrants Act changed its meaning in 1966, or 1972, or 1980, or 1991, it is difficult to see how the ICCPR can advance the construction argument. If, prior to 1966 (or one of the later dates), s 7(1)(d) was limited to words intended to provoke, or likely to provoke, unlawful violence, then the ICCPR adds nothing. If it was not so limited earlier, the suggestion that it came later to be so limited, without any intervention by the Queensland Parliament, raises a topic of potentially wide constitutional significance....

25. I turn to the issue that divided the Court of Appeal of Queensland, and that formed the basis of the appellant's case in this Court. The appellant contended that s 7(1)(d) of the Vagrants Act, in its application to the facts of the present case, was invalid for the reason that it was inconsistent with the freedom of political communication conferred by implication by the Commonwealth Constitution.

26. It was common ground in argument in this Court that the appellant's contention is to be considered by reference to the principles stated in *Lange v Australian Broadcasting Corporation*, [(1997) 189 C.L.R. 520, 562–63, 567], and that a law of the Queensland Parliament will infringe the relevant constitutional freedom where it effectively burdens communication about governmental or political matters, and either the object of the law is incompatible with the maintenance of the constitutional system of representative and responsible government or the law is not reasonably appropriate and adapted to achieving its object.

27. It was accepted by the Attorney-General of Queensland that s 7(1)(d) is capable of having a practical operation that, in some circumstances, may burden communication about governmental or political matters, whatever the precise ambit of the concept of governmental or political matters may be. That is true in the sense that threatening, abusive, or insulting words might be used in the course of communicating about any subject, including governmental or political matters. The same could be said about all, or most, of the other forms of conduct referred to in s 7. However, the object of the law is not the regulation of discussion of governmental or political matters; its effect on such discussion is incidental, and its practical operation in most cases will have nothing to do with such matters. The debate concentrated on the question whether the law, in its application to this case, is reasonably appropriate and adapted to achieving its object.

28. The facts of the case illustrate the vagueness of concepts such as "political debate," and words spoken "in the course of communication about governmental or political matters." The appellant was carrying on what the

magistrate described as a personal campaign against some individual police officers, including the first respondent. Let it be accepted that his conduct was, in the broadest sense, "political." It was not party political, and it had nothing to do with any laws, or government policy. Because the constitutional freedom identified in *Lange* does not extend to speech generally, but is limited to speech of a certain kind, many cases will arise, of which the present is an example, where there may be a degree of artificiality involved in characterising conduct for the purpose of deciding whether a law, in its application to such conduct, imposes an impermissible burden upon the protected kind of communication. The conduct prohibited by the relevant law in its application to the present case involved what the magistrate was entitled to regard as a serious disturbance of public order with personal acrimony and physical confrontation of a kind that could well have caused alarm and distress to people in a public place. As was noted above, almost any conduct of the kind prohibited by s 7, including indecency, obscenity, profanity, threats, abuse, insults, and offensiveness, is capable of occurring in a "political" context, especially if that term is given its most expansive application. Reconciling freedom of political expression with the reasonable requirements of public order becomes increasingly difficult when one is operating at the margins of the term "political."...

31. [T]he Court will not strike down a law restricting conduct which may incidentally burden freedom of political speech simply because it can be shown that some more limited restriction "could suffice to achieve a legitimate purpose." This is consistent with the respective roles of the legislature and the judiciary in a representative democracy.

32. Legislation creating public order offences provides a good example of the reason for this difference in functions. The object of such legislation is generally the same: the preservation of order in public places in the interests of the amenity and security of citizens, and so that they may exercise, without undue disturbance, the rights and freedoms involved in the use and enjoyment of such places. The right of one person to ventilate personal grievances may collide with the right of others to a peaceful enjoyment of public space. Earlier, I gave an example of a mother who takes her children to play in a public park. Suppose that she and her children are exposed to threats, abuse and insults. Suppose, further, that the mother is an immigrant, that the basis of such threats, abuse and insults includes, either centrally or at the margin, an objection to the Federal Government's immigration policy, and that the language used is an expression, albeit an ugly expression, of an opinion on that matter. Why should the family's right to the quiet enjoyment of a public place necessarily be regarded as subordinate to the abusers' right to free expression of what might generously be described as a political opinion? The answer necessarily involves striking a balance between competing interests, both of which may properly be described as rights or freedoms. As the Solicitor-General of Queensland pointed out in the course of argument, it is often the case that one person's

freedom ends where another person's right begins. The forms of conduct covered by s 7 all constitute an interference with the right of citizens to the use and enjoyment of public places. As the survey of legislation made earlier in these reasons shows, the balance struck by the Queensland Parliament is not unusual, and I am unable to conclude that the legislation, in its application to this case, is not suitable to the end of maintaining public order in a manner consistent with an appropriate balance of all the various rights, freedoms, and interests, which require consideration.

Notes

1. *The changing constitutional context in Commonwealth countries—the United Kingdom and the Human Rights Act of 1998.* Although most Commonwealth countries continue to exist without written constitutions, note the references in Justice Kirby's *Coleman* opinion to the fact that this is beginning to change, even in the United Kingdom itself. Although the United Kingdom has not adopted a written constitution, it has enacted the Human Rights Act 1998, which among other things makes it unlawful for a public authority to act in a way that is incompatible with a right contained in the European Convention for the Protection of Human Rights and Fundamental Freedoms (Section 6 (1)). To enforce this obligation, the Human Rights Act provides domestic judicial remedies (including damages) for violations of the Convention (Section 8 (1)). The Act also states that any "court or tribunal determining a question which has arisen in connection with a Convention right must take into account any judgment, decision, declaration or advisory opinion of the European Court of Human Rights" (Section 2 (1)(a)). There are limits to the British courts' power to enforce the Human Rights Act, however. Although the Act instructs courts to "read and give effect [to legislation] in a way which is compatible with the Convention rights," the Act does not give the British courts the authority to strike down incompatible legislation. When faced with such legislation, the higher British courts "may make a declaration of that incompatibility," which "does not affect the validity, continuing operation or enforcement of the provision" and "is not binding on the parties to the proceedings in which it is made" (Section 4 (2) & (6)).

   Note, however, that even in the absence of explicit protections of free speech in its written constitution or a statute such as the British Human Rights Act, the High Court of Australia was willing to engage in extensive judicial review of a parliamentary act, which culminated in a significant narrowing of the statute and an acquittal of someone charged under the previous, overbroad version of the law. The court was not only willing to apply general theories of free expression to assist it in interpreting the proper meaning and scope of the act, but was also willing to delve into American constitutional precedents and international agreements such as the ICCPR.

2. *One-on-one incitements and public decorum regulations: the American approach.* Two groups of American First Amendment cases are relevant to the issues addressed by the High Court of Australia in *Coleman*. The first group of American cases is actually mentioned in some of the *Coleman* opinions. These are the so-called fighting words cases. The fighting words category arose from a reference in *Chaplinsky v. New Hampshire*, 315 U.S. 568 (1942) to constitutionally unprotected classes of

speech. One of the unprotected classes of speech listed in the *Chaplinsky* opinion was so-called fighting words, defined by the Court to include words "which by their very utterance inflict injury or tend to incite an immediate breach of the peace." *Id.* at 572. In recent years, the Court has tended to narrow the category of fighting words to include only those words that tend to incite an immediate breach of the peace. The facts of the most prominent modern fighting words decision are similar to the facts of *Coleman*. *See Gooding v. Wilson*, 405 U.S. 518 (1972). In *Gooding*, the defendant was part of a group of students protesting the Vietnam War outside a military installation. When the police tried to move the students away from the entrance to the building, the defendant said to one of the policeman, "White son of a bitch, I'll kill you" and "You son of a bitch, I'll choke you to death." *Id.* at 519 n.1. The defendant was charged with violating a statute that made it a crime to use "opprobrious words or abusive language, tending to cause a breach of the peace." The Supreme Court overturned his conviction on the ground that the statue was unconstitutionally overbroad. The Court ruled that individuals engaged in face-to-face verbal confrontations could be prosecuted only if the government could prove that there was a "likelihood that the person addressed would make an immediate violent response." *Id.* at 528. This standard is similar to the one applied by the majority in *Coleman*, and is also similar to the standard applied under the First Amendment of the United States Constitution to cases involving political advocacy and incitement. Under both the American fighting words and incitement standards, the key is that the government must prove that the speech is likely to produce an immediate response of physical violence or public disorder.

The other category of American First Amendment law that applies to scenarios similar to *Coleman* is the category that deals with public decorum and free expression. The most famous case in this category is *Cohen v. California*, 403 U.S. 15 (1971), in which the U.S. Supreme Court held that the First Amendment protected an individual's right to walk around in public wearing a jacket with the inscription "fuck the draft." Like the Australian court in *Coleman*, the U.S. Supreme Court held that the constitutional protection of free speech extended to abrasive and even offensive speech. The Court held that the government had no authority to dictate the manner of speech to protect the sensibilities of the majority of the general public.

> [W]hile the particular four-letter word being litigated here is perhaps more distasteful than most others of its genre, it is nevertheless often true that one man's vulgarity is another's lyric. Indeed, we think it is largely because governmental officials cannot make principled distinctions in this area that the Constitution leaves matters of taste and style so largely to the individual. (*Id.* at 25)

13

Regulation of Hate Speech

Michel Rosenfeld

In a well-functioning democracy, the vindication of free speech rights depends primarily on the effective protection of unpopular and even offensive views. Indeed, widely shared views or even those held by a bare majority are unlikely to be suppressed, and even if they were occasionally trampled upon, it stands to reason that majoritarian politics would eventually inevitably come to their rescue. For example, in a democracy in which a majority strongly embraces a particular religious ideology, it would be unwise for those in power to seek to suppress expressions of that ideology as that would anger the political majority and prompt them to use their democratic rights to vote out those currently in power in favor of others, who would act more sympathetically to the ideology in question. On the other hand, it is easy to imagine how a political majority may be mobilized to legislate against views it deems repugnant or threatening to its established way of life. The minority religion that promotes a belief system and morality that the majority deems repugnant; the political dissidents who launch a radical attack (by means that most feel amount to mere propaganda) against the prevailing institutional order; and, the proponents of alternative lifestyles that are perceived as profoundly threatening to the traditions and way of life of the vast majority of citizens all loom as prime candidates for becoming the targets of majority-backed laws aimed at curtailing or suppressing their respectively held views. Accordingly, to the extent that these unpopular minority views are nonetheless constitutionally protected, it seems more likely that they will be consistently shielded by unelected judges than by those accountable to electoral majorities.

There is a serious and difficult question concerning whether limits on the protection of minority held views deemed repugnant or pernicious are appropriate, and if appropriate, what those limits ought to be. Can those views be as repugnant or disruptive to the polity as constructed and conceived by the overwhelming majority of its members as to warrant exclusion from free speech protection? Should the line be drawn at speech that poses a "clear and present" danger of violence or injury (e.g., falsely shouting "fire!" in a crowded theater)? Or should protection also be withheld from speech that profoundly upsets, disrupts, or disgusts an overwhelming majority of citizens?

The case of "hate speech"—that is, speech designed to convey or promote hatred on the basis of race, religion, or ethnic origin—is particularly vexing in this context as often a minority group historically subject to much vilification and discrimination becomes the target of vicious group slander that mirrors or reinforces deeply seated prejudices. Significantly, there are widely divergent jurisprudences on the protection of hate speech under constitutional free speech rights. The United States stands apart from most other Western democracies in affording protection to hate speech so long as it does not constitute an incitement to violence. These other democracies do not extend protection to hate speech that incites to racial, religious, or ethnic-based hatred. What accounts for this difference? Is the U.S. approach better or worse? Is the difference explained by ideological, historical, political, or constitutional divergences?

A comparative approach to adjudication of hate speech cases promises to afford crucial insights into these issues, and to allow for a better understanding and assessment of the American approach to the subject. The Canadian Supreme Court decision excerpted below is particularly instructive in this respect for a number of reasons. Chief among these are that Canada like the United States is a North-American common law jurisdiction with a written constitution containing a comparable free speech provision; that the Canadian Court was familiar with the free speech jurisprudence of the United States and that it discussed it extensively in its opinion; and, that the Canadian Court rejected the American approach after a thorough evaluation of its strengths and weaknesses.

Regina v. Keegstra

Supreme Court of Canada
[1990] 3 S.C.R. 697 (Can.)

Dickson, C.J.C. (Wilson, L' Heureux-Dubé, and Gonthier, JJ. concurring)

2. ...Keegstra was a high school teacher...from the early 1970s until his dismissal in 1982. In 1984, Mr. Keegstra was charged under s. 319(2) (then 281.2[2]) of the Criminal Code with unlawfully promoting hatred against an identifiable group by communicating anti-Semitic statements to his students. He was convicted by a jury in a trial before McKenzie J of the Alberta Court of Queen's Bench.

3. ...He taught his classes that...Jews [were] "treacherous," "subversive," "sadistic," "money-loving," "power hungry" and "child killers"... [and that Jews] "created the Holocaust to gain sympathy"...and expected his students to reproduce his teachings in class and on exams. If they failed to do so, their marks suffered.

[After conviction, Keegstra appealed, claiming that s. 319(2) of the Criminal Code unjustifiably infringed his freedom of expression as guaranteed by s. 2(b) of the Charter.[1]]

Criminal Code:

8. 319...

(2) Every one who, by communicating statements, other than in private conversation, wilfully promotes hatred against any identifiable group is guilty of

(a) an indictable offence.

(3) No person shall be convicted of an offence under subsection (2)

(a) if he establishes that the statements communicated were true;

(b) if, in good faith, he expressed or attempted to establish by argument an opinion upon a religious subject;

(c) if the statements were relevant to any subject of public interest, the discussion of which was for the public benefit, and if on reasonable grounds he believed them to be true; or

(d) if, in good faith, he intended to point out, for the purpose of removal, matters producing or tending to produce feelings of hatred towards an identifiable group in Canada....

318(4)..."identifiable group" means any section of the public distinguished by colour, race, religion or ethnic origin.

...

V. The History of Hate Propaganda Crimes in Canada...

23. ...Following the Second World War and revelation of the Holocaust, in Canada and throughout the world a desire grew to protect human rights,

---

[1] [Editor's Note] The Canadian Charter of Rights and Freedoms, 1982 provides as follows:
Section 1 [Limitation of Rights]
The Canadian Charter of Rights and Freedoms guarantees the rights and freedoms set out in it subject only to such reasonable limits prescribed by law as can be demonstrably justified in a free and democratic society.
Section 2 [Freedom of Religion, Speech, Association]
Everyone has the following fundamental freedoms:
(a) freedom of conscience and religion;
(b) freedom of thought, belief, opinion and expression, including freedom of the press and other means of communication;
(c) freedom of peaceful assembly; and
(d) freedom of association.

and especially to guard against discrimination. Internationally, this desire led to the landmark Universal Declaration of Human Rights in 1948, and, with reference to hate propaganda, was eventually manifested in two international human rights instruments....

VI. Section 2(b) of the *Charter*—Freedom of Expression...

35. ...Communications which wilfully promote hatred against an identifiable group without doubt convey a meaning, and are intended to do so by those who make them. [Hate speech is expression protected under 2(b). It is not a form of violence.]

VII. Section I Analysis of s. 319(2)

A. General Approach to Section I...

49. Obviously, a practical application of s. 1 requires more than an incantation of the words "free and democratic society." These words require some definition, an elucidation as to the values that they invoke. To a large extent, a free and democratic society embraces the very values and principles which Canadians have sought to protect and further by entrenching specific rights and freedoms in the Constitution, although the balancing exercise in s. 1 is not restricted to values expressly set out in the Charter....

C. Objective of s. 319(2)...

(i) Harm caused by expression promoting the hatred of identifiable groups

63. Looking to the legislation challenged in this appeal, one must ask whether the amount of hate propaganda in Canada causes sufficient harm to justify legislative intervention of some type.

64. ...[T]he presence of hate propaganda in Canada is sufficiently substantial to warrant concern. Disquiet caused by the existence of such material is not simply the product of its offensiveness, however, but stems from the very real harm which it causes. Essentially, there are two sorts of injury caused by hate propaganda. First, there is harm done to members of the target group. It is indisputable that the emotional damage caused by words may be of grave psychological and social consequence....

65. In my opinion, a response of humiliation and degradation from an individual targeted by hate propaganda is to be expected. A person's sense of human dignity and belonging to the community at large is closely linked to the concern and respect accorded to the groups to which he or she belongs.... The derision, hostility and abuse encouraged by hate

propaganda therefore have a severely negative impact on the individual's sense of self-worth and acceptance....

66. A second harmful effect of hate propaganda which is of pressing and substantial concern is its influence upon society at large.... It is thus not inconceivable that the active dissemination of hate propaganda can attract individuals to its cause, and in the process create serious discord between various cultural groups in society. Moreover, the alteration of views held by the recipients of hate propaganda may occur subtly, and is not always attendant upon conscious acceptance of the communicated ideas....

(ii) International human rights instruments

69. ...I would also refer to international human rights principles...for guidance with respect to assessing the legislative objective.

70. Generally speaking, the international human rights obligations taken on by Canada reflect the values and principles of a free and democratic society, and thus those values and principles that underlie the Charter itself.... Moreover, international human rights law and Canada's commitments in that area are of particular significance in assessing the importance of Parliament's objective under s. 1....

71. No aspect of international human rights has been given attention greater than that focused upon discrimination....

72. In 1966, the United Nations adopted the *International Convention on the Elimination of All Forms of Racial Discrimination,* Can. TS 1970, No. 28 (hereinafter CERD). The Convention, in force since 1969 and including Canada among its signatory members, contains a resolution that States Parties agree to

> ...adopt all necessary measures for speedily eliminating racial discrimination in all its forms and manifestations, and to prevent and combat racist doctrines and practices in order to promote understanding between races and to build an international community free from all forms of racial segregation and racial discrimination.

Article 4 of the CERD is of special interest, providing that

> States Parties condemn all propaganda and all organizations which are based on ideas or theories of superiority of one race or group of persons of one colour or ethnic origin, or which attempt to justify or promote racial hatred and discrimination in any form, and undertake to adopt immediate and positive measures designed to eradicate all incitement to, or acts of, such discrimination and, to this end, with due regard to the principles embodied in the *Universal Declaration of Human Rights* and the rights expressly set forth in article 5 of this Convention, inter alia:
>
> a. Shall declare an offence punishable by law all dissemination of ideas based on racial superiority or hatred, incitement to racial discrimination, as well as all acts of violence or incitement to such acts against any race or group of persons of another colour or ethnic origin, and also the provision of any assistance to racist activities, including the financing thereof....

73. Further, the *International Covenant on Civil and Political Rights*, 999 UNTS 171 (1966) (hereinafter ICCPR), adopted by the United Nations in 1966 and in force in Canada since 1976... guarantees the freedom of expression [in Art. 19] while simultaneously prohibiting the advocacy of hatred:... Article 20 [states]: "1. Any propaganda for war shall be prohibited by law. 2. Any advocacy of national, racial or religious hatred that constitutes incitement to discrimination, hostility or violence shall be prohibited by law."...

(iii) Other provisions of the Charter

78. Significant indicia of the strength of the objective behind s. 319(2) are gleaned not only from the international arena, but are also expressly evident in various provisions of the Charter itself... Most importantly for the purposes of this appeal, ss. 15 and 27 represent a strong commitment to the values of equality and multiculturalism, and hence underline the great importance of Parliament's objective in prohibiting hate propaganda....

(iv) Conclusion respecting objective of s. 319(2)

85. In my opinion, it would be impossible to deny that Parliament's objective in enacting s. 319(2) is of the utmost importance. Parliament has recognized the substantial harm that can flow from hate propaganda, and in trying to prevent the pain suffered by target group members and to reduce racial, ethnic and religious tension in Canada has decided to suppress the wilful promotion of hatred against identifiable groups.

D. Proportionality...

87. ...[T]he interpretation of s. 2(b) under *Irwin Toy* gives protection to a very wide range of expression. Content is irrelevant to this interpretation, the result of a high value being placed upon freedom of expression in the abstract. This approach to s. 2(b) often operates to leave unexamined the extent to which the expression at stake in a particular case promotes freedom of expression principles. In my opinion, however, the s. 1 analysis of a limit upon s. 2(b) cannot ignore the nature of the expressive activity which the state seeks to restrict. While we must guard carefully against judging expression according to its popularity, it is equally destructive of free expression values, as well as the other values which underlie a free and democratic society, to treat all expression as equally crucial to those principles at the core of s. 2(b)....

91. From the outset, I wish to make clear that in my opinion the expression prohibited by s. 319(2) is not closely linked to the rationale underlying s. 2(b)....

92. At the core of freedom of expression lies the need to ensure that truth and the common good are attained, whether in scientific and artistic endeavors or in the process of determining the best course to take in our political

affairs. Since truth and the ideal form of political and social organization can rarely, if at all, be identified with absolute certainty, it is difficult to prohibit expression without impeding the free exchange of potentially valuable information.... Taken to its extreme, this argument would require us to permit the communication of all expression, it being impossible to know with absolute certainty which factual statements are true, or which ideas obtain the greatest good. The problem with this extreme position, however, is that the greater the degree of certainty that a statement is erroneous or mendacious, the less its value in the quest for truth. Indeed, expression can be used to the detriment of our search for truth; the state should not be the sole arbiter of truth, but neither should we overplay the view that rationality will overcome all falsehoods in the unregulated marketplace of ideas. There is very little chance that statements intended to promote hatred against an identifiable group are true, or that their vision of society will lead to a better world. To portray such statements as crucial to truth and the betterment of the political and social milieu is therefore misguided....

[Chief Justice Dickson recognizes that self-fulfillment is also an important free speech objective. However, this self-fulfillment is realized in a community and it must "therefore be tempered insofar as it advocates with inordinate vitriol an intolerance and prejudice which views as execrable the process of individual self-development and human flourishing among all members of society."]

94. Moving on to a third strain of thought said to justify the protection of free expression, one's attention is brought specifically to the political realm. The connection between freedom of expression and the political process is perhaps the linchpin of the s. 2(b) guarantee, and the nature of this connection is largely derived from the Canadian commitment to democracy. Freedom of expression is a crucial aspect of the democratic commitment, not merely because it permits the best policies to be chosen from among a wide array of proffered options, but additionally because it helps to ensure that participation in the political process is open to all persons....

95. ...I am aware that the use of strong language in political and social debate (indeed, perhaps even language intended to promote hatred) is an unavoidable part of the democratic process. Moreover, I recognize that hate propaganda is expression of a type which would generally be categorized as "political," thus putatively placing it at the very heart of the principle extolling freedom of expression as vital to the democratic process. Nonetheless, expression can work to undermine our commitment to democracy where employed to propagate ideas anathemic to democratic values. Hate propaganda works in just such a way....

96. Indeed, one may quite plausibly contend that it is through rejecting hate propaganda that the state can best encourage the protection of values central to freedom of expression, while simultaneously demonstrating dislike for the vision forwarded by hate-mongers....

(ii) Rational connection

102. ...[I]t would be difficult to deny that the suppression of hate propaganda reduces the harm such expression does to individuals who belong to identifiable groups and to relations between various cultural and religious groups in Canadian society.

103. Doubts have been raised, however, as to whether the actual effect of s. 319(2) is to undermine any rational connection between it and Parliament's objective. As stated in the reasons of MCLACHLIN J., there are three primary ways in which the effect of the impugned legislation might be seen as an irrational means of carrying out the Parliamentary purpose. First, it is argued that the provision may actually promote the cause of hate-mongers by earning them extensive media attention. In this vein, it is also suggested that persons accused of intentionally promoting hatred often see themselves as martyrs, and may actually generate sympathy from the community in the role of underdogs engaged in battle against the immense powers of the state. Second, the public may view the suppression of expression by the government with suspicion, making it possible that such expression—even if it be hate propaganda—is perceived as containing an element of truth. Finally, it is often noted...that Germany of the 1920s and 1930s possessed and used hate propaganda laws similar to those existing in Canada, and yet these laws did nothing to stop the triumph of a racist philosophy under the Nazis.

104. ...I recognize that the effect of s. 319(2) is impossible to define with exact precision—the same can be said for many laws, criminal or otherwise. In my view, however, the position that there is no strong and evident connection between the criminalization of hate propaganda and its suppression is unconvincing....

105. It is undeniable that media attention has been extensive on those occasions when s. 319(2) has been used. Yet from my perspective, s. 319(2) serves to illustrate to the public the severe reprobation with which society holds messages of hate directed towards racial and religious groups. The existence of a particular criminal law, and the process of holding a trial when that law is used, is thus itself a form of expression, and the message sent out is that hate propaganda is harmful to target group members and threatening to a harmonious society....

106. In this context, it can also be said that government suppression of hate propaganda will not make the expression attractive and hence increase acceptance of its content....

108. [I] therefore conclude that the first branch of the proportionality test has been met...

(iii) Minimal impairment of the s. 2(b) freedom...

110. The main argument of those who would strike down s. 319(2) is that it creates a real possibility of punishing expression that is not hate

propaganda. It is thus submitted that the legislation is overbroad, its terms so wide as to include expression which does not relate to Parliament's objective, and also unduly vague, in that a lack of clarity and precision in its words prevents individuals from discerning its meaning with any accuracy. In either instance, it is said that the effect of s. 319(2) is to limit the expression of merely unpopular or unconventional communications. Such communications may present no risk of causing the harm which Parliament seeks to prevent, and will perhaps be closely associated with the core values of s. 2(b). This overbreadth and vagueness could consequently allow the state to employ s. 319(2) to infringe excessively the freedom of expression or, what is more likely, could have a chilling effect whereby persons potentially within s. 319(2) would exercise self-censorship. Accordingly, those attacking the validity of s. 319(2) contend that vigorous debate on important political and social issues, so highly valued in a society that prizes a diversity of ideas, is unacceptably suppressed by the provision....

111. ...In order to...determine whether s. 319(2) minimally impairs the freedom of expression, the nature and impact of specific features of the provision must be examined in some detail....

118. ...The problem is said to lie in the failure of the offence to require proof of actual hatred resulting from a communication, the assumption being that only such proof can demonstrate a harm serious enough to justify limiting the freedom of expression under s. 1. It was largely because of this lack of need for proof of actual hatred that KERANS J.A. in the Court of Appeal held s. 319(2) to violate the Charter.

119. ...First, to predicate the limitation of free expression upon proof of actual hatred gives insufficient attention to the severe psychological trauma suffered by members of those identifiable groups targeted by hate propaganda. Second, it is clearly difficult to prove a causative link between a specific statement and hatred of an identifiable group. In fact, to require direct proof of hatred in listeners would severely debilitate the effectiveness of s. 319(2) in achieving Parliament's aim....

124. The factors mentioned above suggest that s. 319(2) does not unduly restrict the s. 2(b) guarantee....

131. ...I should comment on a final argument marshalled in support of striking down s. 319(2) because of overbreadth or vagueness. It is said that the presence of the legislation has led authorities to interfere with a diverse range of political, educational and artistic expression, demonstrating only too well the way in which overbreadth and vagueness can result in undue intrusion and the threat of persecution. In this regard, a number of incidents are cited where authorities appear to have been overzealous in their interpretation of the law, including the arrest of individuals distributing pamphlets admonishing Americans to leave the country and the temporary holdup at the border of a film entitled *Nelson Mandela* and Salman Rushdie's novel *Satanic Verses* (1988).

132. That s. 319(2) may in the past have led authorities to restrict expression offering valuable contributions to the arts, education or politics in Canada is surely worrying. I hope, however, that my comments as to the scope of the provision make it obvious that only the most intentionally extreme forms of expression will find a place within s. 319(2). In this light, one can safely say that the incidents mentioned above illustrate not over-expansive breadth and vagueness in the law, but rather actions by the state which cannot be lawfully taken pursuant to s. 319(2). The possibility of illegal police harassment clearly has minimal bearing on the proportionality of hate propaganda legislation to legitimate Parliamentary objectives, and hence the argument based on such harassment can be rejected.

c. *Alternative modes of furthering Parliament's objective*

133. ... [I]t is said that non-criminal responses can more effectively combat the harm caused by hate propaganda....

134. Given the stigma and punishment associated with a criminal conviction and the presence of other modes of government response in the fight against intolerance, it is proper to ask whether s. 319(2) can be said to impair minimally the freedom of expression. With respect to the efficacy of criminal legislation in advancing the goals of equality and multicultural tolerance in Canada, I agree that the role of s. 319(2) will be limited....

135. In assessing the proportionality of a legislative enactment to a valid governmental objective, however, s. 1 should not operate in every instance so as to force the government to rely upon only the mode of intervention least intrusive of a Charter right or freedom. It may be that a number of courses of action are available in the furtherance of a pressing and substantial objective, each imposing a varying degree of restriction upon a right or freedom. In such circumstances, the government may legitimately employ a more restrictive measure, either alone or as part of a larger programme of action, if that measure is not redundant, furthering the objective in ways that alternative responses could not, and is in all other respects proportionate to a valid s. 1 aim....

138. I thus conclude that s. 319(2) of the *Criminal Code* does not unduly impair the freedom of expression....

[With respect to the third branch of the proportionality test, Chief Justice Dickson emphasizes the enormous importance of the objective of s. 319(2): "Few concerns can be as central to the concept of a free and democratic society as the dissipation of racism, and the especially strong value which Canadian society attaches to this goal must never be forgotten in assessing the effects of an impugned legislative measure." He then concludes that in light of that objective, the effects of s. 319(2), "involving as they do the restriction of expression largely removed from the heart of free expression values, are not of such a deleterious nature as to outweigh any advantage gleaned from the limitation of s. 2(b)." The infringement of freedom of expression is therefore upheld as a reasonable limit under s. 1.]

[Justice McLachlin (Justice Sopinka concurring), dissenting, finds lack of rational connection and refers to the chilling effects of the criminal provision.]

[Appeal allowed.]

Notes and Questions

1. *Hate speech in context and American exceptionalism.* "Hate speech"—defined as speech designed to promote hatred on the basis of race, religion, ethnicity, or national origin—has been subject to regulation since the end of the Second World War. Prompted by the obvious links between racist propaganda and the Holocaust and animated by the aim of rejecting the Nazi experience and of preventing its resurgence, the trend toward excluding hate speech from constitutionally protected expression spread worldwide. This trend was reflected in international covenants as well as in the constitutional jurisprudence of numerous individual countries, such as Germany, *see* Friedrich Kübler, *How Much Freedom for Racist Speech? Transnational Aspects of a Conflict of Human Rights*, 27 Hofstra L. Rev. 335, 340–47 (1998), and in the decade immediately following the war even the United States, *see Beauharnais v. Illinois*, 343 U.S. 250 (1952) (5–4 decision upholding the constitutionality of a statute criminalizing group defamation based on race or religion). Although never repudiated by the U.S. Supreme Court, *Beauharnais* is fundamentally inconsistent with later decisions on the subject, which frame the confines of American exceptionalism regarding the constitutional status of hate speech.

   A large number of international covenants call for, or condone, the criminalization of hate speech. The 1966 *U.N. Covenant on Civil and Political Rights* provides in article 20(2) that "[a]ny advocacy of national, racial or religious hatred that constitutes incitement to discrimination, hostility or violence shall be prohibited by law" (999 U.N.T.S. 171, entered into force 1976). The European Convention on Human Rights and Fundamental Freedoms (ECHR) (1950) has also been interpreted as authorizing criminalization of hate speech. *See, e.g., Jersild v. Denmark*, 19 Eur. Ct. H.R. Rep. 1 (1995) (Danish courts' conviction of racist youths for calling immigrants "niggers" and "animals" upheld as consistent with ECHR Art. 10(2)). A particularly strong stand against hate speech, which includes a command to states to criminalize it, is promoted by the 1965 International Convention on the Elimination All Forms of Racial Discrimination (CERD). Its Article 4 cited by the Court in *Keegstra* requires that states criminalize incitements to racial hatred and that they prohibit organizations that promote and incite racial discrimination. The United States attached a reservation to its ratification of CERD on the grounds that compliance with article 4 would contravene current American free speech jurisprudence. *See* Kübler, *supra*, at 357.

   Most Western constitutional democracies follow Canada in refusing constitutional protection to hate speech. Germany has enacted both civil and criminal laws against hate speech, and has for understandable reasons focused particularly on restricting or punishing anti-Semitic expression. Under current German law, criminal liability can be imposed for incitement to hatred, or for attacks on human dignity against individuals or groups determined by nationality, race, religion, or ethnic origin. *See* Kübler, *supra*, at 344. In addition, in the most notorious and controversial offshoot of its attempt to combat hate speech, Germany has prohibited denying the Holocaust or, to use a literal translation of the German expression, to engage in the "Auschwitz lie". *See Holocaust Denial Case* (German Constitutional Court) 90 BVerfGE 241 (1994) (upholding constitutionality of criminalization of Holocaust denial). Furthermore, other Western European democracies, such as the United Kingdom, Germany, and France, also have extensive regulations including criminal laws, against hate speech. *See* Michel Rosenfeld, *Hate Speech in Constitutional Jurisprudence: A Comparative Analysis*, 24 CARDOZO L. REV. 1523, 1544–47, 1555–56 (2003). (The United Kingdom does not have a written constitution but adheres to broad, firmly entrenched constitutional norms and affords freedom of expression statutory protection. *See* The Human Rights Act 1998.)

In contrast, contemporary American free speech jurisprudence protects hate speech so long as the speech does not *incite violence*. *See Brandenburg v. Ohio*, 395 U.S. 444 (1969). The *Brandenburg* standard was applied subsequently to extend constitutional protection to a Neo-Nazi march in full SS uniform with swastikas in a Chicago suburb where many Holocaust survivors resided, *see Smith v. Collin*, 436 U.S. 953 (1978) and to a cross-burning inside the fenced yard of an African American family by young white supremacists, *see R.A.V. v. City of St. Paul*, 505 U.S. 377 (1992).

Is it preferable to have a single standard for all speech? Or are multiple standards better attuned to discourage, and convey official state reprobation against pernicious racist invective or oppressive verbal assault singling out targeted victims on the basis of their religious affiliation?

Does not the concerted incitement to racial hatred, as was seen in Nazi Germany prior to Second World War, often lead to race-based violence? *See* FRANKLIN S. HAIMAN, SPEECH AND LAW IN A FREE SOCIETY 87 (1981) (arguing that Nazi extermination of Jews might not have been possible in the absence of massive anti-Semitic propaganda designed to desensitize the German people). And, even if intense and concentrated racial or religious hatred does not eventually lead to violence, it is not likely to become so demeaning, humiliating, and oppressive as to cause victim groups profound social and psychological injuries that are comparable in severity with some of the consequences of physical violence? *See* Mari J. Matsuda, *Public Response to Racist Speech: Considering the Victim's Story*, 87 MICH. L. REV. 2320 (1989) (stressing that vicious hate propaganda causes physiological symptoms and emotional distress in victims).

2. *The constitutional treatment of hate speech: Text vs. context.* Is the contrast between *Keegstra* and U.S. cases such as *Collin* and *R.A.V.* explainable in textual terms given differences between the two countries' constitutions? Article 1 of the Canadian Constitution cited in *Keegstra* makes explicit provision for limitation of constitutional rights, including free speech rights. There is nothing comparable in the U.S. Constitution. The First Amendment provides for protection of speech in categorical terms, stating, in relevant part, that "Congress shall make no law... abridging the freedom of speech...". Compare article 5(2) of the German Basic Law (as the German Constitution is referred to) which limits freedom of expression "for the protection of youth and... the right to inviolability of personal honor." Similarly, article 10 of the European Convention of Human Rights protects the right to freedom of expression but specifies, inter alia, in 10(2) that such a right is "subject to restrictions... necessary in a democratic society... for the protection of health and morals, for the protection of the reputation or rights of others...".

   In addition to these textual differences, there are stark contextual ones between the United States and other countries due to history, culture, and ideology. Perhaps the sharpest contrast is that between how Nazi propaganda is constitutionally protected in the United States, *see Smith v. Collin, supra* and consistently subject to criminal punishment in Germany. Besides the historical fact that Germany spread Nazism and that the United States went to war against it, the fear of a recurrence and the constant need for explicit repudiation is paramount in Germany. *See* the *Lüth* case (German Constitutional Court) 7BverFGE 198 (1958) and the *Holocaust Denial* case, *supra*. In the United States, on the other hand, as evinced by the events and ultimate resolution of the controversy over the Neo-Nazi march litigated in *Collin*, the Neo-Nazis were completely isolated and marginalized and the larger public overwhelmingly unsympathetic to their cause. *See* Michel Rosenfeld, *Hate Speech in Constitutional Jurisprudence, supra*, at 1536–40. More specifically, both in terms of the targeted victims of the hate speech involving Jews in the United States versus Jews in Germany (*Cf.* the *Holocaust Denial Case* where the German Constitutional Court asserted that the Nazi "Nuremberg Laws" paving the way to the extermination of the Jews "puts Jews in the Federal Republic in a special, personal relationship vis à vis their fellow citizens; what happened then is also present in this relationship today") and in terms of possibly swaying the nonvictim targeted audience (American versus German non-Jews), Nazism looms as a rather minor preoccupation in the United States and clearly as a major one in Germany.

Do the textual differences mentioned above ultimately matter that much? Consider that although the First Amendment is expressed in categorical terms, the U.S. Supreme Court has interpreted it as allowing the imposition of some limitations on speech. Is not the American jurisprudence just like its Canadian counterpart, ultimately dependent on balancing or proportionality analysis? Does the difference boil down to the United States granting greater weight to speech—including hate speech—than Canada? Or, is it rather that the United States grants less weight to the pain and humiliation of the targeted victims of hate speech? *Cf.* Matsuda, *supra*. Or both?

The contextual differences between anti-Semitism in Germany and the United States are obviously vast. Arguably, the more relevant comparison should be between American racism and German anti-Semitism. The burning of a cross on the lawn of an African American family, as in *R.A.V.*, often done to discourage middle-class African Americans from moving into white neighborhoods, *see* Rosenfeld, *supra*, at 1540, may well amount to expression that seems as threatening to present-day African Americans as Holocaust denial seems to contemporary German Jews. *Cf. Virginia v. Black*, 538 U.S. 343 (2003) (because cross-burnings were frequently followed by beatings, lynchings, shootings, or killings of African Americans, they may in some cases constitute "incitements to violence"). Does U.S. constitutional jurisprudence fail to properly account for the contextual parallels noted above? Or is the difference between the German treatment of anti-Semitic expression and the American treatment of race-based hate speech better understood in terms of different conceptions of free speech?

3. *The dichotomy between fact and opinion, fighting words and the distinction between hate speech in form and in substance.* One of the most important line-drawing problems regarding hate speech involves sorting out crude, purely insulting race or religion based invective from views that may be abhorrent or despicable but that nonetheless should not be barred from the marketplace of ideas. Mere racist name calling may not be worth protecting, *cf. Chaplinsky v. New Hampshire*,

315 U.S. 568 (1942) (insults amounting to "fighting words" not constitutionally protected), but what about sincerely held ideological political or religious views? Should not the views of those who view a particular religion as amounting to Paganism or Satanism be fully protected? Or those of advocates of racial segregation as the means to a better society (even if only to be more vigorously and more thoroughly discredited)?

One possible way to draw the line in question is by relying on the distinction between fact and opinion. This is the approach taken in Germany. Thus, the German Constitutional Court justified its decision in the *Holocaust Denial Case* by stressing that spreading proven factual falsehoods to fuel racial or religious hatred makes no genuine contribution to discovery of the truth and has no legitimate role in opinion formation. Can the fact/opinion distinction used by the German Court serve to draw a workable line? Does Holocaust denial present a unique and completely exceptional set of circumstances? *See* the German Court's decision in the *Historical Fabrication Case,* 90 BVerfGE 1 (1994), where a book claiming that Germany was not responsible for the outbreak of the Second World War as that war was thrust upon it by its enemies was held to involve "opinion" and to be therefore within the realm of protected speech. Is the distinction tenable? What about the claim that the Holocaust did take place coupled with the assertion that the Jews brought it on themselves. Is that an "opinion" or a patently false "fact"? *See also* the *Tucholsky I Case,* 21EUGRZ (1994), where a lower German court held a bumper sticker stating "soldiers are murderers" at the time of the 1991 Gulf War to involve a statement of fact amounting to unprotected group defamation. The Constitutional Court, however, interpreted the slogan as expressing an opinion to the extent that when placed in context its message may well have been: "Don't send young Germans to war and force them to become killers."

In *Chaplinsky,* the U.S. Supreme Court held that "fighting words" addressed at individuals are not protected as they are more likely to provoke a violent reaction by the addressee than to lead to further discussion. More generally, the judicial limitations on free speech imposed in the United States, be they based on the "fighting words" rationale, the "clear and present danger" standard, or the "incitement to violence" one, seem justifiable under the same broad principle. If speech is most likely to be followed by violence or high risk of physical injury virtually barring the chance of further discussion, then such speech is not constitutionally protected. Underlying this principle is the belief, based on the views of the nineteenth century English philosopher John Stuart Mill, *see* his *On Liberty* (1859), that the best way to counter false statements of fact or pernicious opinions is through further speech. Mill was optimistic that truth would ultimately best false ideas. That view was challenged by the Canadian Supreme Court in *Keegstra, supra,* at 3 S.C.R. at 797: "The success of modern advertising, the triumph of impudent propaganda such as Hitler's have qualified sharply our belief in the rationality of man... We act irresponsibly if we ignore the way in which emotion can drive reason from the field." Are the Millian assumptions behind American free speech jurisprudence therefore no longer justified? In the case of "fighting words" or of crude racist or anti-Semitic slogans it may be clear that emotion drives away reason. But what about in other cases? Who should decide? Could any cogent lines be drawn? Is it always undesirable to rely on emotion, even if it risks overriding reason? For example, what about an advertisement relying on images of a dying medically uninsured child cancer victim to counter the reasoned arguments of fiscal conservatives against adoption of universal health insurance?

Assuming that fighting words can be reasonably well distinguished from other kinds of utterances, it may seem desirable to rely on the distinction between hate speech in form and hate speech in substance, and to deny protection to the former while affording it to the latter. Thus, a statement that all members of a particular minority are "vermin," "thieves," "rapists," and so on would not be protected, *see Beauharnais, supra*. But the statement that "based on employment statistics, members of a particular minority group are clearly less capable and less enterprising than the rest of society as they have a much greater unemployment rate," would be protected. This would be the case even if that statement were uttered by an invidious hater of the group, and even if because of massive discrimination in employment and massive denial of educational opportunities to members of that group, any reasonable person would conclude that the employment rate discrepancy is above all the result of discrimination, and that the reasons advanced in the above statement are purely speculative and very likely contrary to fact.

Is the distinction between hate speech in form and in substance, even if sufficiently clear for line-drawing purposes, ultimately desirable? Are not pseudo-scientific factually couched demeaning assertions more harmful in the long run than crude insults? Are not both the members of the vilified minority and the rest of society more likely to be influenced by what appears to be factual scientifically grounded assertions than by sweeping insults?

Beauharnais, *Keegstra*, and cases in Germany and many other countries treat group defamation similarly to individual defamation. Being falsely accused of being a thief in one's individual capacity or because of one's membership in a reviled and discriminated against group seems equally injurious to one's honor, dignity, well-being, and ability to engage in the pursuit of happiness under the same conditions as fellow citizens not within one's group. Yet, *Beauharnais* has not been followed in the United States, and the defamation standard has given way to the incitement to violence standard, *see Collin, R.A.V., supra*. Is that justified? Defamation, even involving public figures, is not protected in the United States when directed against individuals, *see New York Times Co. v. Sullivan*, 376 U.S. 254 (1964) (in case of a public figure, defamatory statement must not only be false but uttered with knowledge of its falsity or in reckless disregard of the truth). What may justify not extending this rule to groups? Is it that group defamation is never *completely* false as, for example, every group of a certain size is bound to include some thieves? Or is it that it is not likely to be taken literally? Indeed, if an individual is defamed as being a thief, his or her personal reputation is likely to suffer as a result. Most people, however, do not really believe that every single member of a group defamed as being made up of thieves is in fact a thief. Is that ultimately relevant? Is it not an equal or even greater affront to dignity to be systematically suspected of being dishonest because of one's group affiliation? May be the best justification for treating group defamation differently than individual defamation is based on the argument that group defamation is better handled through the political process and public debate than through adjudication. Should a country with a large majority that is highly prejudiced against a small minority have a different hate speech standard than a multiracial, multiethnic, multicultural country with no clear or dominant majority?

3. *Slippery slopes, pragmatism, equality, and individual regarding versus group-regarding concerns.* One argument prevalent in the United Stated against regulation of hate speech except when it incites to violence is that such regulation inevitably leads to a "slippery slope" bound to result in unwarranted suppression of legitimate speech. Foreign regulation under an incitement to hatred standard does lend some support to this argument. For example, in *Regina v. Malik* [1968] 1 All E.R. 582 (C.A. 1967) (United Kingdom), a black defendant was convicted under the British Race Relations Act of 1965 and sentenced to a year in prison for asserting, inter alia, that whites are "vicious and nasty people" and that "white savages" beat "black women." The court was unswayed by the defendant's assertion that his speech was in response to the evils that whites had perpetuated against blacks. Should there have been an exception for victims of racism who use hate speech to get back at their victimizers? Or does this British case lend support to leaving it to the marketplace of ideas to deal with hate speech that falls short of incitement to violence? Are judicial decisions based on whether the target group of hate speech is a dominant or subordinate one particularly dangerous or inappropriate?

On the other hand, the British experience also lends some support to the proposition that criminalizing hate propaganda can be both salutary and effective. Indeed, pursuant to legislation adopted in 1936, Public Order Act, 1936, 1 GEO. 6, C.6 § 5, the United Kingdom waged a successful campaign against the spread of British Fascism prior to, and during, the Second World War. *See* Nathan Courtney, *British and U.S. Hate Speech Legislation: A Comparison*, 19 BROOK. J. INT'L. L. 727, 731 (1993). Moreover, even if it had not been that successful, does not outlawing hateful Fascist propaganda and prosecuting it play an important moral role in furtherance of human dignity for all within the polity? Is not official intolerance of Fascist propaganda supported by large majorities among the citizenry likely to boost the morale of the intended victims of that propaganda? Is it not also likely to have a positive effect on those who do not share the Fascist ideology, but might otherwise eventually become influenced by it? Or, on the contrary, notwithstanding the British experience with Fascist propaganda, would banning such hate speech be more likely than not to gain many more new adherents to the Fascist cause?

Even if the slippery slope danger is substantial, is it really that much different in the area of hate speech than in other areas where limitations on free speech seem more readily accepted? Are there countervailing dangers that ought to outweigh slippery slope concerns in the area of hate speech? Arguably, the United States best avoids the slippery slope problem by drawing sharp lines, such as those set by the incitement to violence standard, and by strong adhesion to the principle of viewpoint neutrality. In contrast, Germany relies on distinctions that are more difficult to handle, such as the fact/opinion one, and does embrace some patent viewpoint biases, such as its particularly strong intolerance regarding anti-Semitic expression. *See* Friedrich Kübler, *How much Freedom for Racist Speech? supra*, at 344. For all its profound commitment to viewpoint neutrality, however, the U.S. jurisprudence has not been able to avoid excluding speech based on the particular viewpoint expressed. *See, e.g., Dennis v. United States*, 341 U.S. 494, 544–45 (1951) (Frankfurter, J., concurring) (characterizing clearly political speech of members of the U.S. Communist Party advocating—but not inciting to violence or creating any imminent danger of—the violent overthrow of the government as speech that ranks "low" "on any scale of values which we have hitherto recognized"). This confuses the *category* of speech involved, namely political speech, which has traditionally been ranked as the highest, and the *content* of the speech, which the vast majority of Americans strongly repudiate. Does this mean that biases inevitably creep into any free speech jurisprudence regardless of how or where the relevant lines are drawn? Consider in this respect that, over the years, American jurisprudence has been much more prone to exclude from protection extremist speech coming from the left whereas Western European jurisprudence has been much less tolerant of extremist speech coming from the right. *See* NORMAN DORSEN et al., COMPARATIVE CONSTITUTIONALISM: CASES AND MATERIALS 920 (2003).

The American approach to hate speech has been defended on pragmatic grounds. From a Millian standpoint, the greater the freedom of speech the more likely it becomes that the truth will ultimately prevail. So long as speech is not immediately likely to be followed by violence, further speech will edge us closer to the truth. In the case of hate speech, this presumably means that countering and condemning the hate message will ultimately lead the overwhelming majority of those exposed to the hate message to firmly repudiate it. Justice Holmes adopted a position similar to that of Mill, but for very different reasons. *See* Rosenfeld, *supra*, at 1534. Holmes was highly skeptical and pessimistic, believing establishment of the truth to be highly unlikely. Accordingly, he believed on pragmatic grounds that greater freedom of speech would less likely result in the entrenchment of falsehoods and would prompt people to adopt a healthy measure of self-doubt rather than stubbornly holding on to worthless or harmful ideas. *See Abrams v. United States*, 250 U.S. 616, 630 (1919) (Holmes, J., dissenting). In other words, Mills believed that pragmatically greater freedom of speech maximized benefits whereas Holmes was of the view that it minimized harm.

Is the Canadian approach embraced in *Keegstra* ultimately as pragmatic as its U.S. counterpart if one factors in the contrast between U.S. individualism and Canada's more group-oriented constitutional culture? As Will Kymlicka has argued, although both the United States and Canada are multiethnic and multicultural polities, the United States has embraced an individualist assimilationist ideal symbolized by the metaphor of the "melting pot" whereas Canada has placed greater value on group identity, cultural diversity, and has promoted the ideal of an "ethnic mosaic." WILL KYMLICKA, MULTICULTURAL CITIZENSHIP: A LIBERAL THEORY OF MINORITY RIGHTS 14 (1995). Consistent with Kymlicka's views, could not the U.S. and Canadian approaches be equally pragmatic, with the U.S. approach affording the best practical means to advance an individualistic culture and its Canadian counterpart the best practical means to promote coexistence and mutual respect among groups? Can individual-regarding and group-regarding concerns be cogently kept apart in the context of hate speech? Or are they in the last analysis inextricably bound together? And if that is so, does not greater emphasis on one or the other become solely dependent on cultural or ideological predispositions?

14

Regulation of Campaign Finance

Richard L. Hasen

Free and fair elections are a hallmark of the modern democratic polity. Candidates, parties, or both (depending on a particular jurisdiction's rules) compete for votes in public campaigns for office. Other individuals and groups attempt during the campaign period to influence public opinion about who deserves to be elected. Eligible voters cast ballots that are counted by elections officials, who announce the results. Once the results are finalized, incumbent officeholders peacefully transfer power to the declared winners (or remain in office if the incumbents have won election). This chapter considers the regulation of money that is used to fund these campaigns for office and the limitations, if any, that each polity's constitutional principles impose on that regulation.

Harper v. Canada (Attorney General), [2004]

Supreme Court of Canada
1 S.C.R. 827, 2004 SCC 33 (Can.)

The Canada Elections Act, 2000 S.C., ch. 9 (Can.), sets limits for spending on advertising for individuals and groups. Section 350 provides:

> 350. (1) A third party shall not incur election advertising expenses of a total amount of more than $150,000 during an election period in relation to a general election.
>
> (2) Not more than $3,000 of the total amount referred to in subsection (1) shall be incurred to promote or oppose the election of one or more candidates in a given electoral district, including by
>
> (*a*) naming them;
> (*b*) showing their likenesses;
> (*c*) identifying them by their respective political affiliations; or
> (*d*) taking a position on an issue with which they are particularly associated.

[Stephen Harper, who was then head of a conservative political group opposed to campaign finance regulation, brought suit against the government, claiming the law infringed sections (2)(b) and (d) and section (3) of the Canadian Charter of Rights and Freedoms. (Harper later became a member of the Canadian Parliament and eventually the leader of the Conservative Party and the 22nd Prime Minister of Canada.) The Canadian statute refers to independent individual and groups as "third parties," to distinguish them from candidates and political parties. In the United States, such independent individuals and groups are referred to as entities making "independent expenditures." The term "third party" in the United States refers instead to minor parties, such as the U.S. Libertarian or Green parties.

[Section 1 of the Charter expressly provides for a balancing of rights and interests in cases such as this one. ("The *Canadian Charter of Rights and Freedoms*... guarantees the rights and freedoms set out in it subject only to such reasonable limits prescribed by law as can be demonstrably justified in a free and democratic society.") Section 2 of the Charter provides that "Everyone has the following fundamental freedoms:... (b) freedom of thought, belief, opinion and expression, including freedom of the press and other media of communication; [and] (d) freedom of association." Section 3 provides that "Every citizen of Canada has the right to vote in an election of members of the House of Commons or of a legislative assembly and to be qualified for membership therein." The Court of Queen's Bench, where the initial challenge was filed, agreed that Section 350 of the Canadian Elections Act (along with other provisions) violated the Charter. The Alberta Court of Appeals affirmed. The Supreme Court of Canada, by a 6-3 vote, reversed, upholding section 350 against constitutional challenge. Although the dissenting opinion of Chief Justice McLachlin appears first in the official report of this case, we have reversed the order of the opinions here for the convenience of the reader.]

Bastarache, J.

I. Introduction

At issue in this appeal is whether the third party spending provisions of the *Canada Elections Act*, S.C. 2000, c. 9, violate ss. 2(*b*), 2(*d*) and 3 of the *Canadian Charter of Rights and Freedoms*. To resolve this issue, the Court must reconcile the right to meaningfully participate in elections under s. 3 with the right to freedom of expression under s. 2(*b*)....

V. Analysis

A. Third Party Electoral Advertising Regime

Numerous groups and organizations participate in the electoral process as third parties. They do so to achieve three purposes. First, third parties may seek to influence the outcome of an election by commenting on the merits and faults of a particular candidate or political party. In this respect, the influence of third parties is most pronounced in electoral districts with "marginal seats," in other words, in electoral districts where the incumbent does not have a significant advantage. Second, third parties may add a fresh perspective or new dimension to the discourse surrounding one or more issues associated with a candidate or political party. While third parties are true electoral participants, their role and the extent of their participation, like candidates and political parties, cannot be unlimited. Third, they may add an issue to the political debate and in some cases force candidates and political parties to address it.

Third party spending limits in Canada have a long and litigious history…Parliament enacted new third party spending limits as part of a larger third party electoral advertising regime in the 2000 *Canada Elections Act*. Part 17 of the Act, ss. 349 to 362, creates a scheme that limits the advertising expenses of individuals and groups who are not candidates or political parties. The scheme also requires such expenses to be reported to the Chief Electoral Officer….

This case represents the first opportunity for this Court to determine the constitutionality of the third party election advertising regime established by Parliament. This Court has however previously considered the constitutionality of limits on independent spending in the regulation of referendums in *Libman* [[1997] 3 S.C.R. 569].

B. Libman v. Quebec (Attorney General)

In *Libman*, the Court was asked to determine the constitutionality of the independent spending limits set out in Quebec's referenda legislation, the *Referendum Act*, R.S.Q., c. C-64.1. The impugned provisions of the *Referendum Act* circumscribed groups' or individuals' participation in a referendum campaign by requiring that they join the national committee supporting their position or by affiliating themselves with it. Only the national committees and the affiliated groups were permitted to incur "regulated expenses," which were effectively advertising expenses. Mr. Libman did not wish to endorse either position advocated by the national committee. Rather than supporting the "yes" or "no" position, Mr. Libman advocated in favour of abstaining from the vote. Mr. Libman argued that the impugned provisions infringed his rights to freedom of political expression and freedom of association because they restricted campaign expenditures conducted independently of the national committees.

The Court agreed that the limits on independent spending set out in the *Referendum Act* were not justified. The Court did, however, endorse spending limits as an essential means of promoting fairness in referenda and elections which the Court held were parallel processes….

The Court's conception of electoral fairness as reflected in the foregoing principles is consistent with the egalitarian model of elections adopted by Parliament as an essential component of our democratic society. This model is premised on the notion that individuals should have an equal opportunity to participate in the electoral process. Under this model, wealth is the main obstacle to equal participation; *see* C. Feasby, "*Libman v. Quebec (A.G.)* and the Administration of the Process of Democracy under the *Charter*: The

Emerging Egalitarian Model" (1999), 44 *McGill L.J.* 5. Thus, the egalitarian model promotes an electoral process that requires the wealthy to be prevented from controlling the electoral process to the detriment of others with less economic power. The state can equalize participation in the electoral process in two ways; *see* O. M. Fiss, The Irony of Free Speech (1996), at p. 4. First, the State can provide a voice to those who might otherwise not be heard. The Act does so by reimbursing candidates and political parties and by providing broadcast time to political parties. Second, the State can restrict the voices which dominate the political discourse so that others may be heard as well. In Canada, electoral regulation has focussed on the latter by regulating electoral spending through comprehensive election finance provisions. These provisions seek to create a level playing field for those who wish to engage in the electoral discourse. This, in turn, enables voters to be better informed; no one voice is overwhelmed by another. In contrast, the libertarian model of elections favours an electoral process subject to as few restrictions as possible.

The current third party election advertising regime is Parliament's response to this Court's decision in *Libman*. The regime is clearly structured on the egalitarian model of elections. The overarching objective of the regime is to promote electoral fairness by creating equality in the political discourse. The regime promotes the equal dissemination of points of view by limiting the election advertising of third parties who, as this Court has recognized, are important and influential participants in the electoral process. The advancement of equality and fairness in elections ultimately encourages public confidence in the electoral system. Thus, broadly speaking, the third party election advertising regime is consistent with an egalitarian conception of elections and the principles endorsed by this Court in *Libman*.

In determining the constitutionality of the third party advertising regime, the lower courts failed to follow this Court's guidance in *Libman*. First, they did not give any deference to Parliament's choice of electoral model. Second, they discarded the findings of the Lortie Commission [established by Parliament to make recommendations on campaign finance reform]....

C. Election Advertising Expense Limits

(1) Freedom of expression

The appellant rightly concedes that the limits on election advertising expenses infringe s. 2(*b*) of the *Charter*. Most third party election advertising constitutes political expression and therefore lies at the core of the guarantee of free expression. As discussed below, in some circumstances, third party election advertising may be less deserving of constitutional protection where it seeks to manipulate voters.

(2) The right to vote

The respondent also alleges that s. 350 infringes the right to vote protected by s. 3 of the *Charter* on the basis that it guarantees a right to unimpeded and unlimited electoral debate or expression. The respondent effectively equates the right to meaningful participation with the exercise of freedom of expression. Respectfully, this cannot be. The right to free expression and the right to vote are distinct rights. The more appropriate question is: how are these rights and their underlying values and purposes properly reconciled?...

This case engages the informational component of an individual's right to meaningfully participate in the electoral process. The right to meaningful participation includes a citizen's right to exercise his or her vote in an informed manner. For a voter to be well informed, the citizen must be able to weigh the relative strengths and weaknesses of each candidate and political party. The citizen must also be able to consider opposing aspects of issues associated with certain candidates and political parties where they exist. In short, the voter has a right to be "reasonably informed of all the possible choices."...

The question, then, is what promotes an informed voter? For voters to be able to hear all points of view, the information disseminated by third parties, candidates and political parties cannot be unlimited. In the absence of spending limits, it is possible for the affluent or a number of persons or groups pooling their resources and acting in concert to dominate the political discourse. The respondent's factum illustrates that political advertising is a costly endeavour. If a few groups are able to flood the electoral discourse with their message, it is possible, indeed likely, that the voices of some will be drowned out. Where those having access to the most resources monopolize the election discourse, their opponents will be deprived of a reasonable opportunity to speak and be heard. This unequal dissemination of points of view undermines the voter's ability to be adequately informed of all views. In this way, equality in the political discourse is necessary for meaningful participation in the electoral process and ultimately enhances the right to vote. Therefore, contrary to the respondent's submission, s. 3 does not guarantee a right to unlimited information or to unlimited participation.

Spending limits, however, must be carefully tailored to ensure that candidates, political parties and third parties are able to convey their information to voters. Spending limits which are overly restrictive may undermine the informational component of the right to vote. To constitute an infringement of the right to vote, these spending limits would have to restrict information in such a way as to undermine the right of citizens to meaningfully participate in the political process and to be effectively represented....

(3) The s. 1 justification applicable to the infringement of freedom of expression

The central issue at this stage of the analysis is the nature and sufficiency of the evidence required for the Attorney General to demonstrate that the limits imposed on freedom of expression are reasonable and justifiable in a free and democratic society. The Attorney General of Canada alleges that the lower courts erred in requiring scientific proof that harm had actually occurred and, specifically, by requiring conclusive proof that third party advertising influences voters and election outcomes, rendering them unfair....

The legislature is not required to provide scientific proof based on concrete evidence of the problem it seeks to address in every case. Where the court is faced with inconclusive or competing social science evidence relating the harm to the legislature's measures, the court may rely on a reasoned apprehension of that harm....

[T]he nature of the harm and the efficaciousness of Parliament's remedy in this case is difficult, if not impossible, to measure scientifically. The harm which Parliament seeks to address can be broadly articulated as electoral unfairness. Several experts, as well as the Lortie Commission, concluded that unlimited third party advertising can undermine election fairness in several ways. First, it can lead to the dominance of the political discourse by the wealthy. Second, it may allow candidates and political parties to circumvent their own spending limits through the creation of third parties. Third, unlimited third party spending can have an unfair effect on the outcome of an election. Fourth, the absence of limits on third party advertising expenses can erode the confidence of the Canadian electorate who perceive the electoral process as being dominated by the wealthy. This harm is difficult, if not impossible, to measure because of the subtle ways in which advertising influences human behaviour; the influence of other factors such as the media and polls; and the multitude of issues, candidates and independent parties involved in the electoral process. In light of these difficulties, logic and reason assisted by some social science evidence is sufficient proof of the harm that Parliament seeks to remedy....

(iii) Subjective fears and apprehension of harm

Perception is of utmost importance in preserving and promoting the electoral regime in Canada. Professor Aucoin emphasized that "[p]ublic *perceptions* are critical precisely because the legitimacy of the election regime depends upon how citizens assess the extent to which the regime advances the values of their electoral democracy" (emphasis in original). Electoral fairness is key. Where Canadians perceive elections to be unfair, voter apathy follows shortly thereafter.

Several surveys indicate that Canadians view third party spending limits as an effective means of advancing electoral fairness. Indeed, in *Libman*... the Court relied on the survey conducted by the Lortie Commission illustrating that 75 per cent of Canadians supported limits on spending by interest groups to conclude that spending limits are important to maintain public confidence in the electoral system.

(iv) The nature of the infringed activity: political expression

Third party advertising is political expression. Whether it is partisan or issue-based, third party advertising enriches the political discourse. As such, the election advertising of third parties lies at the core of the expression guaranteed by the *Charter* and warrants a high degree of constitutional protection....

In some circumstances, however, third party advertising will be less deserving of constitutional protection. Indeed, it is possible that third parties having access to significant financial resources can manipulate political discourse to their advantage through political advertising....

Under the egalitarian model of elections, Parliament must balance the rights and privileges of the participants in the electoral process: candidates, political parties, third parties and voters. Advertising expense limits may restrict free expression to ensure that participants are able to meaningfully participate in the electoral process. For candidates, political parties and third parties, meaningful participation means the ability to inform voters of their position. For voters, meaningful participation means the ability to hear and weigh many points of view. The difficulties of striking this balance are evident. Given the right of Parliament to choose Canada's electoral model and the nuances inherent in implementing this model, the Court must approach the justification analysis with deference. The lower courts erred in failing to do so. In the end, the electoral system, which regulates many aspects of an election, including its duration and the control and reimbursement of expenses, reflects a political choice, the details of which are better left to Parliament....

(b) Limits prescribed by law

The respondent argues that the entire third party advertising expense regime is too vague to constitute a limit prescribed by law on the basis that the legislation provides insufficient guidance as to when an issue is "associated" with a candidate or party. Thus, it is unclear when advertising constitutes election advertising and is subject to the regime's provisions. This argument is unfounded. The definition of election advertising in s. 319, although broad in scope, is not unconstitutionally vague....

(d) Rational connection

At this stage of the analysis, the Attorney General "must show a causal connection between the infringement and the benefit sought on the basis of reason or logic"...The lower courts erred by demanding too stringent a level of proof, in essence, by requiring the Attorney General to establish an empirical connection between third party spending limits and the objectives of s. 350. There is sufficient evidence establishing a rational connection between third party advertising expense limits and promoting equality in the political discourse, protecting the integrity of the financing regime applicable to candidates and parties, and maintaining confidence in the electoral process....

(e) Minimal impairment

To be reasonable and demonstrably justified, the impugned measures must impair the infringed right or freedom as little as possible...[T]he impugned measures need not be the least impairing option....

The $3,000 limit per electoral district and $150,000 national limit allow for meaningful participation in the electoral process while respecting the right to free expression. Why? First, because the limits established in s. 350 allow third parties to advertise in a limited way in some expensive forms of media such as television, newspaper and radio. But, more importantly, the limits are high enough to allow third parties to engage in a significant amount of low cost forms of advertising such as computer generated posters or leaflets or the creation of a 1-800 number. In addition, the definition of "election advertising" in s. 319 does not apply to many forms of communication such as editorials, debates, speeches, interviews, columns, letters, commentary, the news and the Internet which constitute highly effective means of conveying information. Thus, as the trial judge concluded, the limits allow for "modest, national, informational campaigns and reasonable electoral district informational campaigns"...

The Chief Justice [for herself and two other Justices, dissenting]

This Court has repeatedly held that liberal democracy demands the free expression of political opinion, and affirmed that political speech lies at the core of the *Canadian Charter of Rights and Freedoms'* guarantee of free expression. It has held that the freedom of expression includes the right to attempt to persuade through peaceful interchange. And it has observed that the electoral process is the primary means by which the average citizen participates in the public discourse that shapes our polity. The question now before us is whether these high aspirations are fulfilled by a law that effectively denies the right of an ordinary citizen to give meaningful and effective expression to her political views during a federal election campaign.

The law at issue sets advertising spending limits for citizens—called third parties—at such low levels that they cannot effectively communicate with their fellow citizens on election issues during an election campaign. The practical effect is that effective communication during the writ period is confined to registered political parties and their candidates. Both enjoy much higher spending limits. This denial of effective communication to citizens violates free expression where it warrants the greatest protection—the sphere of political discourse. As in *Libman,* the incursion essentially denies effective free expression and far surpasses what is required to meet the perceived threat that citizen speech will drown out other political discourse. It follows that the law is inconsistent with the guarantees of the *Charter* and, hence, invalid....

Section 350(2)(*d*) is particularly restrictive. It prohibits individuals from spending more than the allowed amounts on any issue with which a candidate is "particularly associated". The candidates in an election are typically associated with a wide range of views on a wide range of issues. The evidence shows that the effect of the limits is to prevent citizens from effectively communicating their views on issues during an election campaign.

The limits do not permit citizens to effectively communicate through the national media. The Chief Electoral Officer testified that it costs approximately $425,000 for a one-time full-page advertisement in major Canadian newspapers. The Chief Electoral Officer knows from personal experience that this is the cost of such communication with Canadians, because he used this very method to inform Canadians of the changes to the *Canada Elections Act* prior to the last federal election. It is telling that the Chief Electoral Officer would have been unable to communicate this important change in the law to Canadians were he subject—as are other Canadians—to the national expenditure limit of $150,000 imposed by the law....

Under the limits, a citizen may place advertisements in a local paper within her constituency. She may print some flyers and distribute them by hand or post them in conspicuous places. She may write letters to the editor of regional and national newspapers and hope they will be published. In these and other ways, she may be able to reach a limited number of people on the local level. But she cannot effectively communicate her position to her fellow citizens throughout the country in the ways those intent on communicating such messages typically do—through mail-outs and advertising in the regional and national media. The citizen's message is thus confined to minor local dissemination with the result that effective local, regional and national expression of ideas becomes the exclusive right of registered political parties and their candidates.

Comparative statistics underline the meagerness of the limits. The national advertising spending limits for citizens represent 1.3 percent of the national advertising limits for political parties. In Britain, a much more geographically compact country, the comparable ratio is about 5 percent. It is argued that the British limits apply to different categories of advertising over a greater period, but the discrepancy nevertheless remains significant.

It is therefore clear that the *Canada Elections Act*'s advertising limits prevent citizens from effectively communicating their views on election issues to their fellow citizens, restricting them instead to minor local communication. As such, they represent a serious incursion on free expression in the political realm. The Attorney General raises three reasons why this restriction is justified as a reasonable limit in a free and democratic society under s. 1 of the *Charter*: to ensure the equality of each citizen in elections; to prevent the voices of the wealthy from drowning out those of others; and to preserve confidence in the electoral system. Whether that is so is the question in this appeal.

B. Is the Incursion on Free Speech Justified?

(1) The significance of the infringement

One cannot determine whether an infringement of a right is justified without examining the seriousness of the infringement. Our jurisprudence on the guarantee of the freedom of expression establishes that some types of expression are more important and hence more deserving of protection than others. To put it another way, some restrictions on freedom of expression are easier to justify than others.

Political speech, the type of speech here at issue, is the single most important and protected type of expression. It lies at the core of the guarantee of free expression... The right of the people to discuss and debate ideas forms the very foundation of democracy. For this reason, the Supreme Court of Canada has assiduously protected the right of each citizen to participate in political debate... Section 2(*b*) of the *Charter* aims not just to guarantee a voice to registered political parties, but an equal voice to *each citizen*...

Permitting an effective voice for unpopular and minority views—views political parties may not embrace—is essential to deliberative democracy. The goal should be to bring the views of all citizens into the political arena for consideration, be they accepted or rejected at the end of the day. Free speech in the public square may not be curtailed merely because one might find the message unappetizing or the messenger distasteful....

This is the perspective from which we must approach the question whether the limitation on citizen spending is justified. It is no answer to say that the citizen can speak through a registered political party. The citizen may hold views not espoused by a registered party. The citizen has a right to communicate those views. The right to do so is essential to the effective debate upon which our democracy rests, and lies at the core of the free expression guarantee. That does not mean that the right cannot be limited. But it does mean that limits on it must be supported by a clear and convincing demonstration that they are necessary, do not go too far, and enhance more than harm the democratic process.

(2) The law's objective: is it pressing and substantial?

...[T]he limits are purported to further three objectives: first, to favour equality, by preventing those with greater means from dominating electoral debate; second, to foster informed citizenship, by ensuring that some positions are not drowned out by others (this is related to the right to participate in the political process by casting an informed vote); third, to enhance public confidence by ensuring equality, a better informed citizenship and fostering the appearance and reality of fairness in the democratic process.

These are worthy social purposes, endorsed as pressing and substantial by this Court in *Libman*... Common sense dictates that promoting electoral fairness is a pressing and substantial objective in our liberal democracy, even in the absence of evidence that past elections have been unfair...

C. Proportionality

(1) Rational connection

The Attorney General has offered no evidence to support a connection between the limits on citizen spending and electoral fairness. However, reason or logic may establish the requisite causal link...

The real question in this case is not whether there exists a rational connection between the government's stated objectives and the limits on citizens imposed by the *Canada Elections Act*. It is whether the limits go too far in their incursion on free political expression.

(2) Minimal impairment

...The difficulty with the Attorney General's case lies in the disproportion between the gravity of the problem—an apprehended possibility of harm—and the severity of the infringement on the right of political expression.

It is impossible to say whether an infringement is carefully tailored to the asserted goals without having some idea of the actual seriousness of the problem being addressed. The yardstick by which excessive interference with rights is measured is the need for the remedial infringement. If a serious problem is demonstrated, more serious measures may be needed to tackle it. Conversely, if a problem is only hypothetical, severe curtailments on an important right may be excessive.

Here the concern of the Alberta courts that the Attorney General had not shown any real problem requiring rectification becomes relevant. The dangers posited are wholly hypothetical. The Attorney General presented no evidence that wealthier Canadians—alone or in concert—will dominate political debate during the electoral period absent limits. It offered only the hypothetical possibility that, without limits on citizen spending, problems could arise. If, as urged by the Attorney General, wealthy Canadians are poised to hijack this country's election process, an expectation of some evidence to that effect is reasonable. Yet none was presented. This minimizes the Attorney General's assertions of necessity and lends credence to the argument that the legislation is an overreaction to a non-existent problem.

On the other side of the equation, the infringement on the right is severe. We earlier reviewed the stringency of the limits. They prevent citizens from effectively communicating with their fellow citizens on election issues during a campaign....

There is no demonstration that limits this draconian are required to meet the perceived dangers of inequality, an uninformed electorate and the public perception that the system is unfair. On the contrary, the measures may themselves exacerbate these dangers. Citizens who cannot effectively communicate with others on electoral issues may feel they are being treated unequally compared to citizens who speak through political parties. The absence of their messages may result in the public being less well informed than it would otherwise be. And a process that bans citizens from effective participation in the electoral debate during an election campaign may well be perceived as unfair. These fears may be hypothetical, but no more so than the fears conjured by the Attorney General in support of the infringement.

This is not to suggest that election spending limits are never permissible. On the contrary, this Court in *Libman* has recognized that they are an acceptable, even desirable, tool to ensure fairness and faith in the electoral process. Limits that permit citizens to conduct effective and persuasive communication with their fellow citizens might well meet the minimum impairment test. The problem here is that the draconian nature of the infringement—to effectively deprive all those who do not or cannot speak through political parties of their voice during an election period—overshoots the perceived danger. Even recognizing that "[t]he tailoring process seldom admits of perfection," and according Parliament a healthy measure of deference, we are left with the fact that nothing in the evidence suggests that a virtual ban on citizen communication through effective advertising is required to avoid the hypothetical evils of inequality, a misinformed public and loss of public confidence in the system....

Notes and Questions

1. *A menu of campaign finance regulations.* Nothing requires that democracies impose any rules for the financing of election campaigns, and the range of regulation across democracies is wide. The spectrum in common law countries runs from Australia, with an essentially unregulated *laissez faire* system with public subsidies to political parties (*see* Graeme Orr, *Political Disclosure Regulation in Australia: Lackadaisical Law*, 6 ELECTION L.J. 72 (2007)), to Canada, with strict limits on giving and spending money in elections. *See generally* K.D. EWING AND SAMUEL ISSACHAROFF, PARTY FUNDING AND CAMPAIGN FINANCING IN INTERNATIONAL PERSPECTIVE 1 (K.D. Ewing & Samuel Issacharoff eds., Hart Publishing 2006) [hereinafter "PARTY FUNDING"]. On the menu of possible regulations:
   - (a) *Spending limits.* Some countries (or subcountry units, such as states or provinces) impose limits on how much may be spent on elections by candidates, parties, or those acting independent of candidates and parties (so-called "third party" spending).
   - (b) *Contribution limits.* Some polities limit how much individuals or groups may contribute to candidates or parties.
   - (c) *Disclosure requirements.* In some polities, those who give or spend money on political campaigns must disclose such giving or spending in a timely manner, and the government disseminates such information in a timely manner to the public. In other democracies, such as Australia, only sketchy and incomplete information on giving and spending is available, sometimes not until well after the election. *See* Orr, *supra.*
   - (d) *Subsidies.* Some polities provide for public funding of campaigns, or at least for campaigns of parties or candidates from larger parties. Other polities require broadcasters to provide free or deeply discounted advertising time to parties or candidates.

   Australia imposes almost no regulation and Canada imposes very strict regulation. Is one of these countries more "democratic" than the other? What kinds of differences in the quality of campaigns would you expect to see in the two countries?

2. *Why campaign finance regulation?* Supporters of campaign finance regulations have offered a number of rationales for such regulations. Three commonly advanced rationales for regulation are
   - (a) *Corruption prevention.* In advanced democracies, campaigns for office—especially national office—are expensive, and the government may offer no

subsidies or inadequate subsidies for campaign expenses such as the cost of television advertising. Candidates or parties could be tempted to exchange political benefits for large campaign contributions or spending, benefiting the candidate or party.

(b) *Political equality*. Modern elections are premised on the idea of political equality, where each voter has a roughly equal say in the choice of candidates. This ideal of political equality is in tension with a free-market system of campaign financing, because wealth is not distributed equally among individuals. A rich person and a poor person may have the same intensity of preference for a candidate, but the rich person can devote more financial resources than the poor person to help assure the choice of candidates or parties or to gain access to those candidates or parties. A government might impose caps or grant subsidies to equalize resources available for voters, candidates, or parties.

(c) *Public confidence*. Supporters of campaign finance regulation sometimes posit that regulation is necessary to assure public confidence in the electoral process. Public confidence in the electoral process in turn assures that the democratic system of government maintains legitimacy and the polity remains stable. Public confidence ties into the other two rationales for regulation: large campaign spending or contributions may signal to voters that politicians (or parties) are corrupt or that the political system is inegalitarian, allowing the rich to have more influence over elections (or public policy) than the poor. If there is no *actual* corruption or inequality, is campaign finance regulation justified based on misguided public *perceptions*?

3. *Constitutional limitations on campaign finance regulation, the balancing of interests, and the danger of incumbent-protecting laws*. Though campaign finance regulation may prevent corruption, promote political equality, or assure public confidence, regulation comes at a cost in terms of liberty. A law limiting the amount a person may spend to support her preferred candidate, for example, limits that person's freedom to use her resources as she sees fit for expression and association. Even a law requiring disclosure of contributions to candidates (or spending favoring candidates) could have the effect of chilling political activity, particularly if the candidate is controversial or unpopular.

The clash between liberty and the state's interest in corruption prevention, political equality, or preserving public confidence may lead courts, as in *Harper*, to *balance* competing interests. Not every country has the equivalent of the U.S. Constitution's First Amendment, which protects freedom of speech and association, but in many advanced democracies, there is some kind of liberty interest recognized by relevant constitutional law that must be balanced against state interests in regulation. Such balancing is particularly important because of the danger that the state's asserted interests in regulating campaign financing may be *pretextual*: rather than preventing corruption, for example, a campaign finance law passed by a legislative body comprised of once and future political candidates might really be aimed at *protecting incumbents from political competition*.

In reviewing challenges to campaign finance regulations, should constitutional courts balancing interests *defer* to legislative bodies because of their members' expertise in campaigns, or subject such laws to *close scrutiny* because of the potential for partisan entrenchment? The *Harper* Court deferred to the Parliament, and did not require the government to come forward with social science evidence proving that section 350 would promote equality or public confidence in the electoral process. Should it have? If not, should it have inquired into the *motive* of the Parliament to make sure that the law was not passed with an incumbent-protecting intent? *See* Colin Feasby, *Freedom of Expression and the Law of the Democratic Process*, 29 SUP. CT. L. REV.2d 237, 282–89 (2005).

4. *Balancing equality and liberty.* In *Harper*, the Supreme Court of Canada accepted the Canadian government's view that section 350 was justified on political equality grounds, as well as on grounds of promoting public confidence in the electoral process. In a country, like the United States, where courts have rejected the equality rationale for campaign finance limits (*see Buckley v. Valeo*, 424 U.S. 1, 48–49 (1976)), could a law like section 350 be justified on anticorruption grounds when balanced against liberty interests?

In Australia, the Australian government sought to justify a law (modeled after a law in the United Kingdom) banning paid broadcast advertising and granting political parties regulated free broadcast advertising on grounds that such laws would prevent corruption by limiting the need for large campaign contributions as well as promote equality by "eliminat[ing] the privileged status of the few in the community who could afford the high cost of such advertising and 'place all in the community on an equal footing so far as the use of the public airways in concerned.'" *Australian Capital Television Pty. Ltd. v. The Commonwealth of Australia*, (1992) 177 C.L.R. 106 (opinion of Chief Justice Mason, ¶¶ 19, 22). The Australian High Court rejected the ban on paid advertising, holding it violated freedom of communication impliedly protected by the Australian Constitution:

> [T]he overseas experience does not refute the proposition that [the law] impairs freedom of discussion of public and political affairs and freedom to criticize federal institutions in the respects previously mentioned. Thus, the Commonwealth's claim that [the law] introduces and maintains a "level playing field" cannot be supported if that claim is to be understood as offering equality of access to all in relation to television and radio. It is obvious that the provisions of [the law] regulating the allocation of free time give preferential treatment to political parties represented in the preceding Parliament or legislature which are contesting the relevant election with at least the prescribed number of candidates. Their entitlement amounts to 90 per cent of the total free time. Others must of necessity rely on the exercise of discretion by the [Australian Broadcasting] Tribunal. As among the political parties, the principle of allocation to be applied will tend to favour the party or parties in government because it gives weight to the first preference voting in the preceding election....The provisions of [the law] manifestly favour the status quo. More than that, the provisions regulating the allocation of free time allow no scope for participation in the election campaign by persons who are not candidates or by groups who are not putting forward candidates for election. Employers' organizations, trade unions, manufacturers' and farmers' organizations, social welfare groups and societies generally are excluded from participation otherwise than through the means protected by [the law]. The consequence is that freedom of speech or expression on electronic media in relation to public affairs and the political process is severely restricted by a regulatory regime which evidently favours the established political parties and their candidates without securing compensating advantages or benefits for others who wish to participate in the electoral process or in the political debate which is an integral part of that process.

Id. at ¶ 22; *see also* Graeme Orr, Byran Mercurio, & George Williams, *Australian Electoral Law: A Stocktake*, 2 ELECTION L.J. 383, 384–85 (2003).

The term "equality" is imprecise. In the campaign finance arena, it may mean one of at least three different concepts: (1) equality of arms, or "equal campaign spending between the political parties;" (2) equality of "political influence among citizens;" or (3) equality "of access in the so-called marketplace of ideas." Lori A. Ringhand, *Concepts of Equality in British Election Financing Reform Proposals*, 22 Oxford J. Legal Stud. 253, 257 (2002). Which concept of equality was the Canadian Parliament trying to foster with the passage of Section 350? Should the Parliament instead have tried to foster a different concept of equality, or no concept of equality at all? Are broadcast subsidies for election-related advertising, as in Australia (where the amount of party funding tracks prior voter support for the parties), a better way to promote political equality than limits?

5. *Public confidence and voter "manipulation."* The *Harper* majority writes that "it is possible that third parties having access to significant financial resources can manipulate political discourse to their advantage through political advertising." What evidence, if any, does the Court point to on the possibility of manipulation? *See* Andrew Geddis, *Liberté, Egalité, Argent: Third Party Election Spending and the Charter*, 42 Alberta L. Rev. 429, 458 (2004) (positing that nothing more than "common sense reasoning" underlies the Court's analysis on this point).

6. *The line between election-speech and other political speech and the problem of issue advocacy.* The Canadian law at issue in *Harper* barred "third party" advertising during the election period costing more than 3000 CAD per electoral district that "promote[s]" or "oppose[s]" candidates or parties. Such advertising need not expressly advocate the election or defeat of the candidate or party. It is enough that the advertising "tak[es] a position on an issue with which [the candidate or party] are particularly associated." Such a broad definition is bound to include some advertising not intended to affect the outcome of an election and put a great deal of discretion into the hands of whoever administers this law. Should the court have held the law unconstitutional on grounds it was vague or overbroad? Feasby, 29 Sup. Ct. L. Rev.2d 237 at 288, so suggests: "The Court in *Harper* failed to cabin its deference and was uncritical of Parliament's regulation of pure issue advocacy." *See also* Janet L. Hiebert, *Elections, Democracy and Free Speech: More at Stake than an Unfettered Right to Advertise*, 269, 281, in Party Funding, *supra*. Meanwhile, New Zealand election spending limits appear ineffective because they apply *only* to express advocacy. Andrew Geddis, *The Regulation of Campaign Funding in New Zealand: Practices, Problems and Prospects for Change*, 13, 22, in Party Funding, *supra*. In the United States drawing the line between election spending and other spending has proven to be a problem as well. The U.S. Supreme Court upheld new limits on corporate and union spending for some election-related advertising in *McConnell v. FEC*, 540 U.S. 93 (2003). But only a few years later the Court, with two new members, appeared to create a large hole in the statutory scheme on First Amendment grounds. *FEC v. Wisconsin Right to Life, Inc.*, 127 S.Ct. 2652 (2007). *See* Richard L. Hasen, *Beyond Incoherence: The Roberts' Court's Deregulatory Turn in* FEC v. Wisconsin Right to Life, 92 Minn. L. Rev. 1064 (2008).

7. *How low can you go?* In campaign finance law, the devil is often in the details. New Zealand law, for example, imposes spending limits on parties, but they are so generous that "no party has ever reported expending the full amount under the legislation." Geddis, *supra*, at 19.

   At the other end of the spectrum is the United Kingdom, which imposed a £5 limit on "third party" election-related spending. An antiabortion activist successfully challenged the limit as violating the freedom of expression guaranteed in Article 10 of the European Convention on Human Rights. The European Court of Human Rights agreed it was necessary to balance the government's interests in promoting political equality with freedom of expression, and that in this balance Mrs. Bowman, the complaining party, should prevail:

> [T]he Court finds that [the spending limits] operated, for all practical purposes, as a total barrier to Mrs Bowman's publishing information with a view to influencing the voters of Halifax in favour of an anti-abortion candidate. It is not satisfied that it was necessary thus to limit her expenditure to [£] 5 in order to achieve the legitimate aim of securing equality between candidates, particularly in view of the fact that there were no restrictions placed upon the freedom of the press to support or oppose the election of any particular candidate or upon political parties and their supporters to advertise at national or regional level, provided that such advertisements were not intended to promote or prejudice the electoral prospects of any particular candidate in any particular constituency. It accordingly concludes that the restriction in question was disproportionate to the aim pursued.

Bowman v. United Kingdom, 1 Eur. Ct. H.R. 47 (1998). Britain followed up by raising the limit to £500. "No one knows whether the £500 is higher than required to meet the requirements of the *Bowman* judgment, or is too low." K. D. EWING, THE COST OF DEMOCRACY: PARTY FUNDING IN MODERN BRITISH POLITICS 150 (Hart Publishing 2007).

8. *The special role of political parties in a campaign financing regime*. Political parties play a special role in choosing candidates and organizing the government in many polities. Should political parties be subject to special restriction on their finances? Should they receive special subsidies, such as free broadcast advertising? For a survey of approaches to political party campaign financing rules, *see* Karl-Heinz Nassmacher, *Regulation of Party Finance, in* HANDBOOK OF PARTY POLITICS 446–55 (Richard S. Katz & William Crotty eds., SAGE Publications 2006); PARTY FUNDING, *supra*.

15

Religious Freedom

Alan E. Brownstein

The Free Exercise Clause of the U.S. First Amendment has been conceptualized by the Supreme Court and many commentators in all-or-nothing terms. The Court has tended to either apply "strict scrutiny" to burdens on religious exercise—in which case the government's justifications for imposing the burden are rigorously reviewed—or instead, as of late, to apply a minimalist test that asks only whether government burdens on religion are motivated by antireligious sentiment. As the following materials and notes illustrate, other jurisdictions have tried to chart more nuanced middle-ground approaches. Whether balancing tests such as Canada's, discussed below, are workable—there or more generally—is for readers to decide.

Note that Canada, unlike the United States, has no explicit nonestablishment provision in its Charter. And yet, as the materials below suggest, Canada has incorporated many of the principles of religious equality on which much of the U.S. Establishment Clause jurisprudence has been built on. Perhaps Canada's textual protection for multiculturalism has been an adequate vehicle in this regard. After reading the materials, consider whether the Fourteenth Amendment's Equal Protection Clause could or should do more work in U.S. disputes implicating religious equality.

The Canadian Charter of Rights and Freedoms (1982) includes the following provisions:

> 1. The *Canadian Charter of Rights and Freedoms* guarantees the rights and freedom set out in it subject only to such reasonable limits prescribed by law as can be demonstrably justified in a free and democratic society.
> 2. Everyone has the following fundamental freedoms:
>   (a) freedom of conscience and religion;
>
> . . .
>
> 27. This Charter shall be interpreted in a manner consistent with the preservation and enhancement of the multicultural heritage of Canadians.

R. v. Big M Drug Mart Ltd.

Supreme Court of Canada
[1985] 1 S.C.R. 295 (Can.)

Dickson, J., (Beetz, McIntyre, Chouinard, and Lamer, JJ., concurring)

[2] Big M has challenged the constitutionality of the Lord's Day Act [which prohibits work or commercial activity on Sunday]...in terms of...the Canadian Charter of Rights and Freedoms....

V(B) The Historic Underpinnings

[52] Historically, there seems little doubt that it was religious purpose which underlay the enactment of English Lord's Day legislation. From early times the moral exhortation found in the Fourth Commandment (Exodus 20: 8–11), "Remember the Sabbath day, to keep it holy", increasingly became a legislative imperative....

[54] The [English] Sunday Observance Act of 1677 served as a model for Canadian pre-Confederation legislation, especially An Act to prevent the Profanation of the Lord's Day, commonly called Sunday, 1845...which substantially re-enacted the English law with only minor alterations....

V(C) The American Authorities

[74] The United States Supreme Court has sustained the constitutionality of Sunday observance legislation against First Amendment challenges...Despite the undoubted religious motivation of the state laws in question at the time of their passage and their clear origin in the religiously coercive statutes of Stuart England, Warren, C.J., writing for the majority, found that those statutes had evolved to become purely secular labor regulation....

VI Purpose and Effect of Legislation

[79] A finding that the Lord's Day Act has a secular purpose is...simply not possible. Its religious purpose, in compelling sabbatical observance, has been long established and consistently maintained by the courts of this country....

[85] If the acknowledged purpose of the Lord's Day Act, namely, the compulsion of sabbatical observance, offends freedom of religion, it is then unnecessary to consider the actual impact of Sunday closing upon religious freedom. Even if such effects were found inoffensive... this could not save legislation whose purpose has been found to violate the Charter's guarantees....

[89] Both [the trial judge] and the American Supreme Court... suggest that the purpose of legislation may shift, or be transformed over time by changing social conditions... A number of objections can be advanced to this "shifting purpose" argument.

[90] First, there are the practical difficulties. No legislation would be safe from a revised judicial assessment of purpose. Laws assumed valid on the basis of persuasive and powerful authority could, at any time, be struck down as invalid....

[91] Furthermore, the theory of a shifting purpose stands in stark contrast to fundamental notions developed in our law concerning the nature of "Parliamentary intention". Purpose is a function of the intent of those who drafted and enacted the legislation at the time, and not of any shifting variable....

[93] While the effect of such legislation as the Lord's Day Act may be more secular today than it was in 1677 or in 1906, such a finding cannot justify a conclusion that its purpose has similarly changed. In result, therefore, the Lord's Day Act must by characterized as it has always been, a law the primary purpose of which is the compulsion of sabbatical observance....

VII Freedom of Religion

[95] Freedom can primarily be characterized by the absence of coercion or constraint... Coercion includes not only such blatant forms of compulsion as direct commands to act or refrain from acting on pain of sanction, coercion includes indirect forms of control which determine or limit alternative courses of conduct available to others....

[97] To the extent that it binds all to a sectarian Christian ideal, the Lord's Day Act works a form of coercion inimical to the spirit of the Charter and the dignity of all non-Christians. In proclaiming the standards of the Christian faith, the Act creates a climate hostile to, and gives the appearance of discrimination against, non-Christian Canadians. It takes religious values rooted in Christian morality and, using the force of the state, translates them into a positive law binding on believers and non-believers alike. The theological content of the legislation remains as a subtle and constant reminder to religious minorities within the country of their differences with, and alienation from, the dominant religious culture.

[98] Non-Christians are prohibited for religious reasons from carrying out activities which are otherwise lawful, moral and normal. The arm of the state requires all to remember the Lord's Day of the Christians and to keep it holy. The protection of one religion and the concomitant non-protection of others imports disparate impact destructive of the religious freedom of the collectivity.

[99] [T]o accept that Parliament retains the right to compel universal observance of the day of rest preferred by one religion is not consistent with the preservation and enhancement of the multicultural heritage of Canadians....

(i) The Absence of an "Establishment Clause"

[103] Much of the argument before this court on the issue of the meaning of freedom of conscience and religion was in terms of "free exercise" and "establishment"....

[104] It is the appellant's argument that, unlike the American Bill of Rights, the Canadian Charter of Rights and Freedoms does not include an "establishment clause." He urged therefore that the protection of freedom of conscience and religion extends only to the "free exercise" of religion....

[105] In my view this recourse to categories from the American jurisprudence is not particularly helpful in defining the meaning of freedom of conscience and religion under the Charter. The adoption in the United States of the categories "establishment" and "free exercise" is perhaps an inevitable consequence of the wording of the First Amendment. The cases illustrate, however, that these are not two totally separate and distinct categories, but rather, as the Supreme Court of the United States has frequently recognized, in specific instances "the two clauses may overlap."...

[122] What unites enunciated freedoms in the American First Amendment, s. 2(*a*) of the Charter and in the provisions of other human rights documents in which they are associated is the notion of the centrality of individual conscience and the inappropriateness of governmental intervention to compel or to constrain its manifestation....

[134] In my view, the guarantee of freedom of conscience and religion prevents the government from compelling individuals to perform or abstain from performing otherwise harmless acts because of the religious significance of those acts to others....

VIII Section 1 of the Charter

[138] Is the Lord's Day Act, and especially s. 4 thereof, justified on the basis of s. 1 of the Canadian Charter of Rights and Freedoms?

[142] [It is argued] that everyone accepts the need and value of a universal day of rest from all work, business and labor and it may as well be the day traditionally observed in our society.... The first and fatal difficulty with this argument is, as I have said, that it asserts an objective which has never been found by this court to be the motivation for the legislation....

[143] The characterization of the purpose of the Act as one which compels religious observance renders it unnecessary to decide the question of whether s. 1 could validate such legislation whose purpose was otherwise....

Edwards Books and Art Limited v. R; R. v. Nortown Foods Limited

Supreme Court of Canada
[1986] 2 S.C.R. 713 (Can.)

Dickson, C.J.C. (Chouinard and Le Dain, JJ. concurring):

II. The Legislation

[7] The...Retail Business Holidays Act...defines "holiday" to include Sundays and various other days, including some days which are of special significance to Christian denominations, and some which are clearly secular in nature....

[9] Sections 3 and 4 contain a diverse array of exceptions. Most "corner store" operations are exempted...Pharmacies, gas stations, flower stores and, during the summer months, fresh fruit and vegetable stores or stands are excluded...[as are] educational, recreational or amusement services. Prepared meals, laundromat services, and boat and vehicle rentals and service are permitted...[and] a municipality [may] create its own scheme of exemptions where necessary for the promotion of the tourist industry.

[10] Section 3(4)...applies to businesses which, on Sundays, have seven or fewer employees engaged in the service of the public and less than 5,000 square feet used for such service. Its effect is to exempt these businesses from having to close on Sunday if they closed on the previous Saturday...

V. C. The Legislative Purpose of the Retail Business Holidays Act

[63] [T]he Retail Business Holidays Act was enacted with the intent of providing uniform holidays to retail workers. I am unable to conclude that the Act was a surreptitious attempt to encourage religious worship. The

title and text of the Act, the legislative debates and the Ontario Law Reform Commission's Report on Sunday Observance Legislation all point to the secular purposes underlying the Act....

[67] The report recommends...that a uniform weekly pause day be enacted in Ontario. Amongst the factors leading the commission to advocate uniform or common holidays were: (i) the problems of co-ordinating holidays amongst family and friends in a staggered holiday system (especially for families with children of school age); (ii) the difficulty of holding community events under an alternative regime; and (iii) the expressed preference of most people to spend their days off with family, friends or even among crowds.

[68] The report then turned to the question which day of the week ought to be selected as a weekly pause day....The report concluded...that Sunday was the best choice, but for secular reasons....

VI. Freedom of Conscience and Religion under s. 2(a)

[82] What I have said above regarding the legislative purpose of the Retail Business Holidays Act...applies...to the Charter....The Act has a secular purpose which is not offensive to the Charter guarantee of freedom of conscience and religion.

[83] The court held, in the *Big M Drug Mart* case...that both the purposes and the effects of legislation are relevant to determining its constitutionality. Even if a law has a valid purpose, it is still open to a litigant to argue that it interferes by its effects with a right or freedom guaranteed by the Charter....

A. The Constitutional Protection from State-Imposed Burdens on Religious Practices and Religious Non-Conformity

[86] [The United States Supreme Court has consistently upheld the constitutionality of Sunday closing laws against free exercise and establishment clause challenges.] In considering these cases it is important to bear in mind the differences between the Canadian and American constitutions, not just in respect of the wording of the provisions relating to religion, but also regarding the absence of a provision such as s. 1 of the Canadian Charter in the American instrument....

[88] Of particular interest to the present appeals...is the United States Supreme Court's discussion of the "free exercise clause" of the First Amendment. In *Braunfeld v. Brown*,...the appellants were Orthodox Jews engaged in the retail business. They contended that a Pennsylvania statute

prohibiting retail sales on Sundays, which [lacked any exemption], compelled them to either forego their Sabbath or suffer a substantial economic loss, to the benefit of non-sabbatarian competitors.

[89] The opinion of Warren C.J.... was that the law operated "so as to make the practice of their religious beliefs more expensive"... According to the majority, however, it did not necessarily follow that the laws were unconstitutional. The Chief Justice wrote...:

> [I]f the State regulates conduct by enacting a general law within its power, the purpose and effect of which is to advance the State's secular goals, the statute is valid despite its indirect burden on religious observance unless the State may accomplish its purpose by means which do not impose such a burden.

[90] Applying this test, the Chief Justice affirmed the validity of the objective of providing a general day of rest, and assessed the alternative means by which the state's objectives might be achieved without the imposition of such a burden. He was not satisfied with any of the alternatives, including the possibility of a sabbatarian exemption, and accordingly upheld the legislation.

[96] The court [in *Big M*] was concerned... with a direct command, on pain of sanction, to conform to a particular religious precept. The appeals with which we are now concerned are alleged to involve two forms of coercion. First, it is argued that the Retail Business Holidays Act makes it more expensive for retailers and consumers who observe a weekly day of rest other than Sunday to practice their religious tenets. In this manner, it is said, the Act indirectly coerces these persons to forego the practice of a religious belief. Second, it is submitted that the Act has the direct effect of compelling non-believers to conform to majoritarian religious dogma, by requiring retailers to close their stores on Sunday.

[97] The first question is whether *indirect* burdens on religious practice are prohibited by the constitutional guarantee of freedom of religion. In my opinion indirect coercion by the state is comprehended within the evils from which s. 2(*a*) may afford protection... It matters not, I believe, whether a coercive burden is direct or indirect, intentional or unintentional, foreseeable or unforeseeable. All coercive burdens on the exercise of religious beliefs are potentially within the ambit of s. 2(*a*).

[98] This does not mean, however, that every burden on religious practices is offensive to the constitutional guarantee of freedom of religion. It means only that indirect or unintentional burdens will not be held to be outside the scope of Charter protection on that account alone... [L]egislative or administrative action which increases the cost of practicing or otherwise manifesting religious beliefs is not prohibited if the burden is trivial or insubstantial....

[99] [T]he second form of religious coercion allegedly flowing from the Act... involves, not the freedom affirmatively to practice one's religious

beliefs, but rather the freedom to abstain from the religious practices of others. The Retail Business Holidays Act prevents some retailers from selling their products on Sundays. [It is argued]... that the Act thereby requires retailers to conform to the religious practices of dominant Christian sects.

[100] [T]he freedom to express and manifest religious non-belief and the freedom to refuse to participate in religious practice... are governed by somewhat different considerations than the freedom to manifest one's own religious beliefs. Religious freedom... is not necessarily impaired by legislation which requires conduct consistent with the religious beliefs of another person. One is not being compelled to engage in religious practices merely because a statutory obligation coincides with the dictates of a particular religion. I cannot accept, for example, that a legislative prohibition of criminal conduct such as theft and murder is a state-enforced compulsion to conform to religious practices merely because some religions enjoin their members not to steal or kill. Reasonable citizens do not perceive the legislation as requiring them to pay homage to religious doctrine....

[101] The majority judgment of the court in *Big M Drug Mart* was careful, in defining the freedom from conformity to religious dogma, to restrict its applicability to circumstances when the impugned legislation was motivated by a religious purpose....

B. The Impact of the Retail Business Holidays Act

[103] The Act has a different impact on persons with different religious beliefs....

(ii) Sunday Observers:

[107] The Act has a favorable impact on Sunday observers. By requiring some other retailers to refrain from trade on a day of special religious significance to Sunday observers, the latter are relieved of a loss of market share to retailers who would have been open for business on Sunday in the absence of the Act. The cost of religious observance has been decreased for Sunday observers by the enactment of the legislation....

(iii) Saturday Observers:

[110] ...In the absence of legislative intervention, the Saturday observer and the Sunday observer would be on a roughly equal footing in competing for shares of the available consumer buying power. Both might operate for a maximum of six days each week. Both would be disadvantaged relative to non-observing retailers who would have the option of a seven-day week. On this account, however, they would have no complaint cognizable in law, since the disability would be one flowing exclusively from their religious tenets...But, exemptions aside, the Retail Business Holidays Act

has the effect of leaving the Saturday observer at the same natural disadvantage relative to the non-observer and adding the new, purely statutory disadvantage of being closed an extra day relative to the Sunday observer. Just as the Act makes it less costly for Sunday observers to practice their religious beliefs, it thereby makes it more expensive for some Jewish and Seventh-Day Adventist retailers to practice theirs....

VII. Section 1 of the Charter

[117] Two requirements must be satisfied to establish that a limit is reasonable and demonstrably justified in a free and democratic society. First, the legislative objective which the limitation is designed to promote must be of sufficient importance to warrant overriding a constitutional right. It must bear on a "pressing and substantial concern." Second, the means chosen to attain those objectives must be proportional or appropriate to the ends. The proportionality requirement, in turn, normally has three aspects: the limiting measures must be carefully designed and rationally connected to the objective; they must impair the right as little as possible; and their effects must not so severely trench on individual or group rights that the legislative objective, albeit important, is nevertheless outweighed by the abridgment of rights. The court stated that the nature of the proportionality test would vary depending on the circumstances. Both in articulating the standard of proof and in describing the criteria comprising the proportionality requirement the court has been careful to avoid rigid and inflexible standards.

[118] In the present appeals, the only evidence [as to the importance of the legislature's objective] available to the court which relates to s. 1 of the Charter is the Report on Sunday Observance Legislation. It would have been preferable to have had more recent evidence....

[121] [In any case] I regard as self-evident the desirability of enabling parents to have regular days off from work in common with their child's day off from school and with a day off enjoyed by most other family and community members...I am satisfied that the Act is aimed at a pressing and substantial concern. It therefore survives the first part of the inquiry under s. 1.

[122] The requirement of rational connection calls for an assessment of how well the legislative garment has been tailored to suit its purpose....

[126] A...difficult question—and one which goes to the heart of this litigation—is whether the Retail Business Holidays Act abridges the freedom of religion of Saturday observers as little as is reasonably possible. Section 3(4) has the effect, and was intended to have the effect, of very substantially reducing the impact of the Act on those religious groups for whom Saturday is a Sabbath. What must be decided, however, is whether there is some reasonable alternative scheme which would allow the province to achieve its objective with fewer detrimental effects on religious freedom.

[127] One suggestion was that the objective of protecting workers from involuntary Sunday labor could be achieved by legislation which focused on the employee rather than the employer. There could, for example, be an enactment conferring on workers a right to refuse Sunday work. But such a scheme would...fail to recognize the subtle coercive pressure which an employer can exert on an employee...A scheme which requires an employee to assert his or her rights before a tribunal in order to obtain a Sunday holiday is an inadequate substitute for the regime selected by the Ontario legislature....

[128] The other alternative would be to retain the basic format of the Retail Business Holidays Act, but to replace s. 3(4) with a complete exemption from s. 2 for those retailers who have a sincerely-held religious belief requiring them to close their stores on a day other than Sunday. The province of New Brunswick has such an exemption....

[130] The most difficult questions stem from the different impacts of these exemptions on Saturday-observing *retailers*....[T]he legislation before [the United States Supreme Court in *Braunfeld v. Brown*]...contained no exemption clause of any kind aimed at alleviating its deleterious impact on Saturday-observing retailers. Nevertheless, the majority upheld the legislation. Warren C.J. considered,...whether a sabbatarian exemption ought to have been provided:

> [While] [a] number of States provide such an exemption...reason and experience teach that to permit the exemption might well undermine the State's goal of providing a day [of rest]....
>
> Additional problems might also be presented by [an exemption]. To allow only people who rest on a day other than Sunday to keep their businesses open on that day might well provide these people with an economic advantage over their competitors who must remain closed on that day; this might cause the Sunday observers to complain that their religions are being discriminated against. [Some retailers], in order to keep their businesses open on Sunday, [might] assert that they have religious convictions which compel them to close their businesses on [a less] profitable day. This might make necessary a state-conducted inquiry into the sincerity of the individual's religious beliefs, a practice which a State might believe would itself run afoul of the spirit of constitutionally protected religious guarantees....

[132] I see [no] merit [in] the contention that a sabbatarian exemption would discriminate against retailers who do not observe Saturday as a religious day of rest. There is no evidence before this court to suggest that Sunday is *generally* a preferable day for retailers to do business...Alleged discrimination flowing from one day of the weekend being more profitable for particular retailers than the other day of the weekend would be of an entirely different order of magnitude from the disadvantage experienced by retailers who cannot open their stores on a weekend at all.

[133] I am impressed, however, with the concerns...of the United States Supreme Court in two respects. The first relates to the balancing of an

indirect burden on the religious freedom of a retail store owner against the interests of his or her perhaps sometimes numerous employees. The second relates to the undesirability of state-sponsored inquiries into religious beliefs.

[134] With respect to the first concern, I agree with the... United States Supreme Court that it is legitimate for legislatures to be concerned with minimizing the disruptive effect of any exemption on the scope and quality of the pause day....

[135] What cannot be forgotten is that the object of the legislation is to benefit retail employees by making available to them a weekly holiday which coincides with that enjoyed by most of the community....

[136] The economic position of these employees affords them few choices in respect of their conditions of employment. It would ignore the realities faced by these workers to suggest that they stand up to their employer or seek a job elsewhere if they wish to enjoy a common day of rest with their families and friends....

[137] [T]he second factor which... contributes to the justification of the legislation under review... [relates to a] concern about state-conducted inquiries into religious beliefs. The striking advantage of the Ontario Act is that it makes available an exemption to the small and mid-size retailer without the indignity of having to submit to such an inquiry. In my view, state-sponsored inquiries into any person's religion should be avoided wherever reasonably possible, since they expose an individual's most personal and private beliefs to public airing and testing in a judicial or quasi-judicial setting. The inquiry is all the worse when it is demanded only of members of a non-majoritarian faith, who may have good reason for reluctance about so exposing and articulating their non-conformity.

[138] I do not mean to suggest that a judicial inquiry into the sincerity of religious beliefs is unconstitutional.... Judicial inquiries into religious beliefs are largely unavoidable if the constitutional freedoms guaranteed by s. 2(*a*) are to be asserted before the courts.... There will, however, be occasions when a substantial measure of religious freedom can be achieved without mandating a state-conducted inquiry into personal religious convictions, and the legislatures ought to be encouraged to do so, if a fair balance is struck.

[139] [T]he evidence indicates that the overwhelming majority of Saturday-observing retailers are capable of complying with the requirements of s. 3(4).... In my view, there exists to some degree a trade-off between a scheme which provides complete relief from burdens on religious freedom to most Saturday-observing retailers by avoiding a distasteful inquiry and, on the other hand, an alternative scheme which provides substantial relief from burdens on religious freedom to *all* Saturday-observing retailers.... It is far from clear that one scheme is intrinsically better than the other....

[141] Nevertheless, while the number of detrimentally-affected retailers may be small, no legislature in Canada is entitled to do away with any of the religious freedoms to which these or any other individuals are entitled without strong reason. In my view, the balancing of the interests of more than seven employees to a common pause day against the freedom of religion of those affected constitutes justification for the exemption scheme selected by the province of Ontario, at least in a context wherein any satisfactory alternative scheme involves an inquiry into religious beliefs.

[142] I might add that I do not believe there is any magic in the number seven as distinct from, say, five, ten, or 15 employees as the cut-off point for eligibility for the exemption. In balancing the interests of retail employees to a holiday in common with their family and friends against the s. 2(*a*) interests of those affected the legislature engaged in the process envisaged by s. 1 of the Charter, a "reasonable limit" is one which... it was reasonable for the legislature to impose. The courts are not called upon to substitute judicial opinions for legislative ones as to the place at which to draw a precise line.

[143] Having said this, however, I do not share the views of the majority of the United States Supreme Court that no legislative effort need be made to accommodate the interests of any Saturday-observing retailers. In particular, I would be hard pressed to conceive of any justification for insisting that a small, family store which operates *without any employees* remain closed on Sundays when the tenets of the retailer's religion require closing on Saturdays. In my view... it [is] incumbent on a legislature which enacts Sunday closing laws to attempt very seriously to alleviate the effects of those laws on Saturday observers....

[146] ...I have little difficulty in applying the third element of the proportionality test. The infringement is not disproportionate to the legislative objectives. A serious effort has been made to accommodate the freedom of religion of Saturday observers, insofar as that is possible without undue damage to the scope and quality of the pause day objective. It follows that I would uphold the Act under s. 1.

Notes and Questions

1. In *Big M Drug Mart*, the Canadian Supreme Court concludes that a law serving an impermissible religious purpose is unconstitutional—without regard to the law's effect. The U.S. Supreme Court has never struck down a law for violating the Free Exercise Clause of the First Amendment solely because the law served an impermissible purpose.

   The U.S. Supreme Court has, however, held that a law violates the Establishment Clause if it lacks a secular purpose, *see, e.g., Wallace v. Jaffree*, 472 U.S. 38 (1985) (striking down a law authorizing a moment of silence for meditation or voluntary prayer because it was "entirely motivated by a purpose to advance religion.") The Canadian Charter does not have an Establishment

Clause. Is a purpose analysis more appropriate for adjudicating an Establishment Clause case than a Free Exercise Case? Is it ever appropriate for adjudicating a Free Exercise case?

2. While the Canadian Charter does not have an Establishment Clause, it does provide in Section 27 that the Charter "shall be interpreted in a manner consistent with the preservation and enhancement of the multicultural heritage of Canadians." Arguably this provision captures one of the key aspects of the Establishment Clause—the goal of religious equality; government must treat people of different faiths as persons of equal worth who are deserving of equal respect. If the Establishment Clause was not incorporated into the Fourteenth Amendment and made applicable to the states, as some commentators have argued, would this purpose be adequately served by the Equal Protection Clause? *See* Akhil Amar, The Bill of Rights 246–57 (1998).

3. In *Big M Drug Mart*, the Canadian Court rejects the U.S. Supreme Court's argument in *McGowan v. Maryland*, 366 U.S. 420 (1961) that a law may have an impermissible purpose when it is originally enacted, but that purpose may shift over time to one that is constitutionally acceptable. If the Lord's Day Act were enacted initially to serve the religious purpose of compelling adherence to the Christian Sabbath, that purpose cannot change over time to one that serves a secular goal.

   In *Edwards Books and Arts Limited*, however, the Canadian Supreme Court upheld the recently enacted Sunday closing law, the Retail Business Holiday Act, because this law was adopted to serve the secular purpose of providing for a uniform day of rest. Does this mean that the state cured the constitutional defect in the Lord's Day Act of the law serving an impermissible purpose by re-enacting the law under a new name for an allegedly different, secular purpose? Is there any reason why this approach to the problem should be preferred over the evolving purpose analysis applied in *McGowan*?

4. Neither American nor Canadian constitution law considers fundamental rights to be absolute. American courts create standards of review to determine when the state's interest justifies the infringement of a right. Section 1 of the Canadian Charter explicitly recognizes that rights are subject to "reasonable limits... demonstrably justified in a free and democratic society." The Canadian Supreme Court has interpreted that section in a way that bears some parallel to American standards of review (*Edwards Books*,)

   When reviewing laws serving secular goals that incidentally, but substantially, burden the exercise of religion, the Canadian and American cases include four standards that differ as to the rigor of the review they require:

   Employment Division v. Smith, 494 U.S. 872 (1990), describes current American doctrine. Neutral laws of general applicability that substantially burden a religious practice, such as the observance of the Sabbath, will be upheld without review. No accommodations of religious practice are constitutionally mandated.

   Braunfeld v. Brown, 366 U.S. 599 (1961) applied a lenient standard of review to Sunday closing laws. This standard did not reject all free exercise claims without review as does the holding in *Smith.* Instead, the Court suggested that even indirect burdens on religious practice may be unconstitutional if the state could accomplish its objective without imposing such burdens on religious individuals.

Sherbert v. Verner, 374 U.S. 398 (1963) and *Wisconsin v. Yoder*, 406 U.S. 205 (1972) applied rigorous review or strict scrutiny to neutral and general laws that substantially burdened the exercise of religion. Although formally distinguished, those cases were given an extremely narrow reading in, and all but overruled by, the decision in *Smith*.

Edwards Books applies a standard of review of intermediate rigor. The legislature must accommodate religious practices if it is reasonable to do so. While the Canadian Supreme Court allows the government some flexibility in determining the nature and scope of such accommodations, it will balance the extent to which an accommodation undermines the state interests against the burden the failure to accommodate imposes on religious individuals.

Consider the virtues and disadvantages of these different standards of review for the adjudication of free exercise claims. Does the degree of balancing of interests engaged in by the Canadian Supreme Court in *Edwards Books* provide too indeterminate and subjective a basis for constitutional decision making? Is the Court usurping the legislature's function with its analysis? Alternatively, does the current approach of the U.S. Supreme Court provide too little protection to religious freedom? The Canadian Supreme Court in *Edwards Books* suggested that it could not imagine a justification for the state refusing to exempt a small, family business owned by a Saturday Sabbath observer from the requirements of a Sunday closing law. Under current American doctrine, the failure to grant such an exemption would be summarily upheld without the state having to justify its decision in any way.

5. The Canadian Supreme Court suggests that it is preferable to cast a religious accommodation in secular terms (e.g., the size of a store) rather than drafting the exemption to apply only to individuals who adhere to particular religious beliefs. *Edwards Books.* An accommodation that employs secular criteria avoids the problem of the state inquiring into an individual's religious beliefs—which might be experienced as intrusive, particularly for members of minority faiths. Is this a realistic concern? Many religious exemptions, ranging from excusing children from public school to observe a religious holiday to exempting conscientious objectors from military conscription, routinely require the person seeking the exemption to explain the religious basis for their claim to an accommodation. Does religious freedom subsume a right to religious privacy?

6. The Court in *Edwards Books* was concerned that an expanded religious exemption would undermine the benefits of having a uniform day of rest—particularly for employees of businesses that remained open on Sunday. If those interests are so important, however, how can the Court explain the range of nonreligious exemptions recognized by the statute which include pharmacies, gas stations, flower stores, fruit and vegetable stores, educational, recreational, and amusement services, laundromats, boat and vehicle rentals, and additional exemptions needed to promote the tourist industry? Should the number of secular exemptions provided by the statute have any impact on the way a court reviews the legislature's refusal to provide an accommodation for religious individuals whose ability to practice their faith is burdened by a law? *See* Judge, now Justice, Alito's opinion in *Fraternal Order of Police v. City of Newark*, 170 F.3d 359 (3d Cir. 1999).

16

The State Action Doctrine

Frank I. Michelman

The "state action" rule in U.S. constitutional law—as represented by cases such as *The Civil Rights Cases*, 109 U.S. 3 (1883), *Flagg Brothers, Inc. v. Brooks*, 436 U.S. 149 (1978), and *Moose Lodge No. 7 v. Irvis*, 407 U.S. 163 (1972)—limits the reach of the Constitution's guarantees of individual rights in two respects. First, these guarantees do not ordinarily impose any legal responsibility on nonofficial parties engaged in the conduct of nongovernmental affairs. Second, they do not ordinarily impose any responsibility on the state to control the conduct of nonstate parties—the state's own liabilities typically being limited to cases of rights-invasive conduct by the state itself, acting through its officers and agents. In a lingo often used by jurists outside the United States, our state action rule is said to deny any purely "horizontal" (private-on-private), as opposed to "vertical" (government-on-private), application or effect to those constitutional guarantees to which it attaches. (The salient exception is the Thirteenth Amendment's prohibition against slavery and involuntary servitude. *See, e.g., Jones v. Alfred H. Mayer Co.*, 392 U.S. 409 (1968).)

The American state action rule is plainly a product of a congeries of factors and considerations. Historically, the American constitutional guarantees of individual rights are widely understood to have sprung from fears of oppression by *governmental* power; they were part of a program to create limited *government*. Conversely, a subjection of all private affairs and market relations to the same demands for nondiscrimination, say, or due process, that the Fourteenth Amendment is read to impose on state governments seems out of keeping with American constitutionalism's core commitments to personal freedom and private ordering. (Am I under constitutional obligation not to choose my house guests on the basis of sex, religion, or race? Should our Constitution be read to make it impossible for willing parties, in any circumstances, to conclude a strictly at-will employment contract?) No doubt some government regulation of discrimination and process in private sector and market affairs is in order—civil rights legislation, for example, abounds in the United States—but here a second core commitment of American constitutionalism kicks in. Within the American scheme of federalism, the policy choices involved in fashioning such regulation are felt to be primarily reserved for lawmakers at the state level, as opposed to the federal Supreme Court or Congress. The federalism theme is manifest, for example, in *The Civil Rights Cases*. The state action rule draws additional support from American separation-of-powers sensibilities, which point toward letting legislatures—not courts—decide how far nonstate parties should be required by law to respect the values and interests that animate the Bill of Rights.

Perhaps few would object to these evident commitments of American constitutionalism to private ordering, federalism, and the separation of powers. While raising no doubts about their general rightness and wisdom, the following judgments—one from the Federal Constitutional Court of Germany, the other from the European Court of Human Rights, both arising out of the same invasion-of-privacy complaint from a European public personage—prompt questions about whether a rule ostensibly focusing on the presence or absence of state action is a necessary, a desirable, or even a conceptually viable way of giving these commitments effect in constitutional law. These judgments also illustrate how the "state action" problem is knit together with two others that typically crop up in comparative constitutional studies: (1) Is a constitutional Bill of Rights best written and read to impose only negative restrictions on state conduct, or also to impose active duties of aid or protection? (2) What is (or ought to be) the effect, if any, of Bill-of-Rights provisions on the content of the general, background law (of tort and contract, say) that typically governs private transactions and relationships?

Von Hannover v. Germany

Application no. 59320/00

European Court of Human Rights (Third Section) (2004)

[The background to the case is as follows: The applicant, Caroline von Hannover, is a daughter of Prince Rainier III of Monaco. As a member of Prince Rainier's family, she acts as head of certain humanitarian and cultural foundations, and she sometimes represents the ruling family at public events. She does not perform any governmental function in or for the State of Monaco.

[Since the early 1990s, Applicant had, with mixed success, been suing publishers in civil courts in a number of European countries, seeking injunctive relief against publication in the tabloid press of photos about her private life. (For example, one photo at issue in this case "shows the applicant at the Monte Carlo Beach Club, dressed in a swimsuit and wrapped up in a bathing towel, tripping over an obstacle and falling down." Another, bearing the caption "These photos are evidence of the most tender romance of our time," shows Applicant "with the actor Vincent Lindon at the far end of a restaurant courtyard" in Provence.)

Having failed to obtain all the relief she sought in a series of actions and appeals in the civil courts of Germany—those courts issued injunctions against publication of some but not all of the photos at issue—Applicant sued Germany before the European Court of Human Rights, sitting in Strasbourg, France (the "Strasbourg Court"). The Court is a creature of the European Convention for the Protection of Human Rights and Fundamental Freedoms ("European Convention"), a multi-state treaty to which Germany is a state party. The Convention empowers the Strasbourg Court to hear claims from private parties against state-party conduct allegedly in violation of the Convention's mandates, and to order relief where violations are found. In this case, Applicant claimed that the German court decisions in her lawsuits had infringed her right to respect for her private and family life as guaranteed by Article 8 of the Convention.] Article 8 provides:

1. Everyone has the right to respect for his private and family life, his home and his correspondence.
2. There shall be no interference by a public authority with the exercise of this right except such as is in accordance with the law and is necessary in a democratic society in the interests of national security, public safety or the economic well-being of the country, for the prevention of disorder or crime, for the protection of health or morals, or for the protection of the rights and freedoms of others.

The German courts had decided Applicant's claims against the publishers—civil tort claims, in essence—by construing and applying various doctrines of German civil and statute law, while taking also into account certain guarantees in Germany's Constitution, known as its *Grundgesetz* or "Basic Law." Provisions of the German Basic Law deemed relevant by the German courts included the following:

Article 1 § 1. The dignity of human beings is inviolable. All public authorities have a duty to respect and protect it.

Article 2 § 1. Everyone shall have the right to the free development of their personality provided that they do not interfere with the rights of others or violate the constitutional order or moral law....

Article 5 §§ 1 and 2.

1. Everyone shall have the right freely to express and disseminate his or her opinions in speech, writing and pictures and freely to obtain information from generally accessible sources. Freedom of the press and freedom of reporting on the radio and in films shall be guaranteed. There shall be no censorship.
2. These rights shall be subject to the limitations laid down by the provisions of the general laws and by statutory provisions aimed at protecting young people and to the obligation to respect personal honour.

[The highest-level judicial judgment in Germany was delivered by the Federal Constitutional Court of Germany (FCC), Germany's highest ranking court with regard to all matters affecting the constitution (Basic Law) and German constitutional law. Here are some passages from the FCC's main judgment in the case.]

Under Article 2 § 1 of the Basic Law, general personality rights are guaranteed only within the framework of the constitutional order. The provisions concerning the publication of photographical representations of persons listed in sections 22 and 23 of the KUG [a German statute dealing with intellectual property] are part of that constitutional order. They ... aim to strike a fair balance between respect for personality rights and the community's interest in being informed ...

Under section 22, first sentence, of the KUG, pictures can only be disseminated or exposed to the public eye with the express approval of the person represented. Pictures relating to contemporary society are excluded from that rule under section 23(1) of the KUG ... Under section 23(2) of the KUG, however, that exception does not apply where the dissemination interferes with a legitimate interest of the person represented. The protection by degrees under these rules ensures that they take account of the need to protect the person being represented as well as the community's desire to be informed and the interest of the media which satisfy that desire....

In the instant case regard must be had, in interpreting and applying sections 22 and 23 of the KUG, not only to general personality rights, but also to the freedom of the press guaranteed by Article 5 § 1, second sentence, of the Basic Law in so far as the provisions in question also affect those freedoms....

The fact that the press fulfils the function of forming public opinion does not exclude entertainment from the functional guarantee under the Basic Law.... Entertainment can also convey images of reality and propose subjects for debate that spark off a process of discussion and assimilation relating to philosophies of life, values and behaviour models....

As regards politicians, this public interest has always been deemed to be legitimate from the point of view of transparency and democratic control. Nor can it in principle be disputed that it exists in respect of other public figures. To that extent it is the function of the press to show people in situations that are not limited to specific functions or events and this also falls within the sphere of protection of press freedom. It is only when a balancing exercise has to be done between competing personality rights that an issue arises as to whether matters of essential interest for the public are involved and treated seriously and objectively or whether private matters, designed merely to satisfy the public's curiosity, are being disseminated ...

[The FCC's judgment went on to identify certain factors that the balancing in this case ought to consider, such as the Applicant's status as a public figure (but not a governmental official), and the degree of reasonable expectation of seclusion from the public eye of various locations in which the Applicant was photographed. The FCC by and large approved the decisions of the lower courts regarding the various photos in issue. In the event, the Applicant obtained some injunctive relief from the German courts, but not nearly all that she had sought.

[Applicant then sued *Germany* for damages in the Strasbourg Court, claiming that Germany, through the acts and decisions of its civil courts, had infringed her rights as guaranteed by Article 8 of the European Convention, quoted above.[1] Arguments before the Court attacked and defended the balance struck by the German courts between the rights and values of personality and privacy advanced by Applicant and those of public information and communicative freedom advanced by the publishers (admitted to the case as intervenors).

[The Strasbourg Court upheld the Applicant's claims against Germany. Following are excerpts from the Court's judgment.]

3. Compliance with Article 8

(a) The Domestic Courts' Position

54. The Court notes that the Federal Constitutional Court interpreted [the applicable German legislation] by balancing the requirements of the freedom of the press against those of the protection of private life, that is, the public interest in being informed against the legitimate interests of the applicant.... The [FCC] attached decisive weight to the freedom of the press, even the entertainment press, and to the public interest in knowing how the applicant behaved outside her representative functions....

(b) General Principles Governing the Protection of Private Life and the Freedom of Expression

56. In the present case the applicant did not complain of an action by the State, but rather of the lack of adequate State protection of her private life and her image.

57. [A]lthough the object of Article 8 is essentially that of protecting the individual against arbitrary interference by the public authorities, it does not merely compel the State to abstain from such interference: in addition to this primarily negative undertaking, there may be positive obligations inherent in an effective respect for private or family life. These obligations may involve the adoption of measures designed to secure respect for private life even in the sphere of the relations of individuals between themselves [citing prior cases of the Strasbourg Court]....

58. That protection of private life has to be balanced against the freedom of expression guaranteed by Article 10 of the Convention....

59. ...The present case does not concern the dissemination of "ideas", but of images containing very personal or even intimate "information" about an individual. Furthermore, photos appearing in the tabloid press are often taken in a climate of continual harassment which induces in the

---

[1] To be precise, Applicant's case against Germany was heard not by the full court ("Grand Chamber"), but by a panel or "chamber" of seven judges.

person concerned a very strong sense of intrusion into their private life or even of persecution....

(c) Application of These General Principles by the Court

61. The Court notes at the outset that in the present case the photos of the applicant in the various German magazines show her in...activities of a purely private nature such as engaging in sport, out walking, leaving a restaurant or on holiday....

63. The Court considers that a fundamental distinction needs to be made between reporting facts—even controversial ones—capable of contributing to a debate in a democratic society relating to politicians in the exercise of their functions, for example, and reporting details of the private life of an individual who, moreover, as in this case, does not exercise official functions....

64. ...The situation here does not come within the sphere of any political or public debate because the published photos and accompanying commentaries relate exclusively to details of the applicant's private life....

68. ...[T]he context in which these photos were taken—without the applicant's knowledge or consent—and the harassment endured by many public figures in their daily lives cannot be fully disregarded....

69. The Court reiterates the fundamental importance of protecting private life from the point of view of the development of every human being's personality....The Court considers that anyone, even if they are known to the general public, must be able to enjoy a "legitimate expectation" of protection of and respect for their private life....

74. The Court therefore considers that the criteria on which the domestic courts based their decisions were not sufficient to protect the applicant's private life effectively....

(d) Conclusion...

79. Having regard to all the foregoing factors, and despite the margin of appreciation afforded to the State in this area, the Court considers that the German courts did not strike a fair balance between the competing interests.

80. There has therefore been a breach of Article 8 of the Convention....

II. Application of Article 41 of the Convention

82. Article 41 of the Convention provides:

> If the Court finds that there has been a violation of the Convention or the Protocols thereto, and if the internal law of the High Contracting Party concerned allows only partial reparation to be made, the Court shall, if necessary, afford just satisfaction to the injured party.

83. The applicant claimed [against the German government] 50,000 euros (EUR) for non-pecuniary damage on the ground that the German courts' decisions prevented her from leading a normal life with her children without being hounded by the media. She also claimed EUR 142,851.31 in reimbursement of her costs and expenses for the many sets of proceedings she had had to bring in the German courts.

84. The Government contested the amounts claimed....

85. The Court considers that the question of the application of Article 41 is not ready for decision. Accordingly, it shall be reserved and the subsequent procedure fixed having regard to any agreement which might be reached between the Government and the applicant....

[Two separate concurring opinions are omitted.]

Notes and Questions

1. In the *von Hannover* case, who performed the acts that the Strasbourg Court found had infringed on the Applicant's interests protected by Article 8 of the Convention? Was it the *paparazzi*? The publishers? Did the Court, then, give horizontal effect to Article 8? Is horizontal application of Article 8 what the language of the Article most naturally suggests?

   If your answer is that the Strasbourg Court's application of Article 8 in *von Hannover* was strictly vertical, then precisely which state officials undertook precisely what acts that the Court found to have contravened Article 8?

   On the theory you have just offered, does a "state action" rule ever have any real bite or make any real difference? Princess Caroline framed her complaint at Strasbourg as one against the German state (including its courts) for failing to enact (or for failing to identify and enforce) state laws providing effective relief against private acts infringing on Convention-protected privacy interests. What is to stop losing parties in U.S. civil disputes from using that same form to frame claims under the U.S. Constitution against some state, whenever they choose to do so?

   Take *Moose Lodge*, for example. In the actual case, Irvis sued the Lodge in federal court for acting in violation of his rights under Fourteenth Amendment's equal protection clause, and lost—or so he was told—because the Lodge is not a state party against whom those rights run. But imagine, for a moment, that Irvis tries instead to follow the lead of Princess Caroline, and so sues *Pennsylvania* for failing to institute and enforce laws protecting him against race-based refusals of service at the Lodge—in violation, he says, of his rights to such laws under the equal protection clause.

   Is the problem that Pennsylvania cannot be sued without its consent under U.S. constitutional rules on state sovereign immunity? (*See generally* R. FALLON ET AL., HART AND WECHSLER'S THE FEDERAL COURTS AND THE FEDERAL SYSTEM 973–1066 (5th ed. 2006). (By comparison, Germany made itself liable to suit under the European Convention by signing it.)) No, because the same effect is easily achieved by a different route: Let Irvis sue the Lodge in a Pennsylvania state court for an alleged state law tort of refusing him service on the basis of race. Let the trial court grant the Lodge's predictable motion to dismiss for failure to state a valid legal claim, because (the court rules) the law of Pennsylvania imposes on the Lodge no duty to serve whomever it chooses not to serve. Let Irvis take the case on appeal to the Supreme Court of Pennsylvania and let that Court affirm the ruling below. Let Irvis now petition for review by the U.S. Supreme Court, claiming that *Pennsylvania, by having the laws its courts say it has,* is acting in violation of his equal protection rights.

Can the U.S. Court *now* brush him off on the ground of "no state action?" If "no" (*but see Flagg Brothers*), then the Court, in order to decide the merits of Irvis's petition, will have to face squarely a question about the Constitution's substantive meanings: Does the equal protection clause, or does it not, impose a positive duty on states to have and enforce laws protecting against race-based refusals of service in establishments resembling the Lodge?

Of course, it is easy to imagine the Supreme Court answering "no" to that question, thus still leaving the *Moose Lodge* plaintiffs without a winning constitutional claim. But note that *von Hannover* is in this respect no different. The balance of privacy and free-speech concerns was obviously debatable in that case, and we can easily imagine the Strasbourg Court agreeing with the balance struck in Germany. Had it done so, it would have denied the Applicant's claim—not for the scrutiny-blocking reason of absence of state action, but for the fully substantive reason that Germany had struck a fair balance between free speech and privacy and thus complied in full with its obligations under the European Convention.

Does it matter at all in such cases whether plaintiffs suffer dismissal of their claims of higher-law violation for lack of substantive merit, or rather for the more technical-looking reason of "no state action"?

2. The state action rule plainly matters in the practical workings of U.S. constitutional law. With the *von Hannover* example before us, how may we explain this fact? Does the key perhaps lie in the Supreme Court's holding in *DeShaney v. Winnebago County Department of Social Services*, 489 U.S. 189 (1989)—to the effect that our Bill of Rights is strictly a negative "limitation on the State's power to act," and not at all a commitment to positive, protective action by the state? Is the crucial line really the one between state *action* and state *inaction*, not the one between *state* action and *nonstate* action? Consider the Strasbourg Court's remark in *von Hannover* that "the applicant did not complain of an action by the State, but rather of the lack of adequate State protection of her private life and her image." Consider also that the Court went on, even so, to decide the merits of Applicant's claim under Convention Article 8 because "there may be positive obligations [on state parties] inherent in an effective respect for private or family life."

   Article I of the European Convention states explicitly that "the High Contracting Parties *shall secure* to everyone within their jurisdiction the rights and freedoms defined in…this Convention." The Strasbourg Court made no mention of Article 1 in its *von Hannover* judgment, but does the article contain important textual support for the Court's finding of a violation of the Convention in that case?

   Compare the Strasbourg Court's 2001 *Case of Z*, (2001) 10 BHRC 384. Z's case resembles *DeShaney* very closely on the facts. The Strasbourg decision imposed liability on the United Kingdom for harms suffered by young children whom British social service agencies had culpably failed to remove from the custody of evidently violence-prone parents. The Court applied Article 3 of the European Convention, providing that "no one shall be subjected to…inhuman or degrading treatment." It did not, however, base liability solely on Article 3. Rather, the judgment relied on Articles 1 and 3 in combination: "The obligation on High Contracting Parties under Article 1...to secure to everyone...the rights and freedoms defined in the Convention," the Court wrote, "taken in conjunction with Article 3, requires States to take measures designed to ensure that individuals...are not subjected to torture or inhuman or degrading treatment, including such ill-treatment administered by private individuals."

Compare South Africa's current Constitution. It provides, in § 7, not only that the state must "respect...the rights in the Bill of Rights," but also that it must "protect, promote, and fulfill" these rights. The Constitutional Court of South Africa relied in part on § 7 in the widely known case of *Carmichele v. Minister of Public Safety and Security*, (2001) 10 BCLR 995 (CC), 2001 SACLR LEXIS 64. State police officials had declined to oppose a bail application by an obviously deranged and dangerous detainee, who assaulted and raped the plaintiff shortly after being released on bail. The lower courts rejected her claim in tort for negligence by the officials. Section 12(1) of South Africa's Constitution grants to everyone the right "to freedom and security of the person," and it specifically includes a right "(c) to be free from all forms of violence from either public or private sources." The Constitutional Court held that this section, bolstered both by § 7 and § 39(2) of South Africa's Constitution, discussed in Note 5 below, required the country's common law judiciary to "develop" the country's common law of tort so that officials performing as the *Carmichele* defendants did will be suable for harms suffered as a result of their negligence. In subsequent proceedings, the lower courts complied and the officials were held liable. In South Africa, *Carmichele* is widely regarded as a leading instance of what is called (by some jurists—usage of this term is contested) "indirect horizontal" application of the Bill of Rights. In your view, did the Constitutional Court apply Constitution § 12(1) horizontally or vertically in *Carmichele*?

Whether or not we class any or all of these cases as instances of horizontal application of constitutional guarantees, the holdings in *von Hannover*, *Z's Case*, and *Carmichele* all obviously rest on a certain sort of conclusion regarding *the substantive content* (as distinct from the agents to whom applicable) of the higher-law guarantees involved in these cases. In all of them, the applicable higher law was found to impose on the governments concerned certain active duties of protection of persons within their territories.

The substantive content of U.S. constitutional law, as construed by the Supreme Court in *DeShaney*, is drastically different. Why? We could say that, unlike the European Convention (Article I) and the South African Constitution (sections 7 and 12(1)(c)), the U.S. Constitution nowhere expressly imposes any active state duty of protection. But are you sure about the equal protection clause? And would this textual difference fully or sufficiently explain the stark difference in the doctrinal outcomes between Europe and South Africa, on the one hand, and the United States on the other?

3. In *New York Times Co. v. Sullivan*, 376 U.S. 254 (1964), the Supreme Court upheld the *Times*'s claim that its constitutionally guaranteed right of free speech was infringed by a large defamation judgment obtained against it in the courts of Alabama by L. B. Sullivan, and so ordered the judgment vacated. Obviously, it was not Alabama but Sullivan, acting in the case as a private party, who made the choice to sue the *Times*. Was it Sullivan, then, who committed the constitutional violation of which the *Times* complained? (Was it the *paparazzi* who committed

the Article 8 violation of which Princess Caroline complained in *von Hannover*?) Did the Supreme Court, then, apply the guarantees of the First and Fourteenth Amendments horizontally in *Sullivan*?

The *Sullivan* Court expressly affirmed that the Fourteenth Amendment is directed only against "state" action, not private action, but it had no difficulty finding state action on which to fasten constitutional scrutiny. "The Alabama courts," the Court explained,

> have applied a state rule of law which petitioners claim to impose invalid restrictions on their constitutional freedoms of speech and press. It matters not that that law has been applied in a civil action and that it is common law only.... The test is not the form in which state power has been applied but, whatever the form, whether such power has in fact been exercised.

In other words: Who made the law that encroached unduly on the free speech of the *Times*? Why, Alabama did, for this law is no less the act and choice of the state of Alabama because it is common law "made" by the state's judiciary than if it had been statute law made by the state's legislature. Such was the Supreme Court's inference, and it seems impossible to resist in our post-*Erie* age. *See Erie R.R. Co. v. Tompkins*, 304 U.S. 64, 79 (1938) (quoting from prior decisions) ("Law in the sense in which courts speak of it today does not exist without some definite authority behind it. The common law so far as it is enforced in a State, whether called common law or not, is not the common law generally but the law of that State existing by the authority of that State...The authority and only authority is the State, and if that be so, the voice adopted by the State as its own [whether it be of its Legislature or of its Supreme Court] should utter the last word.")

In your view, did the Supreme Court give horizontal effect to the U.S. Constitution's freedom-of-speech guarantee in *Sullivan*? If your answer is "no," why is it? (On whom, after all, did the burden of the Court's decision fall? Was it Alabama that suffered being stripped of a damage award, or was it J.B. Sullivan, a private party? If that is not giving horizontal effect to a constitutional guarantee, what would be?) If your answer is "yes," then does it follow that horizontal effect can at least sometimes be found where the act that fails constitutional scrutiny is the act of a state? Would that in fact be an apt summary of what occurred in *von Hannover*?

4. According to the Supreme Court in *Sullivan*, the state action there consisted in Alabama's common law of libel being what it was. Is a state's law being what it is always and necessarily a product of *active* choice (as opposed to mere passivity or nonaction) by a state's legislature or by its courts in common law mode? If the answer is yes, then does every judicial decision in a civil law case—tort, contract, property, and so on—involve state action onto which constitutional scrutiny can fasten? Is *that* what *von Hannover* teaches?

   Consider once again our reconstructed *Moose Lodge* litigation from Note 2. Are not the state courts wielding state law against Irvis? Might not the state's law possibly have been receptive, rather than hostile, to Irvis's claim of a right to race-blind service? If it is not receptive, is not that because someone so *chooses*? Who is that "someone," if not a lawmaking organ of the State of Pennsylvania? (Note again that it does not follow that a choice hostile to Irvis's claim is unconstitutional on the merits. That is a separate question. On the evidence of its *Moose Lodge* opinion, the Supreme Court would certainly uphold Pennsylvania's choice as constitutional.)

5. The judgment of the Strasbourg Court in *von Hannover* clearly reflects an answer to the last question that is characteristic of the constitutional law of Germany, South Africa, and some other countries (including the United States, *per Sullivan*?): A country's or state's law governing private, civil relations is always something for which some official or official body of that state or country is answerable to constitutional requirements, whether that law supports (as in *Sullivan*) or denies (as in *von Hannover*) relief in a given case.

   In South Africa, that stance is arguably dictated by Constitution § 39(2): "When interpreting any legislation, and when developing the common law or customary law, every court, tribunal or forum must promote the spirit, purport and objects of the Bill of Rights." (Several other constitutional clauses affect the result in South Africa, and the exact force of § 39(2) is a matter of ongoing debate, but that debate is not relevant here.) The Constitutional Court—in *Carmichele* and elsewhere—has read § 39(2) as clothing every South African litigant with an entitlement to a check by the trial judge, for harmony with the aims and values of the Bill of Rights, of every common law rule that the judge might apply when deciding against that litigant's claim or defense; and claims of failure or error by trial judges in this regard are reviewable by the Constitutional Court. In *Carmichele*, to illustrate, the responsible police officials eventually were held liable, but not for having violated any duty directly imposed on them by the Constitution. They were rather held liable for commission of the common law tort of negligent causation of harm, *after* the common law of negligence had undergone constitutionally mandated review and reform in order to bring it in line with the "spirit, purport, and objects" of the Bill of Rights. Some South African jurists use the terminology of "indirect horizontal" application of the Bill of Rights to describe such a course of decision. You should be able to see that a constitutional requirement that it be undertaken in every suitable case means, in effect, that no case comes to court in South Africa that is not potentially a constitutional case. Is there something wrong with that? (In *Flagg Brothers*, the U.S. Supreme Court called such a result "intolerable," so maybe there is.)

   In the course of deciding in *Carmichele* that § 39(2) should be given such an effect, the Constitutional Court made reference to a prior, similar development in German constitutional law, under the name of *Drittwirkung* or "third party effect" of constitutional guarantees. The notion is that the guarantees of the German Basic Law are directly and primarily applicable to conduct by the government, but that they also "radiate" throughout the legal order to require civil law modifications as necessary to keep the civil law in tune with constitutional value-orderings.

   The *Drittwirkung* doctrine has its source in the famous case of Eric Lüth, 7 BVerfGe 198 (1958). Lüth was ordered by German lower courts to desist from efforts to organize a public boycott against an anti-Semitic movie, in a lawsuit brought against him by the filmmaker, on the basis of a provision of the German civil code making it tortious to cause damage to another "in a manner offensive to good morals." Lüth successfully complained before the FCC that this ruling was offensive to the principle animating the Basic Law's guaranty of freedom of speech. As the FCC wrote:

   > The primary purpose of Basic Law rights is to safeguard the liberties of the individual against interferences by public authority. They are defensive rights of the individual against the state. This [purpose] follows from... the historical developments leading to the inclusion of basic rights in the constitutions of various countries....

> It is equally true, however, that the Basic Law is not a value neutral document.... Its section on basic rights establishes an objective order of values, and...this value system...must be looked upon as a fundamental constitutional decision affecting all spheres of law. Thus...every provision of private law must be compatible with this system of values, and every such provision must be interpreted in its spirit....In order to determine what is required by [legal] norms such as ["good morals"], one has to consider first the ensemble of value concepts that a nation has developed at a certain point in its...history and laid down in its constitution....
>
> The Constitution requires the judge to determine whether the basic rights have influenced the substantive rules of private law in the manner described.... If he does not apply these standards and ignores the influence of constitutional law on the rules of private law, he violates objective constitutional law by misunderstanding the content of the basic right (as an objective norm); as a public official, he also violates the basic right whose observance by the courts the citizen can demand on the basis of the Constitution.... [Citizens] can bring such a decision before [the FCC] by means of a constitutional complaint.
>
> ...[But it] is not up to [the FCC] to examine decisions of the private-law judge for any legal error he may have committed. Rather, [the FCC] must confine its inquiry to the "radiating effect" of the basic rights on private law. ...(translated by DONALD KOMMERS, THE CONSTITUTIONAL JURISPRUDENCE OF THE FEDERAL REPUBLIC OF GERMANY 363–64 (1989))

You should be able to see the *Lüth* conception at work in the FCC's *von Hannover* judgment, noting that the radiating effect there attaches to a regulatory statute (the KUG) along with the general, background private law contained in the German civil code.

6. *Some sources and further reading:* THE CONSTITUTION IN PRIVATE RELATIONS: EXPANDING CONSTITUTIONALISM (A. Sajó & R. Utz eds., 2005); Stephen Gardbaum, *Where the (State) Action Is*, 4 I•CON 760 (2006); Mark Tushnet, *The Issue of State Action/Horizontal Effect in Comparative Constitutional Law*, 1 I•CON 79 (2003); Frank I. Michelman, *The Protective Function of the State in the United States and Europe, in* EUROPEAN AND AMERICAN CONSTITUTIONALISM (Georg Nolte ed. 2005); Frank I. Michelman, *The Bill of Rights, the Common Law, and the Freedom Friendly State*, 58 U. MIAMI L. REV. 401 (2003) (on South Africa); DAVID P. CURRIE, THE CONSTITUTION OF THE FEDERAL REPUBLIC OF GERMANY 181–89 (1994) (on Germany and Lüth).

TABLE OF CASES

INDEX

www.ingramcontent.com/pod-product-compliance
Ingram Content Group UK Ltd.
Pitfield, Milton Keynes, MK11 3LW, UK
UKHW020924170926
475595UK00031B/50

9 780195 328103